Unintended Consequences

The Ohlin Lectures

Unintended Consequences

The Impact of Factor
Endowments, Culture, and
Politics on Long-Run
Economic Performance

Deepak Lal

The MIT Press
Cambridge, Massachusetts
London, England

This book was set in Palatino on the Monotype "Prism Plus" PostScript Imagesetter by Asco Trade Typesetting Ltd., Hong Kong.

Printed and bound in the United States of America.

Library of Congress Cataloging-in-Publication Data

Lal, Deepak.
    Unintended consequences : the impact of factor endowments,
    culture, and politics on long run economic performance / Deepak Lal.
        p.   cm. — (The Ohlin lectures ; 7)
    "The Ohlin Memorial Lectures 1995, delivered at the Stockholm
School of Economics, 30th and 31st Oct. 1995."
    Includes bibliographical references and index.
    ISBN 0-262-12210-3 (hc. : alk. paper)
    1. Economic history—Congresses.   2. Social history—Congresses.
3. Individualism—Congresses.   4. Applied anthropology—Congresses.
I. Title.   II. Series.
HC13.L35   1998
330.9—dc21   98-38290
                                                              CIP

"Only connect."

E. M. Forster, *Howards End*, chap. 22

"If we could go back to the elements of societies and examine the very first records of their histories, I have no doubt that we should there find the first cause of their prejudices, habits, dominating passions, and all that comes to be called national character."

De Tocqueville, *Democracy*, vol. I, p. 35

"It is no chance matter we are discussing but how one should live."

Plato, *Republic. 8*

Contents

Preface

This book contains a somewhat expanded version of the Ohlin Memorial Lectures I delivered at the Stockholm School of Economics in the autumn of 1995. I am extremely grateful to Staffan Linder and Mats Lundahl for inviting me to deliver these prestigious lectures and for not batting an eyelid when I suggested I would talk on culture and development—a subject that appears to be vague, muddled, and soft-headed to many economists. But it is also one that has been in the air during the last few years, and I had been keeping an eye on the debates that have arisen in that time. The lectures seemed a good opportunity to order my thoughts and do the necessary reading. Little did I realize that I would have to take account of not only what economists had to say on the subject (which is not much) but also of the relevant literatures in history, anthropology, social psychology, evolutionary biology, neurology, macrosociology, and the social and economic histories of the regions and cultures that form Eurasia. Such an interdisciplinary, cross-cultural sweep would have seemed daunting but for the help of many friends.

I was fortunate to have been appointed as the first holder of the James S. Coleman chair in international development studies at the University of California at Los Angeles, where I moved in 1991. Because this is an interdisciplinary chair I have made an effort to engage colleagues from many other disciplines studying developing countries. Many of these colleagues—sometimes unbeknownst to them—have pointed me in the right direction. I hope this book, written wholly at UCLA, will justify the interdisciplinary hopes of the electors to the Coleman chair. My new academic home also has one of the finest research libraries in the world. There were times when the librarians at the Bio-Medical library did look quizzically at an economist's requesting books and journals in biology and neurology. But without these marvelous research library resources this book could not have been written.

I also need to acknowledge another, more longstanding debt—to the Oxford school of Modern Greats (PPE), which was a model of a broad education in the social sciences when I read for it in the early 1960s, after completing a degree in history at St. Stephens College in Delhi. It aroused my interest in all the different social and human sciences, which have sadly become increasingly separated through narrow specialization—and none more so than economics. If this book succeeds in showing, however imperfectly, the relevance of all these branches in understanding our world, it is due to my having kept an interest, first aroused by PPE (the acronym stands for Philosophy—Politics and Economics), in what are now considered to be disparate subjects.

I was also greatly helped by the comments, suggestions for further reading, and general support—badly needed to boost morale when dealing with a theme as broad and contentious as mine—on the first draft of the manuscript from many friends. I would like to thank Robert Boyd, James Buchanan, Stanley Engerman, Nikki Hart, David Henderson, Dharma Kumar, Timur Kuran, Barbara Lal, Leonard Liggio, Justin Lin, Ian Little, Mats Lundahl, Douglass North, Jeffrey Nugent, Richard Rosecrance, Maurice Scott, Robert Skidelsky, Warren Tenhouten, and Martin Wolf. In addition participants at a colloquium I organized on culture and development at UCLA in December 1996 provided much food for thought, in particular Richard Baum, Shmul Eisenstadt, Ronald Findlay, Nathan Glazer, Avner Greif, Bill Jenner, and James Q. Wilson. Parts of the book have also been presented at seminars at UCLA, the University of Southern California, Hong Kong University of Science and Technology, and San Andreas University, Buenos Aires, whose participants' comments have also helped to improve this book.

Last but not least I am again grateful to Lorraine Grams, who has so efficiently produced the various drafts without a hitch, even when our communications were intercontinental.

In reading this book it should be borne in mind that these are lectures. The book is not a treatise. I have, as in any series of lectures, sought to synthesize and summarize the relevant literature—including my own past work—into a coherent story. The notes provide detailed references to the ubiquitous controversies in the different areas I cover. These are essential for the scholar but tedious for the general reader—whose interest I want to solicit. Both will, I hope, find that the story I have to tell is as engrossing, enlightening, and surprising as I found when putting it together.

Introduction

It is a great honor to have been asked to deliver this year's Ohlin Memorial Lectures. I have chosen a topic that combines the two major interests of Bertil Ohlin—economics and politics—and I hope to show how his basic building block, relative factor endowments as the basis for international trade, can also provide a powerful tool in thinking about a topic that is currently very much in the air: the role of culture in human affairs. Thus, recently, Samuel Huntington of Harvard has argued[1] that with the end of the Cold War, international friction in international affairs in the future will be determined by the cultural divide between the great civilizations—Western (with its various subdivisions: Western versus Eastern Christianity, Latin American versus North American), Islamic, Sinic, Hindu, and Japanese—with each vying for power and influence, and each trying to promote or protect traditional values and ways of life.

At the same time, there are many influential voices in East Asia—Lee Kwan Yew of Singapore, Mahatir of Malaysia—as well as numerous Chinese and Japanese politicians who claim that Eastern social and political forms are superior to Western ones. Rather than succumb to Western classical liberal values, which have produced decadence among prosperity in the West, the East, they argue, should stick by its familial and authoritarian cultural and political values as embodied in Confucianism or neo-Confucianism.

In an influential article Hicks and Redding[2] have stated that economists cannot explain the success of the East Asian edge without taking into account various cultural factors associated with their Confucian heritage. Purely economic factors cannot explain their economic "miracles." Even among development practitioners the importance of culture is being emphasized as witness the recent book by a former senior USAID official, Lawrence Harrison, entitled *Who Prospers* (with the subtitle "How Cultural Values Shape Economic and Political Success"). The journalists who have tried to explain the rise of East Asia in cultural terms are myriad—for instance, a recent popular book by Joel Kotkin entitled *Tribes*, whose subtitle "How Race, Religion and Identity Determine Success in the New Global Economy" gives away its message.

Thus in a neat reversal of Max Weber's famous thesis on the role of Protestantism in the rise of Western capitalism, we now have an Eastern "religion"—Confucianism, neo-Confucianism, post-Confucianism—being touted as the source of East Asia's success.[3] Clearly "culture" is in the air.

Some form of extraeconomic, possibly cultural explanation is also supported by the recent explosion of research in the so-called new growth economics. In thinking about growth, which for development economists is rightly the centerpiece of their studies, a useful distinction between *extensive* and *intensive* growth made by Lloyd Reynolds[4] is worth noting. Extensive growth has been fairly common throughout human history, as output has expanded to keep pace with the inexorable growth in the numbers of the human animal. But this form of growth did not permit a sustained rise in per capita income. That occurs only with intensive growth with output growing faster on a sustained basis than population. This—as much recent research, including my own, summarized in a book with Hla Myint called *The Political Economy of Poverty, Equity and Growth*—is the only way to deal with the mass structural poverty that has been humankind's fate in the past. For extensive growth merely provided a level of living not much above subsistence for the mass of humanity, from which particular individuals and whole societies could be periodically toppled by the four horsemen of the Apocalypse. When and how intensive growth has been generated is the central question of development economics, and it is a question to which I hope to provide some answers in these lectures.

There is considerable agreement among economists that the proximate causes of growth are allocative efficiency, the investment rate, and the rate of technical progress. Arthur Lewis, in his famous book *The Theory of Economic Growth*, notes that "the growth of output per head depends on the one hand on the natural resources available and on the other on human behavior.... The enquiry into human actions has to be conducted at different levels, because there are proximate causes of growth, as well as causes of these causes." In the Lal-Myint book we show that both the efficiency and level of investment are the proximate causes of growth in our sample of twenty-one developing countries whose economic histories between 1950 and 1985 formed the basis of the study. Furthermore, the policy regime was crucial in explaining the differences in the efficiency of investment. This is in consonance with the results of the cross-country econometric exercises that have proliferated in recent years, and that try to explain differences in growth rates in the set of countries for which Summers and Heston have put together comparable data for the 1950–1988 period. Thus Sala-i-Martin, commenting on the study by Levine and Renelt that surveyed these econometric exercises, notes that "Levine and Renelt always find some group of policy variables that matter. The problem is that since policies are so highly correlated with each other, the data cannot always tell them apart.... Hence the main message from the Levine and Renelt study is not that nothing matters, but that policy matters. The data cannot really tell exactly which policy is bad." In the Lal-Myint study we could, through our analytical economic histories, at least establish that the classical liberal economic package was conducive to intensive growth. But that pushes the question back to the next stage: Why have all countries not adopted these growth-promoting policies?

This took us into the realm of political economy, and we found that rather than the type of polity, the initial resource endowment, in particular the availability or lack of natural resources, was a major determinant of the political determinants of policies that impinged on the efficiency of investment and thereby the rate of growth. This was basically due to the inevitable politicization of the rents that natural resources yield, with concomitant damage to growth performance. In many cases we found that natural resources had proved to be a "precious bane," as they led to polities which tended to kill the goose that laid the golden eggs (see Chapter 9). Thus the resource-poor countries' economic performance tended to be much better, on average, than that of those with abundant natural resources.

But we had abstracted from cultural influences, which might explain why even within our broad natural resource-based grouping of countries, besides marked differences between the groups, in policy and performance, there was also significant intragroup variation. For example, although both Ghana and Thailand were land-abundant countries in our classification and did not have marked differences in the predatoriness of their polities, they adopted very different policies with dramatically different outcomes.

In these lectures I want to peel the onion explaining growth performance a bit further to see whether and in what way cultural influences might effect economic performance. But, as I shall soon argue, inasmuch as in many cases the cultural variables are subject to long hysteresis, to identify them and see if and how they might change we will often have to go back and trace their origins (*pace* the epigraph from Tocqueville). I found this in my previous foray into this treacherous field in my book on India, *The Hindu Equilibrium*. In these lectures I will be looking at the various influences on economic growth in the very long run—"la longue durée" of the Annales school of French historians, in which, as Braudel has so eloquently shown, "mountains, not monarchs ... come first."[5]

The interaction of factor endowments, culture, and politics in explaining when and why intensive growth occurred is therefore one of the major themes of these lectures. The other major theme is the role of individualism in promoting this growth, and the strange metamorphoses this in turn has caused when we look at the present day interaction between the West and the Rest.

Because economists are persuaded only by formal models, I should also state that the stories I will be telling can be put into four formal models. The factor-endowments story is based on Ester Boserup's model as formalized by Pryor and Maurer and by Locay; the political-economy story is in terms of the formalized model of the predatory state in my *Hindu Equilibrium*; the cultural story about the hysteresis of cultural beliefs is in terms of the dual preference model of Timur Kuran, which he has formalized; and the story about the evolution of institutions tying labor down to land is based on Domar's model of a labor-scarce economy. The Appendix provides brief outlines of these models with brief notes referring to the text to show how various aspects of my story can be fitted into these four frameworks.

1   On Culture

But what is culture? And are economists right to ignore it, in explaining human behavior? Becker and Stigler's manifesto "De Gustibus Non Est Disputandum," and Becker's statement that most aspects of human behavior "in a variety of contexts and situations" can be explained by "the combined assumptions of maximizing behavior, market equilibrium, and stable preferences, used relentlessly and unflinchingly, [which] form the heart of the economic approach" to human behavior, express these attitudes most bluntly.[1]

One way of looking at the difference between economists and sociologists on the role of culture is in terms of an aphorism cited by Jon Elster[2] that when studying a cattle herd structuralists (read sociologists) focus on the "the fence around the cattle," whereas individualists (read economists) focus on "the activity of the cattle within the boundary of the fence." Both are likely to be relevant, of course. But, in the case of human behavior, there is the added complication that the fence itself will have been constructed by "the cattle," and they can, if they choose, shift its alignment! On this more eclectic view, how cultural constraints effect human behavior would be relevant for studying economic performance.

Some economists, most notably Hayek, have seen the importance of the cultural correlates of a market economy as an important element in its functioning, with Hayek even arguing for a form of cultural evolution that has in an unplanned and unintended way led to a move from a Stone Age culture, with its sense of community and shared purpose, to a modern culture where there is respect for abstract rules, such as the rule of law, and "a detachment from communal, cooperative ends." Thus, in addition to the political conditions stressed by classical liberals such as Smith and Hume for the creation and sustenance of an open-market economy, Hayek also stresses the importance of this gradual evolution to a "new" cultural milieu; essentially through the working of the Invisible Hand. In contrast with the East Asian Confucianists, however, he would be on the side of the materialists, who believe that with the recent worldwide move from the plan to the market, the cultural and political correlates of Western market economies—democracy, respect for human rights, and some form of public-welfare system—will inescapably arise in the rest of the world, leading to the victory not just of the West's technology and market institutions but also of its ideology.[3]

The relative roles of factor endowments, culture, and politics in affecting the past and future of humankind comprise an even more highly contested field between other social scientists, historians, and even archaeologists.[4] In these lectures, I am hoping first to clarify these links; second, to see what, if anything, we can say about them on the basis of current research; and third, and most important, to determine if and, if so, how they have led to differences in the current wealth of nations, with some concluding speculations about the future.

Social Equilibria

But before I go any further, I need to define the three terms of my title more precisely. Relative factor endowments—of land, labor, and capital—as I hope to show, remain the most basic building block to explain many surprising outcomes, economic, cultural and political. They are, if you like, the DNA of the story I am going to tell. That is why I hope these lectures will be seen as appropriately honoring the social scientist, Bertil Ohlin, who first emphasized and rigorously demonstrated the importance of this building block, and how its interactions with technology and preferences explained an ancient and important aspect of human interaction—international trade.[5] But, like Ohlin, I would like to suggest that "differences in factor endowments, technology and preferences might be rooted in differences in climate, language, cultural and legal institutions."[6]

I can no longer skirt around a definition of culture. This is contentious.[7] As a first cut it is useful to use one by a leading sociologist and anthropologist Ernest Gellner. He says that "a culture is a distinct way of doing things which characterizes a given community."[8] This may seem too broad and hence meaningless to economists. For Douglass North[9] culture underpins the "rules of the game" in any society, and provides "the informal constraints on human interaction," which in a world of limited information and computational ability reduces the costs of such interaction. Moreover, these behavioral constraints are socially transmitted, "a form of transmission unlike genetic transmission, which does perpetuate acquired characteristics."[10]

But this is still too broad for my purposes. It may be useful, therefore, to see how ecologists view culture. They emphasize that, unlike other animals, the human one is unique because its intelligence gives it the ability to change its environment by learning. It does not have to mutate into a new species to adapt to the changed environment. It learns new ways of surviving in the new environment and then fixes them by social custom.[11]

This definition of culture fits in well with the economists' notion of equilibrium. Frank Hahn[12] describes an equilibrium state as one where self-seeking agents learn nothing new so that their behavior is routinized. It represents an adaptation by agents to the economic environment in which the economy "generates messages which do not cause agents to change the theories which they hold or the policies which they pursue." This routinized behavior is clearly close to the ecologists' notion of social custom, which fixes a particular human niche. On this view, the equilibrium will be disturbed if the environment changes, and so the human agents will—in the subsequent process of adjustment—have to abandon their past theories, as these would now be systematically falsified. To survive, they must learn through a process of trial and error to adapt to their new environment. We will then have a new social equilibrium, which relates to a state of society and economy in which "agents have adapted themselves to their economic environment and where their expectations in the widest sense are in the proper meaning not falsified."[13] This equilibrium need not be unique nor optimal, given the environmental parameters. But once a particular socioeconomic order is established, and proves to be an adequate adaptation to the new environment, it is likely to be stable, as there is no reason for the human agents to alter it in any fundamental manner, unless and until the environmental parameters are altered. Nor is this social order likely to be the result of a deliberate rationalist plan. We have known since Adam Smith that an unplanned but coherent and seemingly planned social system can emerge from the independent actions of many individuals pursuing their different ends and in which the final outcomes can be very different from those intended. All this, I hope, is uncontroversial.

Controversy arises as soon as we start distinguishing between beliefs relating to different aspects of the environment. I would like to distinguish between two major sorts: those related to ways of making a living, which will determine what anthropologists and archaeologists call the material forms of a culture; and those related to understanding the world around us and humankind's place in it which determine how people view their lives—its purpose, meaning, and relationship to others (*pace* the epigraph from Plato). The former are thus beliefs about the material world. I will label these *material* beliefs. The latter can most usefully be labeled *cosmological* beliefs, which is a more neutral term than the much-abused term "ideology."

The primacy of one or the other pole of this distinction has been fiercely contested by two warring factions we can call materialists and idealists. Marxists, with their distinction between the "infrastructure" and "superstructure," believe that the latter is determined by the former, as do many infected with Darwinism in the social sciences. Many anthropologists and sociologists believe exactly the opposite, and contemporary deconstructionists represent the apotheosis of the idealist view. As a good Hindu I naturally believe that the truth lies somewhere in between. But this, as I noted earlier, is likely to get me immediately excommunicated from the Chicago church as an economist.

To see why my middle position is a tenable one, consider the fact that two of the schools—Marxist and Chicago—share the belief that material interests, not ideas, influence human action and that ideas or "ideology" can be explained by interests. But here is the irony: Starting from the same point—the "brute facts" of interest—they end up with different ideologies. With identical materialist views, and access to the same historical facts, they come to diametrically opposed views about social reality.

Nature and Nurture

For the person in the middle this is hardly surprising, because as John Searle has shown in a brilliant book, *The Construction of Social Reality*, "social facts" are different from "brute facts" such as "that is Mount Everest." Brute facts, mainly concerning the physical world, are always there. They cannot be different just because we *say* they are something different. But social facts can be, inasmuch as they are a matter of human construction and interpretation. Moreover, even though, as emphasized by sociobiologists and evolutionary psychologists, in our biological makeup we share many similarities with other higher animals, there is one vital difference (Searle insists), between us and lions and apes, and that is *self*-consciousness, where the emphasis is on the uniqueness of the predicate qualifying the "consciousness," which of course we share with many animal species. The major and unique vehicle of this self-consciousness is language.[14] Just as the modern computer has similarities with the human mind, man is not a computer, and computers can never be human.[15] Similarly, though humans are like animals in many respects they are not *just* animals. In both cases, argues Searle, it is the unique self-consciousness of humans that makes the difference.

Moreover, the recent demonstration by evolutionary psychologists that there are many similarities in behavior between humans and the higher animals, which are explicable in Darwinian terms of serving the "selfish gene,"[16] does not imply that *all* aspects of human behavior particularly those based on our moral sentiments are purely determined by our genes. Such a claim would rest on Hume's famous naturalistic fallacy. This is accepted even by evolutionary biologists.[17] Evolutionary psychologists following Darwin maintain that although biology ensures that we are not *naturally* moral animals, unlike other animals we have the capacity, based on self-awareness, memory, foresight, and judgment, to lead a truly examined life. Hence, as Darwin claimed, humans are the only moral animal. "A moral being is one who is capable of comparing his past and future actions or motives, and of approving or disapproving of them," he wrote. "We have no reason to suppose that any of the lower animals have this capacity."[18] In fact, one of the major functions of cosmological beliefs is to provide social norms that make us moral animals *despite* our instincts. These norms are the essential cement of society, as will be dramatically apparent to any reader of William Golding's novel *Lord of the Flies.*

Evolutionary psychology, based on Darwinian principles, is currently unmasking the origins of these basic instincts.[19] There has been a long-standing dispute among philosophers and social scientists about their nature. Crudely put, there is the position championed by Rousseau that these instincts are healthy and that man is naturally good. It is society that has corrupted humans. They need to throw off its chains to lead the good life.[20] The alternative, much darker view of human nature is that of Hobbes, who saw the necessity of strong social constraints to prevent a "war, as if of every man, against every man" entailed by the social interactions of egotistical and aggressive human beings. What is emerging from evolutionary psychology is a more complex view in which both the darker Hobbesian and sunnier Rousseausque aspects of human nature commingle. It is close to that taken by the sages of the Scottish Enlightenment, Smith and Hume. In the latter's words, "there is some benevolence, however small ... some particle of the dove kneaded into our frame, along with the elements of the wolf and serpent."[21]

As Darwin conjectured, and recent research is confirming,[22] many of these instincts can be explained in terms of the "inclusive fitness" strategies of our thoroughly selfish ancestors, who lived for millennia in bands of hunter-gatherers.[23] Evolutionary psychologists claim that given the time scale of Darwinian processes of "inclusive fitness"—it takes about ten thousand years to produce a new species[24]—much of our current biological nature must have been determined in the distant past, in particular during the hunter-gatherer stage of our development in the Pleistocene.[25] Given the time scale involved in evolutionary processes, it is unlikely that natural selection has since markedly changed these instincts.

Even in the hunter-gatherer environment there were advantages in cooperation.[26] This would lead to some altruism—or sympathy, as Adam Smith called it[27]—even among these selfish beasts. Many of the other moral instincts have also been provided rationales as fruitful strategies to curb, detect, and punish defection in the strategic non-zero sum game of genetic competition with one's fellows, with whom cooperation in various tasks yields direct benefits; but even greater benefits accrue if one can cheat and be a free rider.[28]

These evolved basic instincts (including "reciprocal altruism") would, however, have been determined by repeated social interactions with one's fellows on a "face to face" basis in the hunter-gatherer band. The rise of settled agriculture and urban civilization would have enlarged the scope for opportunistic behavior, because of the relatively larger number of more anonymous social transactions entailed in civilized ways of living. An internalized moral code would then be needed, as individuals came to deal with a host of anonymous "strangers" on an occasional basis.[29] The evolutionary "tit for tat" strategy of supreme egoists, which works in the infinitely repeated prisoner's dilemma game underlying "reciprocal altruism," would not work in this new "one shot" prisoner's dilemma game. The cooperative gains that result from the increasing division of labor in a more complex civilization would not have been available without some mechanism for dealing with the increased potential for defection when social interactions became anonymous and sporadic.

The cosmologies of the ancient civilizations created internalized moral codes to prevent such defection (through, for example, moral prohibitions against our basic instincts to lie and cheat). This is now being recognized even by evolutionary psychologists.[30] Civilizations, through their cosmological beliefs, tamed our basic instincts, or, as Freud would say, repressed them.[31] They promoted "character" for the self-control of the baser instincts. Charles Darwin, Samuel Smiles, and John Stuart Mill in nineteenth-century Britain all realized and emphasized that these culturally acquired higher moral sentiments need to be cultivated against those darker dispositions genetically endowed to us by natural selection. "The truth," Mill wrote, "is that there is hardly a single part of excellence belonging to human *character*, which is not decidedly repugnant to the untutored feelings of human *nature*."[32]

Being based on evolutionary processes, human *nature* will be universal. *Character* will be particular, depending upon the varied processes of cultural socialization. Since the spread of settled agriculture and the emergence of urban civilizations, both nature and nurture will, thus, have determined individual behavior.[33] It is tempting to provide Darwinian explanations, too, for the varied culturally acquired aspects of "character." But it would be fallacious. For the Darwinian view of humans as "fitness maximizers" applies only to the slow-moving biological evolutionary processes. No teleological analogy is valid in explaining the behavior of humankind during the brief period of time that is our recorded history, and during which the processes of natural selection would have had insufficient time to operate.[34]

This is not to deny that functional explanations can be provided for many acquired cultural traits. Most are likely to have arisen with the growing division of labor allowing further gains from cooperation to accrue, even though biologically we are predominantly self-serving opportunists.[35] But over time, these cultural traits could have outlasted their utility. One cannot assume that some current cultural "trait" is functional just because it was so in the past. Cosmological beliefs could survive even when they no longer have any function because of the process of preference falsification (see Appendix).[36] Over time cosmological beliefs do change; we will come across examples in later chapters.[37] But they probably change at a slower rate than do what I have called material beliefs. The latter can change within a generation, as witness the spectacular material changes predicated on such changes in beliefs that have occurred in East Asia over the last thirty years. By contrast, there is likely to be greater hysteresis in cosmological beliefs,as witness the continuing rejection of Darwinian evolution by many intelligent religious people in the West.[38]

Different Social Equilibria

There are thus a number of different processes with their respective equilibria that could explain social outcomes. They can be distinguished by the period of time over which the equilibrating forces work. The quickest working is the market process of supply and demand, which leads to a market equilibrium. The second fastest are the processes leading to an equilibrium regarding material beliefs, which determine the organizational framework within which the market process operates (or, as in controlled economies, does not operate). Changing signals from the environment can alter such material equilibria within the lifetime of a generation. Slower moving are the cultural equilibria associated with cosmological beliefs. These would seem to require at least a generation or two to alter. Finally, there is the evolutionary equilibrium associated with the "selfish gene," which is the slowest-moving of all and for all practical purposes can be ignored in our investigations, except for its legacy on our minds.

Individualism and Communalism

If much of our evolutionary biological legacy can be crudely described as the egotistical individualism underlying parts of human nature, that of the culturally transmitted cosmological beliefs can equally crudely be described as communalist—promoting "brotherly love" among self-seeking opportunists.[39] We would therefore expect that during the period since the rise of the great Eurasian civilizations both "individualism" and "communalism" would be part of civilized man's character.

Some social psychologists have attempted a quantification of these traits and then examined their relative importance across different cultures. That there are marked differences is shown in the survey by Triandis.[40] One important finding is that the West is more individualist than the rest.[41] In this respect the West appears to be closer to many hunter-gatherer societies than to agrarian civilizations, which were primarily communalist.[42] But, inasmuch as the West, too, was initially a part of the ancient agrarian Eurasian civilizations, its current exceptionalism needs some explanation. Why and how this change took place and with what consequences will be a major part of the story that I will be retailing in these lectures.

The Emotions: Shame and Guilt

If the importance of cultural "traits" in the civilizing process is granted, we need also to briefly delineate the mechanisms whereby they are inculcated. There seems fairly general agreement about the role of the emotions in internalizing the "moral codes" embodied in cultural traditions.[43] But there seems to be no agreement whether these emotions are part of our evolved basic human nature or are themselves social constructs. By and large sociologists and anthropologists seem to take the latter view, whereas biologists and neuroscientists seem to take the former.[44] I cannot go into the merits of this dispute in these lectures, particularly as it is not germane to the main point I want to stress, namely that the emotions form an integral part in the socialization process—something on which there seems to be agreement among the warring factions. Ekman and Davidson, summing up this debate, note that "all agree that there is evidence of universality for emotions, that there is less evidence but some, for universals in the antecedents of emotions, and that biology and culture both play a role in accounting for these universals."[45]

Of these emotions, two are of particular importance for the development of a culturally acquired "moral sense." These are *shame* and *guilt*. Unlike the other emotions—disgust, sadness, anger, and fear—the antecedent events that trigger these emotions seem to differ across cultures.[46] For the other emotions there appears to be greater similarity between different cultures in the antecedent events prompting them. This is not surprising. As Ekman and Davidson note, "shame and guilt are emotions in which moral judgments are at issue, and might therefore be ones in which differences in cultural values might have more relevance."[47]

Though many—including Freud, but not Darwin[48]—have failed to note the difference between them, shame and guilt are very different emotions.[49] "Shame is the social emotion, arising as it does out of the monitoring of one's own actions by viewing one's self from the standpoint of others."[50] Or, as Bernard Williams, puts it, "the basic experience connected with shame is that of being seen, inappropriately, by the wrong people, in the wrong condition. It is straightforwardly connected with nakedness, particularly in sexual connections."[51] In shame the internalized figure for the emotion is "a watcher or witness, [in] the case of guilt, the internalized figure is a *victim* or an *enforcer*."[52] In the case of guilt, "the attitude of the internalized figure is anger, while the reaction of the subject is fear *at* anger, rather than fear *of* anger."[53] By contrast, "there is no need with shame that the viewer should be angry or otherwise hostile. All that is necessary is that he should perceive that very situation or characteristic that the subject feels to be an inadequacy, failing or loss of power."[54] Robinson Crusoe without Friday could not have felt shame, but if he believed in a Judeo-Christian God he would have felt guilt![55] Thus, we shall also be looking at the role of shame and guilt as socializing devices in various civilizations, for the internalized moral codes that form the cement of their societies are based on these moral sentiments.[56]

The Anthropological Record

It might seem natural to turn to the specialists in culture—the anthropologists—to answer questions concerning the relative influence of material and cosmological beliefs in effecting long-run economic performance. Unfortunately, most have been infected with idealism.[57] But I doubt if there are many outside sociology and anthropology who still maintain the purely idealist position that material culture is solely determined by ideas and ideology. In fact, there is some evidence from anthropology itself that can be used in support of the middle ground I am attempting to hold. Fredric Pryor[58] put together a database of sixty preindustrial societies scattered across the globe, using several variables found in anthropological studies. His statistical tests fail to confirm many of the idealist propositions about the economy. By and large, he found that cross-cultural differences in modes of production, distribution, and exchange could be satisfactorily explained by standard economic (that is materialist) variables.

Another source of cross-cultural data—the *Ethnographic Atlas* compiled by G. P. Murdock—has been used by both Jack Goody and C. R. Hallpike to test various hypotheses about culture.[59] Goody looks at various systems of marriage and inheritance, the differing status of women, and the differing complexity of the polity, across cultures, by distinguishing them primarily by their material base: the predominance of either hoe or plow agriculture. As economists steeped in the new household economics deriving from Becker's *Treatise on the Family* would expect, the economic determinants of these social customs are statistically significant.

There are a number of other "social" phenomenon of importance for development that can also be explained in materialist terms. Thus, the growing evidence on the economic determinants of the demographic transition[60] shows that even in these intimate matters concerning fertility, the materialist explanations outperform the idealist. Similarly, the rapid diffusion of the Green Revolution technology across a whole host of different peasant cultures attests to the universal power of what Sir John Hicks called the Economic Principle—namely, that "people would act economically; when the opportunity of an advantage was presented to them they would take it."[61]

Hallpike's statistical analysis further confirms the power of this economic principle in determining various aspects of material culture in his cross-cultural sample. He finds that "type of subsistence is an extremely reliable predictor of the degree of permanence"; "population density is

closely related to mode of subsistence; as is community size." But he also
finds that "the predictive value of economy becomes very irregular with
regard to household form, slavery, compactness of settlement, community
integration, (besides the importance of kinship for pastoralists), and community leadership. But many other variables emphasized by anthropologists are not correlated whilst some forms of social organization do
appear to be common."[62] This is hardly surprising. As Hallpike notes, the
data in the *Ethnographic Atlas* come from primitive societies in which "if
one has a simple subsistence economy, with only a few hundred people to
organize, the same few principles of residence, descent, marriage, leadership etc., will work in almost all of them."[63]

His most important claim from the anthropological record concerns
what I have called cosmological beliefs relating, for instance to illness and,
of course, religion. "Rather than ecology, it seems that historical relationships (often indicated by membership of a common language family) is a
more reliable predictor of social organization and religion.... It is often
possible to predict more about a society if we know its language group
than if we know its environment. This is ... because linguistic affiliation is
often good evidence that the societies in question share a common origin."[64] He then goes on to define a society's "core principles" as consisting of "certain rules and categories of a general nature [concerning social
organization], and [which] display a fair degree of internal consistency ...
as well as general cosmological categories.... A society's core principles
are therefore part of a total world view and not purely confined to the
forms of social organization."[65] On the basis of his own and other studies
he claims that "the evidence that societies have core principles is very
substantial. Cross-culturally, we constantly find that groups of societies
with common origins (as shown particularly in membership of the same
language family) share many basic features of organization and world—
view that cannot be explained on adaptive or functional grounds."[66]

This is echoed in Douglass North's account of the differing fortunes of
North and South America, despite the similarities in resource endowments. He lays these at the doors of their differing cultural and political
heritage, molded by sixteenth-century England in North America and by
fifteenth-century Spain and Portugal in South America.[67]

I hope I have now provided sufficient justification for my middle
ground between materialism and idealism. Both on the basis of the epis-
tomological argument given earlier and on the available cross-cultural
empirical evidence, it is clear that both material and cosmological beliefs
will govern human action. Moreover, because material beliefs are most

likely to reflect the economic principle, the material aspects of culture are likely to be rapidly adjusted to the changing material environment, whereas cosmological beliefs are not. Boyd and Richerson survey a large number of ethnographic studies[68] that show that a change in the ecological environment changes material culture but "cosmological beliefs" are more stable. As they put it, "An enormous amount of circumstantial evidence suggests that culturally transmitted traits are stable over time and in the face of changing environments."[69] If, moreover, Hallpike's claim that the language group (and hence) history is a better predictor of "world views" is correct, these cultural traits are only likely to change slowly, if at all, as the material environment changes.

Cosmology, Polity, Economy

But is this hysteresis in "core principles" or "ideologies" of any relevance for the economy, or is it merely an epiphenomenon? Not only the persistence but also the origins of these core principles—the "world view"—is of importance, as we shall see, because in some important cases they directly effect material beliefs and hence the economy, but, more importantly, they influence politics. Though there is a lot of politics that can be explained by the interaction of "personal interests" and hence material factors, an important element cannot: changes in political regimes.

A universal feature of polities is the ubiquitous predatoriness of the State. This merely reflects the necessary monopoly of coercive power and the inevitable maximization of net revenue that self-interested governors will then extract from their subjects. But this purely "interest"-based explanation—which I myself have advanced in the past (and will be using later in these lectures)—ignores one basic fact emphasized by Searle: the attitudes and beliefs of the governed.

The State itself is an institution, and hence a subclass of *social* fact. Unlike brute facts such as mountains, institutions are first of all social facts that, as Searle calls them, are "observer-relative." Unlike mountains, money or the State could not exist without human beings. Second, they are based on what he calls "collective intentionality."[70] Third, institutions are based on what he terms "constitutive rules." These are different from rules that regulate some activity that already exists.[71] Thus institutional facts are a subset of social facts. For both, unlike natural facts, the *attitude* we take constitutes the fact. Thus, as Searle writes of social facts as compared with natural facts, "Something can be a mountain even if no one believes it is a mountain; something can be a molecule even if no one thinks anything at all about it. But for social facts, the attitude that we take toward the phenomenon is partly constitutive of the phenomenon."[72]

These features of institutional facts imply that any State, no matter how tyrannical and predatory, must be based on some general acceptance by the populace of its legitimacy. For, as is evident from the dramatic events of 1989, the role of the military or police in maintaining the institutional structures of the State is greatly exaggerated. Ultimately, like other institutions, any State also depends upon general acceptance of its right to rule. "It is tempting," Searle writes,

> to think that there must be some rational basis for such acknowledgment, that the participants derive some game theoretical advantage or get on a higher indifference curve.... But the remarkable feature of institutional structures is that people continue to acknowledge and cooperate in many of them even when it is by no means obviously to their advantage to do so. When institutions are maintained largely by habit, they can collapse quite suddenly, as when people lose confidence in their currency or cease to recognize their governments as a government.[73]

These conjectures have recently been confirmed in theoretical models by economists,[74] most notably in an impressive book by Timur Kuran called *Private Truths, Public Lies*. He builds a model of preference falsification, where a person's utility depends upon both others' opinion of him or her as well as the traditional sources of his or her own intrinsic utility.[75] In the resulting dual preference model there are multiple equilibria: with a place for groups (the majority) who conform to existing "public" norms as well as for dissenters. But if for some reason there is a move from one of the existing "social" equilibria, then through a bandwagon effect opinion can shift swiftly to the diametrically opposite equilibrium. If these arguments are accepted, then we have a direct route between the society's world view and the polity.

In summary, factor endowments are likely to form an important basis of material culture. Given the operation of the universal economic principle in this sphere, adjustments to changes in the material environment are likely to be fairly swift. By comparison, changes in the other component of culture, cosmological beliefs, are likely to be slower moving and prone to sudden jumps. Both types of cultural views are likely to influence the polity, but world view is likely to be dominant.

What of the effects of the polity on the economy? I can be brief because a whole host of economic historians—for example, Hicks, North, Jones, Rosenberg and Birdzell—have seen the rise of the West, and the economic transformation it represented, as in part stemming from the political changes that accompanied the slowly rolling Industrial Revolution.

Briefly, these tied the hands of governments, stemming if not stifling their predatory instincts. Intensive growth followed. Jones, for one, believes that intensive growth was always bursting to bubble through but was snuffed out by the "rent seeking" of predatory states. Political changes in the West constrained this predatoriness and unleashed the unbound Prometheus that has transformed the world.

These political prerequisites of "capitalism"—as this new mode of production has been named—should, if our argument so far is correct, have had cultural prerequisites. This has been recognized, not least by Max Weber, but with little agreement on their content. I will be returning to some of these debates in the following chapters. But at this stage of my argument, all I hope to have established is that, despite the rival arguments of the fundamentalists on the materialist and idealist sides, given the epistemology of our world, we must take both interests and ideas into account in explaining human behavior. Or to put it differently, there is a general equilibrium system that determines the political and economic outcomes, in which factor endowments, the two components of culture, and the polity interact. In that sense, as we are used to in economics, everything depends upon everything else. But I have suggested that with changes in the material environment (factor endowments, technology, and trading opportunities, determined as much by political factors as changing costs of transportation), aspects of the material culture are likely to react more rapidly than those related to the cosmology, and *mutatis mutandis* of the polity.

In understanding both the past and the present, we therefore need to examine the history of both changes in the material environment and of cosmologies. But because the latter are characterized by considerable hysteresis, we need to go back a long way—at least with the ancient civilizations—to see how these world views arose, as well as their content and consequences for the economy.

The Ancient Civilizations I:
Egypt, Mesopotamia,
Judea

I am now going to take you in a gallop through human history. The purpose is to see if various cultural and political differences in the great civilizations can be explained in material terms or if we also have to bring in cosmological beliefs. I assume that most of the salient features of this history will be known to you. I will, however, pause to emphasize the differences in the material circumstances and the cosmological beliefs of the peoples I will be so hastily surveying, both to support the middle position between materialism and idealism and to develop the story of the determinants of intensive growth I promised at the outset.

Smithian and Promethean Growth

In thinking about intensive growth it is useful to distinguish between two types, as emphasized by the economic historian E. A. Wrigley.[1] He notes that until fairly recently sustained increases in per capita income could not be expected, inasmuch as most economies were agricultural, their growth ultimately bounded by the productivity of land. In such an economy there is a universal dependence on organic raw materials for food, clothing, housing, and fuel. Their supply in the long run is constrained by the fixed factor—land. This also applied to traditional industry and transportation, which depended on animal muscle for mechanical energy and on charcoal (a vegetable substance) for smelting and working crude ores and for providing heat. Thus, in an organic economy, once the land frontier is reached, diminishing returns will take their inexorable toll. With diminishing returns to land, conjoined to the Malthusian principle of population, a long-run stationary state where the mass of people languished at a subsistence standard of living seemed inevitable. No wonder the classical economists were so gloomy. Until the land frontier was reached there could be some extensive growth with both population and output growing at about the same rate, thereafter, the only remedy to prevent immiserization was some form of population control.

But even in an organic economy there was some hope of intensive growth, resulting in a secular increase in per capita incomes. The system of market "capitalism" and free trade outlined and defended by Adam Smith could increase the productivity of an organic economy somewhat over what it was under mercantilism. By lowering the cost of the consumption bundle, it could also provide a rise in per capita income, that is, intensive growth. But if this growth in popular opulence led to excessive breeding, the land constraint would ultimately result in a return to subsistence wages. Technical progress could hold the stationary state at bay, but the land constraint would ultimately prove binding.

The Industrial Revolution led to the substitution of this agriculture-based economy by a mineral-based energy economy. But this fundamental change was only becoming apparent toward the mid-nineteenth century in England, and it was not until Marx was writing that it had become manifest. This new economic regime substituted mineral raw materials for the organic products dependent on land. Coal began to provide most of the heat energy of industry and, with the development of the steam engine, virtually unlimited supplies of mechanical energy. This radically altered the prospects of raising per capita output.[2]

Thus the Industrial Revolution in England was based on two forms of "capitalism," one institutional, namely that defended by Adam Smith because of its productivity-enhancing effects, even in an organic economy, and the other physical: the capital stock of stored energy represented by the fossil fuels which allowed mankind to create a

world that no longer follows the rhythm of the sun and the seasons; a world in which the fortunes of men depend largely upon how he himself regulates the economy and not upon the vagaries of weather and harvest; a world in which poverty has become an optional state rather than a reflection of the necessary limitations of human productive powers.[3]

For much of history, until the rolling Industrial Revolution allowed a substitution of a mineral for an organic economy, the only hope of getting intensive growth was through the increasing division of labor associated with the capitalism of Adam Smith. This I label *Smithian* growth, as contrasted with the "technologically" based, more modern form I call *Promethean* growth.[4] The most likely engine of Smithian growth was an expansion in international trade on the lines outlined in the *Wealth of Nations*, and rigorously demonstrated by Ohlin and his successors.

But even if the prospects of intensive growth were not bright, extensive growth was ubiquitous. We clearly do not have any statistical evidence on the expansion of output keeping up with population, but assuming that, by definition, if the income level fell below subsistence the population would die off, it seems reasonable (as Eric Jones has argued)[5] to assume that where we have evidence for an expansion of population we can assume that extensive growth was occurring. Thus, at least for much of prehistory, world population history is our only source for estimating the extent of extensive growth during the premodern period.

Agriculture, Civilization, and Nomads

We begin our story before the last Ice Age, when our ancestors, who were hunter-gatherers, migrated from their ancestral home in the savannahs of Africa to all corners of the globe. They used the ice bridges that at that time linked all the continents, but that since the ending of the Ice Age have disappeared. This covers the period 100,000 B.C. to 10,000 B.C., when the ice cap melted. During this period McEvedy and Jones estimate that the human population more than doubled to about four million. This expansion of population (and the extensive growth it represented) was due to our hunter-gatherer ancestors' extending the range and limit of the area of human occupation. At the end of this period they had occupied all the world's habitable area in their land-extensive form of making a living. They had reached the land frontier of their type of subsistence economy. Further growth in numbers would mean higher human densities on land.

This increased population density propelled the move to agriculture, as Ester Boserup argues in her brilliant book *The Conditions of Agricultural Progress*: first slash and burn, then bush fallow, short fallow, and annual cropping to multicropping.[6] Each stage of greater intensification of agriculture allowed a greater population to be supported. Thus, at least in those parts of the world where ecological conditions allowed a move from the most primitive—slash and burn—to the most intensive—multicropping—the land frontier became endogenous, in the sense that a growing population could be accommodated by greater intensification. But even in these favored regions, such extensive growth would ultimately be limited by the fixed factor, land, whereas regions that were not so ecologically favored could only support smaller populations in more "primitive" forms of subsistence agriculture.[7]

From about 8000 B.C. settled agriculture spread with the domestication of plants and animals. Probably originating in the hills of northern Iraq or

Kurdistan, where the wild ancestors of wheat and barley grew naturally, it had by 6000 B.C. become established in the area from western Iran to the Mediterranean and across the Anatolian highlands to both sides of the Aegean Sea. It was based on cultivating wheat and barley and herding sheep, goats, pigs, and possibly cattle. It then gradually spread to Egypt, China, Western Europe, and other parts of the Old World.[8]

The invention of agriculture led to momentous changes in the life of humankind. The most important was the growth of ancient civilizations in the river valleys of the Tigris and Euphrates, the Nile, the Indus, and the Yellow. These civilizations were based on fairly intensive cultivation with annual cropping, usually requiring irrigation. A larger population than was previously imaginable could now be supported. This intensive form of irrigated agriculture also required labor cooperation in digging and diking. Civilized complexity developed from the agricultural surplus that was available to support specialists—kings and priests, for example— resulting in the stratification of society that, Gellner notes, is common to all settled agrarian civilizations with "their qualitative division between three orders of men, those who fight, pray and work."[9] Urbanization accompanied this social stratification, and the city (civitas) became the emblem of civilization.

From about 2000 B.C., the invention of the plow allowed civilization to spread to the rain-watered lands around the Mediterranean. In Boserupian terms, the plow permitted a shorter period of fallow than was possible with the slash-and-burn system of primitive agriculture, and thus agriculture developed on rain-fed lands, supporting a larger population than had previously been possible. Civilization, with its need for an agricultural surplus, could now spread beyond the ancient river valleys. This led in time to the emergence of the Greek world.

But there were other parts of the ancient world where the ecological conditions were not favorable for intensive agriculture: the grasslands of the great steppe regions of Eurasia, lying north of the ancient centers of civilization. Unable to practice slash-and-burn agriculture, given the paucity of trees, the hunters of this area, faced with the twin evolution of agriculture and the domestication of animals among their southern neighbors, found their environment particularly well suited to maintaining domestic herds of animals. They became nomadic pastoralists, herding cattle and later horses. Thus, unlike their more sedentary fellows in the emergent agrarian civilizations, these nomads kept a link with the hunter-gatherer past.

In the south of the civilized belt in the Near East in the Arabian peninsula, the ecology also did not permit settled agriculture. Again, pastoralism developed, but it was based on sheep and goats, which are able to
cope with the shortage of summer fodder in this semidesert.[10]

These pastoralists of the north and south, as much as the settled agrarian civilizations on which they preyed, were an essential part of the
dynamic process that has created the modern world. Like hunters, pastoralists depended upon herbivores and wandered over large distances in
search of grass for their animals. These had to be protected from both
other animals and humans. Their lifestyle required a chief who could
command the whole "tribe" and decide its marches. Thus unlike the early
sedentary farming communities which remained fairly peaceful, the pastoralists retained their warlike organizations and violent habits of big
game hunters. This gave them an inherent advantage in their military col-
lision with the farmers. As McNeill notes;

Indeed, pastoralists enjoyed so great an advantage that they were always tempted
to try to domesticate their fellow men by conquering and exploiting them as they
did their animals. The subsequent history of mankind in the Old World turned
upon an interplay between the superior numbers made possible by farming and
the superior politico-military organization required by pastoralism.[11]

The Ancient Near East

We cannot follow the rise and fall of the various Near Eastern empires of
early antiquity, often pressured by the barbarians from the north. But two
points in the history of ancient Mesopotamia and Egypt are worth noting
for my general thesis.

The first is the invention of writing in ancient Sumer around 3000 B.C.
This arose because the bureaucrat priests needed to keep accounts of the
surplus that was sent in to the city from the countryside, with its intensive agriculture. Here material aspects led to a vital higher cultural form.

The second concerns the differences in the types of centralized state
and the related "state" ideology in ancient Mesopotamia and Egypt.
These differences can again be traced back to differences in ecology—
namely material factors. Thus the Chicago scholar of preclassical antiquity, Henri Frankfort, noted in his book *Kingship and the Gods* that despite
superficial similarities the two civilizations differed fundamentally and
profoundly in their conceptions of kingship which both regarded as the
foundation of civilized life.

In Egypt the king was a god, in Mesopotamia merely a "great man":

In Egypt kingship entailed a mystic communion between two generations, between the living son, as Horus, and his dead predecessor, as Osiris. As a god, the king of Egypt had absolute power over the land and its people, yet he could not act arbitrarily and capriciously but only in accordance with *maat*, "right order".... In Mesopotamia ... though the king was considered divinely elected for his office, he had to grope his way through rites, dreams and omens in order to learn how to perform his royal duties.[12]

Both societies reflected the natural rhythms of the seasons in their festivals. But whereas in Mesopotamia they were imbued with a sense of anxiety, with the solemnities moving from deep gloom to exultation, in Egypt they merely reaffirmed that all was well with the world. This was because the Egyptians had a static view of the universe, believing that the cosmic order had been established at its creation.[13]

What accounts for these differences in cosmological beliefs (and thence the nature of the polity) in two of the earliest agrarian civilizations? Frankfort provides an answer in terms of differences in ecology. "This contrast in outlook," he writes,

is curiously in keeping with the physiographical differences between the two countries. The rich Nile Valley lies isolated and protected between the almost empty deserts on either side, while Mesopotamia lacks clear boundaries and was periodically robbed and disrupted by the mountaineers on its east or the nomads on its west. Egypt derived its prosperity from the annual inundation of the Nile, which never fails to rise, even if the floods differ greatly in effectiveness. But Mesopotamia is for much of its grazing, dependent on an uncertain rainfall and possesses in the Tigris an unaccountable, turbulent, and most dangerous river.[14]

Thus, Frankfort provides a material explanation for these differences in cosmologies—with both civilizations being concerned with maintaining life but with the Mesopotamians, accepting the inevitability of death, and concentrating on religious rituals to maintain life on earth by harmonizing it with nature. By contrast, the Egyptians, denying the reality of death, considered life to be everlasting. Humans survived even though the body decayed. But

notwithstanding these beliefs a "soul" could not be abstracted from the body, or rather, man's personality required both at all times; and to gain eternal life, man's surviving part should not be entirely dissociated from the seat of his identity, his body. Hence the rich development of Egyptian sculpture, hence mummification, hence, also, the equipment of the tomb with the necessities of life.[15]

If ecological differences account for these different cosmologies of the two ancient Near Eastern religions, they can also explain that of the third major Near Eastern religion, which has had an even longer life, and (as we shall see) has changed the world—Judaism. The nomadic people who inhabited the borders of civilization, had a third form of kingship which differed from that of the ancient Egyptians and Mesopotamians. This type of polity, as Frankfort notes, "is found among people who acknowledged kinship above every other bond of loyalty and whose coherence derived from a shared nomadic past rather than from what they had achieved as a settled community."[16]

The Hebrews cosmological beliefs were formed in a kingless period when they claim that Jehovah singled them out as the chosen people as a result of Moses' Covenant of Sinai. Their god was a transcendent god who had primacy over any earthly powers. The tribes accepted a king only under exigency. When Ammonite oppression was added to the Philistine menace, the people said, "Nay, but we will have a king over us, that we may also be like all the nations; and that our king may judge us and go before us and fight our battles."[17] Thus where kingship was a function of the gods in Egypt and a divinely ordained political order in Mesopotamia, for the Jews it was an imitation of these others that they themselves had introduced to deal with an emergency.[18] Thus, unlike the kings of the Egyptians and the Mesopotamians, the Hebrew king lacked sanctity. "This relationship with his people was as nearly as secular as is possible in a religious society. Nowhere else in the Near East do we find this dissociation of a people from its leader in relation to the divine." [19]

Two other features of the Hebrew religion were distinctive. Unlike the other people of the region, who had all inherited polytheistic pantheons, the Hebrews developed a transcendental monotheism. According to McNeill, given their history, which itself was influenced by their nomadic past and the geography of the region in which they lived,

monotheism seemed the only [logical] ... explanation in a world in which distant monarchs and unforseeable events originating hundreds of miles away profoundly affected local affairs. In such an age, religious localism no longer accorded with commonsense and everyday experience. Traditional rites rang hollow; only the Hebrews were able to give full expression to the widely felt need for religious universalism. Their definition of ethical monotheism constituted therefore one of the greatest and most enduring achievements of ancient Middle Eastern civilization.[20]

The second important portent for the future was the codification of the Hebrew scriptures into the books of the Old Testament before the fall of

Jerusalem in 587 B.C. This had profound effects. With the subsequent exile of the Jews among many alien peoples, their belief that they were the chosen people, and most importantly their Book, allowed them to retain "the full belief in their religion, reinforcing their hopes by pondering the promises of the holy texts. Religion was thus separated from locality."[21] This was to have profound effects for the world, as we will see.

3

The Ancient Civilizations
II: India and China

We now move on from the Near East, where the first civilizations were founded, to the other great civilizations in India and China. In time, great civilizations also developed autonomously in Mesoamerica and Peru. I will not be discussing them, partly because of my limited knowledge of them, but most important because in Oswald Spengler's words these were "assassinated civilizations" that despite their past glories no longer influence our world in any great measure. Neither will I deal with Africa. This is largely because despite the emergence of a number of African empires with their own distinctive civilizations over the centuries, African economies were never able to generate a sufficient agricultural surplus to allow the social and economic differentiation that has been a hallmark of the Eurasian civilizations. This was largely due to the fragility of the region's soils, which did not permit the adoption of the plow over the hoe and thence the transformation of shifting to settled agriculture.

So I turn to the two great ancient civilizations, the Indian and Chinese, which together with the Western and its close cousin the Islamic have continued to influence the minds and hearts of humans to the present. Together, the people living in the homeland of the Indian and Chinese civilizations comprise over 2 billion of the world's 5.3 billion inhabitants. This does not take account of the substantial diaspora from both India and China, whose cultural beliefs are still largely governed by their parent civilizations.

India

The first civilization in India[1] was built on the floodplain of the Indus valley. It was in full flower by about the beginning of the third millennium B.C. Little is known about the beliefs of this civilization because, to date, the Indus script has not been decoded. Like the Mesopotamian, it relied on the annual inundation of the great river and used flood defenses in the form of burnt-brick walls. It was an urban civilization, dependent on the surplus of a flourishing agriculture, as is attested to by the existence of granaries in its cities.

By about 1500 B.C. the Indus civilization had disintegrated for reasons that still remain obscure. Various tribes, less similar in their ethnic origins than in the common origin of their languages in the Aryan (Indo-European) speech group, started migrating from the northwest passes into what is now Punjab. These were the "Aryan speaking peoples" whose gradual progress across the length and breadth of India led to their gradual evolution from seminomadic cattle-breeding pastoralists into settled agriculturalists, who gradually established another urban civilization (initially) in the Indo-Gangetic plain. In this process they evolved the caste system, which has provided the basic social framework for the daily lives of the people of the subcontinent, now called Hindu. It has survived innumerable foreign invasions—from the barbarians from the north and most recently by sea in the south—internal turmoil, colonization, and economic vicissitudes, so much so that after over two thousand years it still remains of vital importance in understanding the society and politics of India.

The Hindu Social System

The three pillars of the Indian social system were the relatively autarkic village communities, the caste system, and the joint family. It was a decentralized social system that did not require either a centralized political power or a church for its perpetuation. The village communities were not completely autarkic, but their trading links were fairly localized.

The social system consisted of numerous endogamous hierarchically ranked occupations, and often region-specific subcastes (jatis). These were subsumed under the fourfold varna classification, under which there were four broad varnas (castes): Brahmins (priests), Kshatriyas (warriors), Vaishya (merchants), and Shudra (workers and the rural peasantry). Although this scheme is usually identified as the caste system, it merely provided the broad theoretical framework for Hindu society. The interweaving of the hierarchically arranged subcastes were the real fabric of the Indian caste system. These subcastes were based on occupational specialization, but mobility was possible and did occur within the intercaste or intracaste status hierarchy. This vertical mobility was dependent on the whole caste's moving up the social hierarchy. This was usually done by adopting a different occupation, possibly migrating to a new region and demanding a higher ritual status. The very complicated vertical hierarchy of castes also made it easier to absorb new ethnic groups who arrived in successive waves throughout Indian history. Their place in the social hierarchy was determined partly by their occupation and sometimes by their social origins.

I have argued in *The Hindu Equilibrium* that this system arose as the Aryan response to the problem of securing a stable labor supply for the relatively labor-intensive agriculture they came to practice in the Indo-Gangetic plain. Given the ecological circumstances of this large plain (once the primeval forests had been cleared during the Aryan advance), and the primitive forms of transport then available, a major constraint on achieving a political solution for the provision of a stable labor supply, was the endemic political instability among the numerous feuding monarchies. The large, rich, geographically homogenous Indo-Gangetic alluvial plain formed a natural "core area," in Eric Jones's sense, for an Indian state. But given the plain's size and the available military and transport technology, its domination by a single state has been episodic. Though the lodestone of every petty Indian chieftain has been the establishment of a subcontinental empire, these centripetal tendencies have been counterbalanced by the centrifugal forces flowing from geography, and by the ensuing difficulties of communication in holding the subcontinent together.

This endemic political instability meant that various alternative methods of tying down the scarce labor (relative to land) needed for the labor-intensive form of plow agriculture on the plains were not available, such as slavery, poll taxation, indenture, or limitations on migration. For these required the power of a centralized state and its attendant bureaucracy for enforcement. As Domar argues in his theoretical model of slavery, free labor, free land, and a nonworking upper class cannot coexist; of these, any two, but not all three, can coexist. Hence the need to tie down the laborers (see Appendix 4).[2]

The caste system provided a more subtle and enduring answer to the Aryans' problem of maintaining their rural labor supply. It established a decentralized system of control that did not require any overall (and larger) political community to exist for its survival, and it ensured that any attempt to start new settlements outside its framework would be difficult if not impossible. The division of labor by caste and its enforcement by local social ostracism were central to the schema.

The endogamous specialization of the complementary services required as inputs in the functioning of a viable settlement meant that, any oppressed group planning to leave a particular village to set up on its own would find—if it were confined to a single caste group—that it did not have the necessary complementary skills (specific to other castes) to start a new settlement. They would need to recruit members of other complementary castes to join them in fleeing the Aryan settlement. This would have been unlikely. For some of these other complementary castes would already have a high ritual and economic status, with little incentive to move to the more uncertain environment of a new settlement.

Neither could the oppressed lower castes (or individuals in them) acquire the requisite complementary skills themselves and thereby overcome the difficulty of putting together the required coalition to form a new settlement from within a single oppressed caste. This was unlikely to happen because of the social ostracism embedded in the caste system. It would not be profitable for other groups to impart the knowledge of these complementary skills, inasmuch as the ostracism involved in breaking the caste code, either as a consumer or producer (at each level of the caste hierarchy) would entail higher costs than any gains from performing any profitable arbitrage in the labor market that breaking the castewise segmentation of labor might entail.[3]

Moreover, through the process of "preference falsification" modeled by Kuran (see Appendix), the system could continue even in the presence of "hidden dissent." For the system discourages open protests and disagreements; it uses open voting rather than secret ballots at meetings of caste councils to resolve disputes; and it has sanctions against disagreements with the judgment of these councils. Thus a climate of opinion could be maintained that made it virtually impossible for dissenters to reveal themselves and thereby organize caste-breaking coalitions.

Though the labor scarcity that led to this decentralized system of social control had disappeared in the Hindu heartland by the time of independence, the caste system was only slowly undermined, largely under the aegis of democratic elections, but accompanied by much casteist violence. The recent ascent of a leader of the "untouchables" to the chief ministership of Uttar Pradesh is a sign that demography and politics may at last be undermining this ancient Hindu social system, which has provided the cultural stability of the subcontinent for millennia.

The other decentralized element of the Hindu sociopolitical system was the ancient tradition of paying a certain customary share of the village output as revenue to the current overlord, which meant that any new political victor had a ready and willing source of tribute already in place. Given the endemic political instability, the caste system's vocational segregation meant that war was a game for the professionals, which saved the mass of the populace from being inducted into the deadly disputes of their changing rulers. For the latter, however, the ready availability of revenue from the customary local arrangements greatly reduced the effort required to finance their armies and courts. The village communities, for their part, bought relative peace and quiet and could carry on their daily business more or less undisturbed by the continuing aristocratic conflict.

In modern India the resilience of the system of democracy introduced by the British partly reflects these ancient attitudes, with the ballot box providing a less deadly arena for conflict than the battlefield for India's political classes. And the people accept with an ancient resignation that the politicians will take a fixed share of the national income for their own aggrandizement.

It is worth noting, for my present purposes, that one of the supporting pieces of evidence about the labor control-mediated explanation for the caste system was the contrast between the polities and cosmologies of the monarchies of the Indo-Gangetic plain and the republics in the Himalayan foothills in ancient India. The latter's ecology was unsuitable for the development of the labor-intensive agriculture of the plains. Because of geographical barriers, they could also form small natural states. This meant that the ancient tribal traditions of the migrant Aryans, as embodied in the popular assemblies (the "sabha" and "samiti") could be maintained in the foothills, whereas a form of sacral monarchy legitimized by God's intermediaries, the Brahmins, became the common political form among the feuding monarchies in the plains.

Moreover, these republics occupied less fertile hilly ground. The clearing of the foothills and the subsequent system of agriculture practiced thereon was probably based on bush fallow, which would require less labor per acre than the form of cultivation on the plains. They would not need the social control mechanisms of the caste system for their economy. It is not a mere coincidence, therefore, that these republics provided the strongest resistance to the caste-based society developing in the plains. The leaders of the two most important anticasteist religious movements in India—Buddhism and Jainism—were from the republics in the foothills. These sects also provided the vehicle for social escape for the mercantile classes, which had prospered with the growth of trade and commerce in the sixth to fourth centuries B.C. But the economic power of this Vaishya caste was not matched by political power, which was held by the two upper "varnas" of priests and warriors. The rise of the heterodox sects provided them and others oppressed by the caste system with an avenue of escape.

The resulting conflict between tribe and caste and between caste and sect was not settled until the fourth century A.D., when Samudra Gupta destroyed the Licchavi republics and caste triumphed over tribe and sect. Subsequently, until the modern era there was nothing to challenge this social system, which seemed so attuned to the ecological and political circumstances of the subcontinent.

Along with caste and village community, the third pillar of the Indian social system was the joint family, which maintained a close link between brothers, uncles, cousins, and nephews, often living under one roof or group of roofs, and who jointly owned the immovable property of the family. The family, not the individual, was the basic unit of the social system.[4] The dead and the living were linked together through the annual rite of commemorating ancestors, *shradha*, which, as with ancestor worship in China, was a most potent force in consolidating the family.[5] Partition of a large joint family was allowed by the ancient law codified by Manu, with property being divided among the sons, who would then set up their own joint family units. Wills did not exist in ancient India. The eldest son also received no special inheritance, except sometimes a very small weightage of about one-twentieth of the share.[6] The Hindu legal system was hierarchical and holistic. Over time,

apart from the *dharmashastras* (law books), local customs and royal decrees modified the contextual significance of the socially operative legal norms.... Despite these regional and contextual variations the particularistic and hierarchical nature of the Hindu legal system persisted. It continued to be group-oriented and non-egalitarian or ascriptive instead of being individual-oriented and universalistic. The impact of the Muslim culture and administration did not bring about any basic change in the qualitative nature of this legal system.[7]

It was the British Raj, particularly in its pre-Mutiny reforming zeal, which introduced various legal innovations that overturned traditional Hindu law, based as they were on the principles of universalism, rationalism, and individualism.[8] But personal laws, relating to the family, marriage, divorce, adoption, joint family guardianship, minority, legitimacy, inheritance, succession and religious endowments,[9] were largely left untouched.[10] It was only after independence that legal reform of personal and family law picked up where Governor General Bentinck left off. Untouchability was outlawed; bigamy became punishable; divorce, inter-caste marriages, and widow remarriage were permitted; and widows and daughters were given shares in ancestral immovable property. The administration of Hindu temples and monasteries was radically altered by legislation.[11]

Two aspects of this legal modernization under Western influence are of importance for our purpose. The first is that in contrast with the ancient Indian tradition, the British under Cornwallis introduced the novel idea of the separation of the judicial and executive functions of government. "The sociological significance of this system was that even the governmental executive decisions were now contestable in civil courts, thus providing a foundation for *the rule of law* and right of liberty and justice."[12] This has been of profound significance, insofar as it has allowed democracy to flourish, and also despite corruption and the law's delays, a Western legal tradition governing commerce and contracts has taken root. Also unlike many other colonialists, the British powers, since Macaulay's famous minute, encouraged and promoted Western education among their subjects. The legal profession that was created to run the new legal system was largely indigenous and has provided the internalized ballast in the Indian polity to the siren voices from the past.

The second aspect of the westernization of the ancient Indian legal tradition was that, with its emphasis on "equality in the eyes of the law, judicial ignorance of complainants, the ideal that economic relations are based on contract not status, the goal of settling the case at hand and only in that case, and the necessity of a clear-cut decision rather than compromise,"[13] meant that the twin traditional values of hierarchy and holism were undermined. Hierarchy was abolished as the new legal norms disregarded any distinctions based on caste. Holism, whereby the traditional recognition of the Hindu household, clan, subcaste, and caste as social units was undermined when the individual became the only recognized unit in the new legal and administrative system.[14] But it has taken a long time for the potential this created for social egalitarianism to be actualized. Cohn's observation in the 1950s that despite the fact that lower classes at the village level have become more conscious of their legal rights, their attempts to enforce them through the courts have been rarely successful, is sadly still a feature of Indian justice. But the legal infrastructure is in place, and this is in marked contrast to the other ancient civilization—China.

Has this legal modernization, and creeping industrialization and westernization also damaged the traditional joint family system of the Hindus? It is a commonplace of the Western sociological literature (as also of Chicago "household economics") that with industrialization and modernization the extended or joint family associated with agrarian, preindustrial societies will be replaced by the conjugal or nuclear family.[15] India to date belies this prediction, even in the urban areas where modernization and Westernization has been more extensive.

In assessing this continuity, it is important to note that the residential criterion which is commonly used to chart the changing fortunes of the "nuclear" and "joint" family is ambiguous. Thus, as Goody notes, this ambiguity is illustrated by the fact that although members of many so-called "joint undivided families" reside in "nuclear families" their property interests remain "joint" (undivided).[16] Singh notes,

what matters most is not the composition of the residential family group but the nature and quality of social interaction emanating from the supposedly nuclear family which interlinks its sentimental bonds, ritual and economic obligations to other family units in the same place or in other places which too maybe nuclear as [a] residential group but functionally maybe joined in obligational ties with this nuclear family.[17]

Studies by Desai, Kapadia, Kolenda, and Shah support Srinivas's[18] conclusion that despite significant changes in the family system, particularly of the Westernized urban elite group, "it would be a gross oversimplification to suggest that the Indian family system has changed or is changing from the joint to the nuclear type."[19]

Economic Stagnation and the Boserupian Process

Unlike the case of China, we do not have historical records to base any explicit quantitative judgments about the standards of living resulting from this socioeconomic system. There is only inferential evidence about Indian standards of living before the modern era. My summary of it in *The Hindu Equilibrium* concluded that there seems to have been stagnation of per capita income from about 300 B.C. up to the modern era. India thus probably reached a "high level equilibrium trap" during the reign of the Mauryas, who created the first pan-Indian empire and established the first centralized bureaucracy in India. As in the Abbasid Middle East and Sung China much later, this political and ideological unification of the subcontinent could have spurred a period of Smithian intensive growth. We have no hard evidence for this conjecture compared with the firmer evidence we do have for intensive growth in later civilizations. But if reports like those of the Greek traveler Megasthenes, who spoke of India's fabulous wealth, and of subsequent visitors like the Chinese pilgrim Huan Tsiang

(A.D. 606–47) are accurate, India must have attained a standard of living higher than other civilizations of the time well before the beginning of the Christian era. Moreover, if Maddison's estimate that "India's per capita income in 1750 was probably similar to that in 1960, at about $150 at 1965 U.S. prices"[20] is correct, this stagnation was at a fairly high level for "organic" economies, and higher than contemporaneous economies for millennia. It was this relative economic success that, I hypothesize, maintained the Hindu equilibrium.

But as population expanded from an estimate of 100 million in 300 B.C. to 125 million in A.D. 1600 and 300 million by 1911, clearly extensive growth on Boserupian lines was taking place. Some support for this is provided by cross-sectional evidence on the state-level differences in output per acre and average farm size.[21] If the Boserupian process were operating, one would expect to find the states arrayed along a curve described by a rectangular hyperbola—the "Ishikawa curve,"[22] as I called it after the economist who discovered it in his studies of Asian agriculture. These are reproduced as figures 3.1 and 3.2. It can be seen that most Asian countries and most Indian states, apart from Haryana and Punjab (for the time periods represented), seem to be crawling up the Ishikawa curve, much as Boserup's theory would predict. By contrast, the Indian states of Punjab and Haryana, which pioneered the technologically driven "Green Revolution," have clearly broken through this Boserupian mold.

I could find no evidence, despite nationalist hagiography, that there were any prospects for indigenous Promethean growth emerging in medieval India, growth supposedly blocked by British colonialism. In fact, it was under British aegis that India became one of the pioneers of industrialization in the Third World. But because of the ancient animus against trade and commerce and longstanding Brahminical attitudes against the market, this early promise has still not been fulfilled. We take up this more modern story in Chapter 7.

Cosmological Beliefs

But we also need to examine the cosmological beliefs that underpinned the Hindu social system. Two features of the social system and the "core principles" it embodied are worth noting. First is the disjunction between power and status; second is its notion of salvation. The first is obvious, given that the Brahmin (priest) was hierarchically placed above the Kshatriya (warrior). However, we need to look more closely at the second principle.

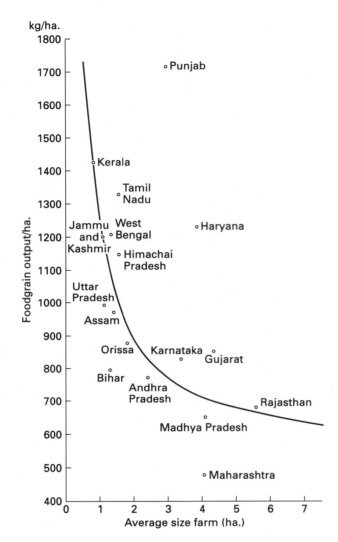

Figure 3.1
Ishikawa curve, India, 1970–1971

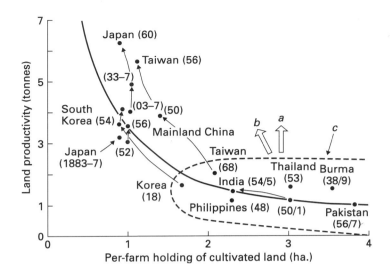

Figure 3.2
Relations between land productivity and per-farm cultivated area, selected Asian countries

Notes:

1. Land productivity is defined in this figure as (per-crop-ha. yield of paddy) × (multiple cropping index).

2. Circle c indicates the location of countries with per-crop-ha. yield of paddy less than 2.3 tonnes.

Source: Ishikawa 1967, p. 78.

For a self-conscious animal, the fact of death needs some explanation, as does humankind's place in the world—which essentially means our relationship to nature. From trying to answer these metaphysical questions, different religions were born. The sociologist of religion Bryan Wilson notes:

The explicit and manifest function of religion is to offer men the prospect of salvation and to provide them with appropriate guidance for its attainment.... Man has conceived of salvation in a wide variety of ways. Sometimes it has been culturally phrased as triumph over death ... [as in] Christianity.... In other cultures, death is regarded as not so romantic an event, and salvation is sought rather than the evil prevalent in earthly life [as in Hinduism].... In less developed religions, salvation may in practice be very much more narrowly conceived, perhaps simply as the curing of disease, or the elimination of witchcraft.[23]

He then distinguishes between the *spiritual* conceptions of salvation— for which no empirical proofs are needed—and *particularistic* conceptions

in which specific help is sought—cures; protection; temporal well being. Though
Hinduism does have the elaborate spiritual conception of the Vedas and Upa-
nishads, for most Hindus given the elasticity of belief allowed it is the particularistic aspects of the religions which impinge on daily life. It is the immanentist
rather than transcendental religiosity which has been the practical religiosity of
the Hindus. (Ibid., p. 73)

Gods coming down to work their miracles still form a part of the daily
beliefs of Hindus—as witness the worldwide hysteria recently surrounding the feeding of milk to statues of the god Ganesh, who then seemed to
drink it.

It was not what a man believed but what he did (following his or her
"dharma") that determined what he would be in his next reincarnation. Best of all, he could escape the endless cycle of rebirth and attain
"moksha"—the Buddhist nirvana. Most of these "right actions," moreover,
were based on rituals. They were in the social world. But at the same time
the "core principles" allowed a form of individualism. The renouncer who
went off into the forest (away from the mundane world) could directly
seek "moksha." We shall observe this "otherworldly" individualism, as
Dumont[24] calls it, in the origins of Western civilization. Most important,
unlike, for instance, the Chinese, the Hindu's salvation was always personal. Through carrying out dharma in the mundane social world, the end
was *personal* salvation; in this the Hindu conception had more in common
with the Western world than the Sinic, as we will see.

But this "individualism" was not of the type now associated with the
West. As Gellner has pointedly noted, Western individualism is incon-
ceivable in Hinduism. He tries to picture a Hindu Robinson Crusoe, a
polyglot called Robinson Chatterjee. "A Hindu Crusoe," he writes,
"would be a contradiction. He would be destined for perpetual pollution:
if a priest, then his isolation and forced self-sufficiency would oblige him
to perform demeaning and polluting acts. If not a priest, he would be
doomed through his inability to perform the obligatory rituals."[25]

One final cultural aspect of importance is the process of socialization,
which is required to provide the essential cement of society. The major
form this takes is through child-rearing practices. Werner has provided
considerable evidence that "differences between societies in presumably
long-standing, traditional child-rearing practices have substantial effects
on the cognitive capabilities and social behavior of children and adults."[26]
One of the major functions of religious traditions has been to provide a
moral conscience. A major difference between the process of socialization
(and the inculcation of an internalized morality) in the Eastern religions

and the Semitic ones is that it is based on *shame* rather than *guilt*. Indian society has always been a "shame" society, and continues to be one.[27] As we will see in Chapter 9 this has very important consequences when we examine the effects of culture on the economy today.

China

It is time to turn to the other ancient civilization that continues to our day, the Sinic. Again we first examine how the material conditions altered. This is the story in terms of factor endowments. We then outline the "core principles" that underlay the culture and polity that emerged.

The Material Base

Chinese civilization began with the rise of agriculture at about the same time as in western Asia. It arose in the Yellow River valley in the north, where from around 6000 B.C. millet was grown on the well-drained lowest terraces of the river valleys.[28] Later rice cultivation spread from its heartland in Southeast Asia. Early dynasties gave way to the Shang, which ruled much of the North China plain and parts of the Yangtze Valley from the sixteenth to the eleventh centuries B.C. Great cities arose. Subsequently empires rose and fell, sometimes with intervening periods of warring states and also anarchy. There was the constant threat of encroaching barbarians from the nomadic steppes to the north. But, when they did intrude, the barbarians were quickly sinified. So a distinct and self-contained culture developed.

Until the collapse of the Han dynasty (206 B.C.–A.D. 220), the material basis of this culture was dry farming based on millet.[29] Large-scale migration of Chinese settlers into the Yangtze River valley began during the fifth and sixth centuries A.D. At first the land was cleared by fire, flooded, and then abandoned. But, gradually, settled farming developed with wet-rice cultivation. This was accompanied by the development of new tools, crop rotations, and new kinds of seeds. Wet rice required a radically different technology from the dry farming in the north. Well before the fourteenth century this new rice technology was fully developed and adopted in all the rice regions of the country. Thereafter, for the six centuries following the founding of the Ming dynasty in A.D. 1368 there were few improvements in these techniques.[30]

With the opening up of the Yangtze Valley, "extensive growth" on Boserupian lines followed. Once the land frontier was reached, per capita food availability remained roughly constant, with rising labor intensity of cultivation, and hence rising output per acre as the population per acre rose. Perkins's detailed history of Chinese agriculture explicitly makes this claim.[31] Like India, China from a much earlier date has traveled up the Ishikawa curve with rising population. "Between 1400 and 1800 China's population rose six-fold from over 65 million persons to about 400 million. . . . The average rate of increase over the four centuries was 0.4–0.5 percent per annum."[32] With per capita income stagnant, from about 1400 until the modern era there was thus modest extensive growth propelled by growth of population.

However, there was a period in China under the Sung in the eleventh century when China had intensive growth, and for the first time population exceeded 100 million. But by the fourteenth century the population was the same size (65 million) as at the end of the Han dynasty (A.D. 220). The drop in population between the twelfth and thirteenth centuries was due to Mongol depredations. The Mongol armies sacked most of North China and parts of the south. Apart from large numbers put to the sword, the destruction of crops and granaries led to further deaths from starvation and disease.[33]

The intensive growth under the Sung was fueled first and foremost by the agricultural revolution that followed the expansion into the southern lands in the Yangtze River valley, and the development of the new wet-rice technology. This was disseminated widely all over China under government sponsorship through manuals utilizing the earlier invention of woodblock printing.

The new technology was fairly labor intensive, and, as in Hindu India, there was the need to tie relatively scarce labor to the greatly expanded area of potential arable land. Medieval Europe also faced this problem when its economic center of gravity shifted from the Mediterranean as the northern forests were cleared. But the technologies differed in the two areas, with the symbols of the advance in Europe being "the axe, the improved plough and efficient horse-harness, in China they were the dam, the sluice-gate, the noria (peripheral pot-wheel) and the treadle water-pump."[34] In both cases the manor provided the institutional solution.

But Chinese manorialism, with rural labor tied down in a form of serfdom, differed profoundly from its European counterpart. This was due to differences in the polity. In politically fragmented medieval Europe, a decentralized feudal system based on fealty and vassalage arose. The associated rights and obligations gave a distinctive degree of autonomy to the various actors in the polity and economy which greatly facilitated the subsequent rise of the West. By contrast, China maintained its centralized imperial unity. The distinctive feature of this "manorialism without feudalism," as Elvin dubs it, was that there was no separate and specialist military class (*regime feodale*) with virtually independent fiefs granted in exchange for military service as in Europe, because the Chinese imperial state retained its control over defense. This was because, unlike the much weaker Western European states that arose after the fall of the Roman empire, the Chinese state had enough of its own resources to provide a centralized defence. Nevertheless, manorialism siphoned off enough wealth to seriously weaken the imperial administration, and this, Elvin argues, explains the paradox of "the astonishing power of the Sung state, and its equally astonishing incapacity to survive unconquered."[35]

The manorial system survived with declining vigor from the Ming (1368–1644) to the earlier part of the Ching (or Manchu) dynasty and was displaced by a new and distinctive rural order. "The landlord and the pawn-broker took the place of the manorial lord; financial relationships displaced those of status."[36] Though Elvin does not give this causal significance, he does note that this decline was associated "with the tremendous demographic upsurge which took the Chinese population from over 200 millions in 1580 to about 410 millions in 1850."[37] With unchanged agricultural techniques and little or no expansion in the cultivated area, this population expansion would have led to a substantial increase in the ratio of labor to land. From being scarce the increasingly abundant labor would no longer need to be tied down to the land, as in medieval times. The frequent serf uprisings, the declining attractiveness of land as an investment,[38] and the lack of primogeniture, with equal inheritance among male heirs, led to the fragmentation of large estates. By the beginning of the nineteenth century, the Chinese countryside had become predominantly a world of small-landowners.[39]

Thus the interactions of changing factor endowments with technology can provide an explanation of changing rural institutions, as in India (and as has been done for medieval Europe). But in all three cases, the problem of tying scarce labor down to the land was dealt in very different ways, mainly due to differences in the polity. These differences in turn were partly the result of the different ecological—geographical—circumstances in the three areas. So far, in the Chinese case "materialism" seems to provide an adequate explanation for both its premodern economy and society.

The Needham Problem

Some doubts about this conclusion emerge as soon as we examine the other sources of intensive growth under the Sung. These were a revolution in water transport[40]; increased monetization, including the introduction of paper money, which by the twelfth century had led to "printing press inflation"[41]; and, based on local markets, the growth of "a national hierarchy of markets linking almost the entire Chinese economy."[42] This linking of the Chinese rural economy with the market converted the Chinese peasantry "into a class of adaptable, rational, profit-oriented petty entrepreneurs."[43] The growing economic interdependence and growth of commerce led to an urban revolution, making medieval China the most urbanized society in the world. But unlike the cities of medieval Europe, which played a historic role in its ascendancy, the Chinese cities did not.[44] This was because of the continued existence of a unified imperial Chinese state. Nevertheless, all these changes taken together could be expected to fuel—as they did—the Smithian form of intensive growth in China under the Sung.

But the really extraordinary aspect of this medieval Chinese spurt was that it was also associated with remarkable scientific and technological advances, such that, as Needham and more recent research by Hartwell has shown, it had all the technical ingredients to devise those technological breakthroughs which are the hallmarks of the Western industrial revolution, and the basis for the Promethean form of intensive growth, which turns an organic into a mineral based economy. The Sung Chinese knew how to use coke instead of charcoal as fuel, and had developed a technique for making iron using coke before the 11th century.

At the peak of coal usage (between 1050 and 1126) it was ... used for smelting, something not paralleled in Europe until the 18th century. Iron output surged up.... Hartwell compares the level of China's output in 1078 with that attained in Europe in 1700. Chinese output then came close to the total production of Europe including Russia (151k–185k tons), and it topped the British output as late as 1788.... In terms of real prices the [price] of iron in terms of grain fell from 632:100 in 997 A.D. to 177:100 by 1080 A.D. The corresponding ratios in England were 223:100 in 1600 and 160:100 in 1700. Only the technical developments of the late 18th century decisively reduced the price of iron in terms of grain in England (down to 54: 100 on the eve of the Napoleonic wars), below the Sung ratios of 700 years earlier.[45]

The subsequent stagnation of the Chinese economy despite this medieval creativity is one of the great historical puzzles. But one set of explanations has some contemporary resonance.[46]

McNeill, Jones, and Lin, for instance, all relate the so-called Needham problem to the creation of the Confucian mandarinate, which was charged with implementing the official doctrine that held that the emperor "should consider the Empire as if it formed a single household,"[47] This household, following Confucian values, despised both soldiers and merchants. The mandarinate's task was to manage both, recognizing that both were needed to maintain the physical integrity of the empire. "Systematic restraint upon industrial expansion, commercial expansion, and military expansion were built into the Chinese system of political administration."[48] The market increased the economy's flexibility, and the resulting

new wealth and improved communications enhanced the practical power Chinese officials had at their disposal.... Discrepancies between the ideals of the market-place and those of government were real enough; but as long as officials could bring overriding police power to bear whenever they were locally or privately defied, the command element in the mix remained securely dominant ... in every encounter the private entrepreneur was at a disadvantage, while officials had the whip hand. This was so, fundamentally, because most Chinese felt that the unusual accumulation of private wealth from trade or manufactures was profoundly immoral ... official ideology and popular psychology thus coincided to reinforce the advantage officials had in any and every encounter with merely private men of wealth.[49]

This form of predatory partnership under the Sung between government and business, which I would label "crony capitalism," is in many ways echoed in the current liberalization in China (see Chapter 7). Just as in Sung times it can be expected to yield intensive growth. But, just as this process was subsequently aborted in medieval China, partly because of the reassertion of atavistic attitudes to trade and commerce as well as the failure to bind the state against its predatory rent seeking instincts, it remains to be seen whether enough has changed today to prevent a repetition of this historical cycle.

Elvin sees the reason for the failure of China to industrialize in the Western manner in the neo-Confucian reorientation of philosophic outlook in the fourteenth century. This reorientation was in part against the imported Buddhism that had made considerable inroads into Chinese culture under the Tang dynasty.

Against the Buddhist assertion of the meaninglessness of life, the neo-Confucians, seeking to establish social order and morality on a firm philosophical basis, developed a form of moral intuitionism that asserted "the reality, the meaningfulness, and the goodness of human life and the nature in which it was embedded." But by moving away from the earlier Chinese view, which emphasized conceptual mastery of external nature, toward the new view, which emphasized introspection, intuition, and subjectivity, "the new emphasis on Mind devalued the philosophical significance of scientific research by draining the reality from the world of sensory experience, though in a less absolute fashion than did Buddhism."[50] Elvin finds

the consequence of this philosophy for Chinese science were disastrous. As the result of a highly sophisticated metaphysics there was *always* an explanation—which of course was no explanation at all—for anything puzzling that turned up.... Given this attitude, it was unlikely that any anomaly would irritate enough for an old framework of reference to be discarded in favor of a better one. Here then was the reason why China failed to create a modern science of her own accord, and the deepest source of resistance to the assimilation of the spirit of Western science both in the 17th century and later.[51].

Cosmological Beliefs

Clearly, cosmological beliefs, as I have labeled them, have been an important determinant of both the polity, and through it of economic outcomes. We therefore need to outline the core cosmological beliefs of Chinese civilization. These are sometimes labeled Confucianism, but there is continuing controversy about whether the ancient sage should really be lumbered with whatever people have seen as the distinctive features of Chinese civilization. However, despite differences on specific points, it is clear that there were certain features of Chinese civilization that were set very early on. The first was its optimism, the second its familialism, the third its bureaucratic authoritarianism.[52]

It should be remembered, as W. J. F. Jenner has pointed out, that these characteristics, particularly the bureaucratic authoritarianism of the Chinese state, developed very early. Thus from the reference manuals of a petty bureaucrat of the Qin (Chin) regime in about 217 B.C. found with his body in December 1975 at Shuihudi in Yunmeng, it appears that the Qing regime "kept detailed, quantified central records of the state of the crops almost field by field in every county of the empire. Maintaining that sort of control would be a daunting task for a government equipped with computers and telecommunications. Doing it before the invention of paper, when all the data had to be gathered and stored on strips of wood or bamboo, would have been impossible without an enormous bureaucracy."[53,54]

Jenner's most original insight is that not merely the Chinese state but the very notion of being Chinese was a bureaucratic creation. Very early on this created the Mandarin "tyranny of history" of Jenner's title. He argues that the people comprising what has historically been claimed to be China were ethnically mixed. They were unified as Hans through the bureaucratic device of writing their names in Chinese characters in a Chinese form. Chinese culture was created and transmitted through a written history compiled by bureaucrats. But

Chinese governments have, for at least 2000 years, taken history much too seriously to allow the future to make its own unguided judgments about them. Thus it is that we have a remarkably well-organized published record, covering systematically the last two millennia, that rarely tells an outright lie but passes on the views of earlier bureaucrats as modified by later bureaucrats, and deals mainly with matters of concern to the monarchy and to officialdom.[55]

History became the accumulated administrative experience.[56] Moreover, although it encourages great awareness of historical events, there is little sense of long-run historical process in Chinese culture.[57] Down to the present Communist regime this official history has perpetuated orthodoxy, maintaining, for example, that, there can be only one legitimate government of the Chinese world at any one time. But by Confucian standards the legitimacy of every dynasty has been questionable. "Hence the extreme sensitivity to anything that may show the founders of one's own dynasty as gangsters,"[58] and the importance of the notion of the mandate of heaven, which justifies how one dynasty legitimately succeeds another.

For the great and the good in China, history has provided the only source of immortality, inasmuch as its high culture has been "this-worldly" without any concern about the afterlife. "History thus plays a role comparable to that of religious texts in other cultures. It is also the Last Judgment. The religion of the Chinese ruling classes is the Chinese state, and it is through history that the object of devotion is to be understood."[59]

The natural question is why the Chinese developed this particular world view, so different from that of the ancient Near East, Hindu India, and ancient Greece. David Keightley cites important ecological reasons. The first is that, unlike ancient Greece and Mesopotamia, Neolithic China was "more peopled," with a greater population density, and "that such peopling is congruent with a less individualistic more group-oriented social ethic."[60] Second, if Egypt's self-confidence was due to the benevolence of the Nile, and the pessimism and anxiety of the Mesopotamians and Greeks to their harsh and uncertain environment, then the "comparatively favorable neolithic climate in China would have encouraged a characteristic optimism about the human condition."[61]

Geography also explains the nonpluralistic nature of Chinese society. The market economy did not have the same strategic value in China as in Mesopotamia and Greece, where the poverty of natural resources in the hinterlands made trade indispensable. No such pressure to trade existed in China. Whatever trade there was followed the major river valleys, which flow from west to east, and traverse regions in the same latitude with similar crops and other products. There was therefore less need for trade and for merchants in China than in Greece and Mesopotamia. As in China it is the north and south, not the east and west, that are ecologically distinct,[62] it was only when these former regions were linked under the Sung that trade became important, and with it the need for merchants. The medieval economic revolution that yielded Smithian intensive growth for a time was thus largely based on the expansion of trade. But given the hysteresis of traditional attitudes to trade and merchants these never acquired the same prestige and power as in the West.[63]

In the fourteenth century the Ming dynasty began to restrict foreign trade and foreign contacts. The navy, which had been successfully built up earlier, was abandoned. The major reason seems to be that once the Grand Canal to Peking had been built in 1411, the transport by sea of grain was abolished in 1415. For the first time the navy had become a luxury rather than a necessity.[64]

The Middle Kingdom thereafter continued in haughty isolation from the rest of the world, till new "barbarians" from the South came knocking at its door, and the ancient Chinese state crumpled. But that is a story I will take up later. It is important to note, however, that from the time of the Ming dynasty, China was in a "high equilibrium trap" much like the one India had probably reached under the Mauryas. From now on there was only extensive growth, with a slowly growing population and a high culture that provided social stability and order but was also intellectually sterile.

What were the means of socialization in this Chinese civilization? Again, as there was no notion of sin in this nontheistic civilization, the socialization process was through shame rather than guilt. As Needham tells us, for the Chinese it was important that

"right" behavior be taught, rather than enforced by paternalistic magistrates. Moral suasion was better than legal compulsion. Confucius had said that if the people were given laws [in the sense of detailed codes] and levelled by punishments, they would try to avoid the punishments but would have *no sense of shame*; while if they were "led by virtue" they would spontaneously avoid disputes and crimes."[65]

The family was naturally the institutional basis for this socialization.[66] "To the extent that it is possible to speak of one strategic custom or institution in the mix of early China's cultural variables—strategic because of its pervasive ability to sanctify all other aspects of life and to legitimate and reinforce the lineage—it would seem to be ancestor worship and its social and political corollaries involving hierarchy, ritual deference, obedience and reciprocity."[67] The family has been the only dependable institution for the Chinese for thousands of years. A lesson which the turbulence of the last century has reinforced. "For better for worse, for richer for poorer, in sickness and in health, in the last resort the family is all there is."[68]

Confucianism and the Market

Though Chinese high culture promoted antimarket and antimerchant attitudes, the role of Confucianism remains controversial. Thus some scholars maintain that Confucian values were not directly antimarket but were against ill-gotten and excessive wealth.[69] The Communist party translated this Confucian disdain for the parvenu into antimerchant and antimarket attitudes. Certain other aspects of Sinic culture—familialism, for example, and the importance of education in conferring status through a mandariante selected by examinations—have, moreover, been identified as being important in the development of the neo-Confucian miracle economies of East Asia.[70] It is also argued that China was not unique in fostering antimarket sentiments. Like other absolutist states, whether in Europe or Asia, the Chinese imperial state restricted trade and expropriated the wealth of its merchants. There was nothing distinctive about China in this respect.

But others see a greater continuity in attitudes and values between the classical imperial state and the Communist one. Thus, Jenner notes,

The communist state is in many ways a reinvention of the bureaucratic monarchy.... The founders of the Communist party were products of Qing China, educated in its schools and culture and soaked in its values. To them it was only natural that the state should be absolute and that a bureaucratic monarchy was the normal form it should take.... Attitudes to state power remain heavily influenced by traditional values. The state's power remains absolute and sacrosanct. Though it can often be got around, it cannot be challenged. Politics at the top is played by the rules of palace struggles, which owe more to the political pundit of the third century B.C. Han Fei than to Marx. (pp. 35–36)

Richard Baum[71] provides a detailed reconstruction of these continuing palace struggles at the top of the Chinese state during the period of Deng's reform.[72]

Finally, in assessing the role of Confucian familial values in explaining the success of the overseas Chinese,[73] it is useful to note the institutional consequences as emphasized recently by Greif. He examines the institutional responses to the familial (collectivist) cultural beliefs of Maghribi traders and the individualist ones of Genoese ones in the Mediterranean trading world of the eleventh century. The very familialism of the Maghribi world, which led to their commercial success, nevertheless prevented institutional innovations like the development of contract and commercial law, which emerged as a matter of necessity in the individualistic Genoese trading world, and which were eventually an important factor in the "rise of the West." Similarly, I would argue, the continuing hold of these atavistic familial values has prevented those legal underpinnings of a modern commercialized market economy from emerging in China.

4   Islam

At the end of first Christian millennium, Hindu civilization was well past its climacteric. But China was about to see extraordinary developments under the Sung dynasty. It had only one other competitor on the world stage: the civilization of Islam, which stretched from the Atlantic to the Indian oceans. This had emerged like a meteor in the seventh century, and for the first few centuries of the next millennium it was to be the dominant civilization in the world. It, too, saw a period of intensive growth under the Abbasids. Its subsequent stagnation and defeat at the hands of the imperialist West in the last two centuries is as puzzling as the failure of China to make good on the promise it had shown under the Sung. Once again politics and culture must form part of the explanation.

The Rise of the Arabs

Patricia Crone writes about the rise of Islam:

Of the Middle East in about A.D. 600 one thing can be said for certain: its chances of being conquered by Arab tribesmen in the name of a new religion were so remote that nobody had even speculated that it might happen. Islam came upon the world as a totally unexpected development, and the factors behind its emergence are still little known and poorly understood.[1]

The Arabs were nomadic pastoralists who were well known as raiders by the Byzantine and Sassanian (Iranian) empires, which then dominated the Near East. But inasmuch as they had been in Arabia for some 1,600 years without staging a major conquest, it was a reasonable assumption in the seventh century that they never would.[2] The nomads whom these sedentary civilizations feared were from the steppes to their north. They had in the past threatened and would until the fifteenth century continue to threaten the ancient civilizations, including the one newly founded by the southern nomads, that of Islam. But in the ultimate encounter between these two sets of nomads, the southern ones triumphed by maintaining their integrity—both cultural and at most times politically—and by converting their northern "cousins" to their religion.

The original Arab empire collapsed after a series of civil wars into a number of different states. But in time, another Islamic empire was recreated under the Turks. Since the religion was born, thus, the peoples of the Middle East have lived in Islamic states for more than a millennium. This success in creating and maintaining statehood is particularly surprising for a people organized in the descent groups known as tribes who derived their security not from a state but from the obligations of kinsmen to protect themselves and their honor.

It was Mohammed who provided the Arabs with a new religion and an embryonic state. In order to protect the religious community (*umma*) in a stateless environment, the umma had to be both a congregation and a state.[3] Despite its peculiarities, as we will see, the Islamic state survives to our day. That in itself is no mean achievement for a stateless people.

The victory of Islam in Arabia can be traced to two factors. The first was its appeal to newly urbanized Arabs who were attracted to Judaism and Christianity as the religions of civilization but who were too proud to accept a foreign faith.[4] The second was that from its inception, with Mohammed's use of the sword to convert and conquer other Arabian rivals, Islam also offered more material rewards to the faithful—booty, in other words. With its subsequent dramatic conquests it appeared that God smiled on Muslims.[5]

The success of the southern barbarians in creating a new civilization in lands of very ancient cultural traditions, however, needs an explanation. For it was unique. Other barbarian conquests have either led to the conquerors' being assimilated by the civilization they conquered, or else to their borrowing a civilization from outside. Islam alone established a new civilization in the lands of antiquity it conquered. Crone and Cook, in a brilliant book, *Hagarism*,[6] provide a stimulating though speculative account for the reasons for their success, by contrasting the fate of these southern barbarians and those from the east (the Germanic tribes) who also threatened the world of antiquity.

Crone and Cook argue that along with this external threat from the barbarians to its north and south, classical civilization faced an internal one from the Jews inside its frontiers. This was a threat to the values of the Greco-Roman world. "Their existence constituted a moral condemnation of civilization: that is to say, they had the values with which to reject the prevailing culture, but even in their own diminutive homeland lacked the force to overthrow it."[7] Neither the barbarians nor the Jews on their own could have provided a new civilization. But "if barbarian force and Judaic values could be brought into conspiracy, it was just possible that they could achieve together what they could not bring about apart."[8]

In both the East and the West, antiquity was destroyed by a combination of barbaric conquest and Judaic values. The difference was that, whereas in the West there was a temporal disjunction in this combination, in the East they were conjoined. For, in the West, by the time the barbarian Germanic tribes began their assault, the ancient world had already been converted to a gentler version of the Judaic creed in the form of Pauline Christianity. This transformation occurred when the early Christians realized that Judaism could only be marketed in the civilized world by coming to terms with it.[9] They did this by abrogating the sanctity of Jewish ethnicity, which allowed the gentiles to become Christians, with the promise of salvation in the next world replacing the Jewish hope of redemption in this one. Thus "Judaism in its Christian form ... converted civilization at the cost of accepting it."[10]

The German threat to the ancient civilized world occurred after it had been converted to Christianity. The Germans were pagans but lacked the cultural resources to create a new civilization based on paganism. Having conquered the western lands of antiquity, they accepted its new religion, Christianity. "The barbarian force of the Germans, like the Judaic values of the Christians, could cross the frontier into civilization only at the cost of succumbing to it."[11]

Mohammed's genius lay in integrating religious insights borrowed from Judaism with a religious articulation of the ethnic identity of his Arab followers.[12] Moreover, this barbarian identity was couched in the intelligible and defensible biblical terms of the world they had conquered.[13] With the subsequent consolidation of their conquest society they ensured the survival of this new but not wholly unfamiliar civilization they created. "Judaic values had acquired the backing of barbarian force, and barbarian force had acquired the sanction of Judaic values: the conspiracy had taken shape."[14] A new civilization was born.

But from its birth Islam was threatened by internal contradictions. The first problem arose after Mohammed's death in A.D. 632. It concerned political legitimacy, an issue that has subsequently haunted Muslim society and states. The prophet's decisions while he was alive could be assumed to reflect the will of Allah; so disobedience was tantamount to impiety. But without the prophet to link it to God, how could divine guidance of the community be maintained?[15] This led to the Sunni split with the Shias, who along with most other Muslims, claimed that the Ummayad caliphate that succeeded Mohammed had usurped power by armed force and perpetuated a hereditary principle supported by neither piety nor tribal custom.[16] The Shias favored the descendants of Ali, Mohammed's son-in-law. The majority Sunnis came to accept a compromise devised in the Abbasid caliphate, which had replaced the Ummayads, again by bloodshed. This, too, in the eyes of true believers was a usurpation. However, through the Abbasid compromise the *ulema* (a body of legal experts) became the true heirs of the prophet by expounding the sacred law and applying it to particular cases.[17]

It might have been expected that the outcome of these constitutional crises in the early years of the Islamic empire would be a rejection of absolute rule for some form of consultative government.[18] But this was unlikely. First, because of the scale of the Arab conquests, its constituent nations could not have been held together without an imperial polity. The polity that emerged was, moreover, one in which the unruly tribal conquerors had to be constantly repressed to maintain order. While they were dependent for their income on state handouts,[19] the tribal nobility was unlikely to have much leverage over the caliph. The distribution of public revenues among those entitled to a share became the locus of disputes, not the allocation of the tax burden among those obliged to pay.[20] The leverage exercised by medieval barons against the impoverished sovereigns of Western Europe, which eventually led to these monarchs' ceding fiscal and later legislative control to various forms of popular assemblies, was not available to the Arab nobility. Thus despotism would seem to have been unavoidable in the new Islamic polity, however much it went against the religion Mohammed had founded.

Mohammed's disputed succession also had other more momentous consequences. To prevent backsliding, a steady inflow of booty was required to maintain the Arab tribal confederation. Their rapid conquest of the civilized world provided the means.[21]

Muslim Conquest and Retreat

The Muslim expansion continued until 715, when the Abbasids were stopped by Turkish intervention in the Oxus region. In 733 the Franks defeated the Muslims in Tours, and, most significantly, in 718 the siege of Byzantium had to be called off. This check to their military expansion ended "the dynamic equilibrium [booty in righteous wars] which had held the Muslim community together ever since Mohammed's Medina days."[22]

Eventually, with growing internal dissent and the pressure from the steppes, Turkish soldiers and adventurers filtering in from the steppe land gradually took over political control in Baghdad. However, they continued to cloak their usurpation of effective authority by keeping members of the Abbasid family on the throne until A.D. 1258. Thereafter, the Ottoman empire was the core of Islamic civilization, but with vital outposts in India, Africa, and South East Asia.

Until the late seventeenth century Islam, in the shape of the Ottoman empire, continued to challenge the Christian world. But its predominance was slipping. With the failure of the siege of Vienna in 1683, the subsequent history of Islam has been a history of defeat and humiliation at the hands of the West.

There have been three responses. One is a fatalistic acceptance by the pious, awaiting a more favorable turn in Allah's will. The other two responses have provided diametrically opposed remedies for the Muslim plight. One is to obtain the technical basis of the West's military prowess, and to surpass it. The other is to purify Islam from all the corruptions that have crept in over the centuries into Muslim lives, and thereby regain Allah's favor.

Champions of each policy made their voices heard early in the 18th century; but it was Islam's misfortune—unlike for example, the Japanese—that the two remedies seemed always diametrically opposed to one another. Reformers efforts therefore tended to cancel out, leaving the mass of Muslim society more confused and frustrated than ever.[23]

As with the other civilizations we need to look at the material factors and cosmological beliefs that might help to explain these outcomes.

Material Factors

The heartland of Islam—what is today called the Middle East—encompassed two of the most ancient civilizations built in the river valleys of the Nile in Egypt and the Tigris and Euphrates in Mesopotamia. Apart from these areas of ancient settled agriculture, the most striking geographic character of the area is its aridity and the vast expanses of wasteland it contains. With meager rainfall and few forests, agriculture requires perennial irrigation and defenses against soil erosion.[24] Most of the Arabian peninsula and Egypt is desert, and the central plateau of Turkey and Iran is mostly desert and steppe, flanked to the north by the vast steppe lands of Eurasia.[25]

Agriculture, where it had been established, depended upon maintaining an infrastructure for irrigation and soil conservation. Especially in the great river valleys it was very productive and provided the agricultural surplus that has fed the cities which have been the mark of civilization in the area for millennia. Lying as it does on the great land and sea routes connecting Europe and Asia, trade has been the second most important activity in the region.

The major economic effect of Islam's rapid conquests in its first two centuries was to unite the trading worlds of the Mediterranean and Indian oceans under a common language and culture. The recurrent conflicts between the Byzantine and Persian empires were replaced by a new Islamic hegemony, which led to a large increase in trade and commerce, and thus to intensive growth of the Smithian variety in the period of the Abbasid caliphate.[26] "In the course of the ninth century," Ashtor concludes

a gigantic economic unit, based on commercial exchanges came into being, a unit never before equalled in the history of the old world. The economic ascendancy of the Abbasid empire over other regions of Asia and Africa, and even more over Western Europe, was overwhelming, and it lasted a relatively long period—about two hundred years.[27]

The economic integration achieved by the Abbasid empire led to increasing trade and specialization in various goods of mass consumption such as "textiles and victuals."[28] This stimulated industry through both the larger market that was created and the exchange of technical knowledge. Better techniques, for instance, in textiles in Egypt were imitated by "the flourishing textile industry of Khuzistan," and new industries introduced, for example, paper from China.[29]

There is not much evidence, however, of any new specifically Muslim technological breakthroughs. Both in science and technology, Islam brokered the transfer of ideas and techniques from the earlier ancient civilizations of Greece, India, and China. The efflorescence of Islamic science in the Abbasid period was largely derivative but notable nevertheless, at least compared with what was to happen in the future. It was the economic integration wrought by Muslim arms and maintained through a common Islamic culture over a vast economic space that accounts for the Smithian intensive growth that occurred, growth that has been described as "a true economic miracle."[30]

This Smithian growth was also fueled by a large influx of precious metals—chiefly gold—partly in the form of booty, as well as through trade with African regions in western Sudan and Ghana,[31] a trade often carried out at very favorable terms. Thus "an Arabic author of the 11th century speaks of tribes who simply exchanged for salt an equal weight of gold."[32]

The Abbasid economic miracle was not based on any great improvement in agricultural productivity. There is evidence of a decrease in cultivated area due to salinization and the soil erosion that resulted from the failure to maintain the terraces that had been a distinctive feature of the region's agriculture since antiquity. Against this erosion there was some attempt to drain swamps and to colonize wasteland. Some new crops were introduced. But by and large the impression of a fairly stagnant agriculture amid a great expansion in trade and industry during the Abbasid efflorescence would not be misplaced.

This trade-based expansion, however, did not outlast the Abbasids. Issawi notes:

From the 12th or 13th century until the 19th, a process of economic deterioration took place, interrupted only by such rallies as those in Egypt and southern Syria in the late 13th and early 14th centuries, Anatolia in the 15th and 16th, northern Syria in the 16th and Iran in the 16th and early 17th. And, except in Iran and very briefly in Turkey, this economic deterioration was accompanied by intellectual and cultural decline. By any economic criteria, the Middle East stood far lower in the 18th century than in the 10th or 11th.[33]

It is unlikely that there was an absolute decline in levels of living—except during periods when the four horsemen of the Apocalypse galloped through the region. But from the thirteenth century onward there was, at best, extensive growth. Both Issawi[34] and Owen[35] find that in the nineteenth century (for which firmer conclusions can be drawn) there was no absolute economic decline, but a decline relative to the growing economies of Europe, a symptom being the decline in Middle Eastern trade caused by a number of exogenous shocks: wars, plagues, and the breakdown of government in many areas of Islamic civilization. Agriculture, always precarious in the region, and dependent upon irrigation works and measures to prevent soil erosion, was particularly hard hit. Population and the cultivated area shrank, reducing the agricultural export capacity of the region.[36]

The output and exports of manufactures also declined, caused in part by these shocks and the region's lack of resources—wood, navigable rivers and water power, and above all minerals, particularly the coal on which the Promethean intensive growth of the West was founded. Issawi also mentions the lack of mechanical inventiveness as well as the predatory nature of the state: private property was insecure, and "the entrepreneurial bourgeoisie, consisting of merchants, craftsmen and their guilds, never had enough power or organization to take its needs and interests into consideration."[37]

The last is particularly striking in view of the finding that in the early Islamic empire "60.6 percent of Moslem theologians in the ninth century were merchants, a third of them being traders in textiles."[38] This did not prevent arbitrary taxation and confiscation of private property. "These confiscations of private property, which became a striking feature of social life in the Muslim world, began in a very early period,"[39] and were due to the unique form of the Islamic predatory state.

The stagnation in technology and predatory government policy are attributed by various authors, including Issawi, to Islamic cosmology and polity. But there are others, most notably Rodinson (1974), who claim that given the protean nature of Islamic economic precepts, Muslims have been able to pick and choose between them, and so Islam is irrelevant in explaining the fluctuating economic fortunes of Muslim societies.[40] To form some judgments on this issue, which is central to the concern of these lectures, we need to examine the cosmology and polity of Islam.

Cosmological Beliefs

Islam's God—Allah—was the same deity who had revealed himself to Jesus and Moses, except that Muhammad as the last prophet claimed to have received God's final word, which superseded the revelations of his Jewish and Christian predecessors.[41] Like its Semitic cousins, Islam was monotheistic and universalist and was opposed to the polytheism that was common among Arab tribesmen, as in the pagan world of antiquity. The new religion's message was simple. Mohammed "proclaimed the existence of one God, Allah, the terror of Allah's impending Day of Judgment, and the duty of each human being to obey the will of Allah as revealed by his prophet."[42] Those who believed in Islam formed the umma. Its sense of identity was maintained by certain rituals—the so-called Pillars of Islam.[43] The first was the affirmation that "there is no god but God, and Mohammed is the Prophet of God." This testimony was all that was required to become a Muslim, and it was repeated in the daily prayers. These prayers were the second pillar and were at "the heart of the Muslim discipline ... prescribed five times a day. Prayer involved a ritual abasement before God."[44] The other pillars were

the duties of almsgiving, of fasting from dawn to dusk in the month of Ramadan, and of ... pilgrimage to [Mecca]. [Mohammed] also prohibited wine drinking and the eating of pork. All this together with rules concerning inheritance, marriage, apportionment of booty, settlement of disputes among believers, and similar practical questions quickly gave the small but growing Moslem community a character and internal discipline uniquely its own.[45]

In time (under the caliph Othman) the utterances of the prophet were gathered into the definitive book, the Koran. The prophet's acts and informal conversations, when reported to a chain of reliable witnesses, along with the deeds and words of his intimate circle of companions[46] became the basis of the *sharia*, the sacred law of Islam. A body of legal experts, the *ulema*, then arose to interpret the law in difficult cases. But unlike Christianity, Islam did not have an established church or priesthood. In this sense it was closer to Hinduism than its Semitic cousins.

In other respects, though, it was close to Judaism and Christianity, which, much to their irritation, Mohammed claimed to have superseded and incorporated in his new revelatory religion. But there were some significant differences. We need to note a few that various commentators have identified and that are relevant for our broader theme.

The first concerns the nature of free will. All monotheistic religions embody a tension between the omnipotence of God and the exercise of human free will. The difference between Islam and its other Semitic cousins, according to Cook,[47] is that in Judaism and Christianity God's omnipotence is cut back, with individuals' having enough moral rope to hang themselves. For otherwise their sins would be God's fault.[48] By contrast, Islam, despite some Islamic proponents of human free will,[49] stood by an omnipotent God, "swamping human free will."[50]

Islam, like Christianity, was the heir to two long established cosmologies, the Hebrew and the Greek, the former with their world ruled by a personal, jealous and arbitrary God, the latter with their gods put in perspective in a conceptual universe.[51] These two cosmologies were so different that they were difficult to reconcile. Christianity found a compromise by taking a softer line than its Judaic lineage on concepts, combining it with the Greek tradition of the Stoics, who took a softer line on gods.[52] Islam never resolved this dilemma.[53] When the rationalist Mutazila movement threatened to be winning, the "ulema" counterattacked and won by a form of conceptual Luddism that was no part of the intellectual tradition: the elegant concepts of the impersonal universe were reduced to an anti-conceptual occasionalism, a bizarre fusion of theistic voluntarism and atheistic atomism in defence of the sovereignty of a Hebraic god against the wiles of Hellenic causality.[54]

In practice, living in a world of some causal autonomy, they had to come to terms with at least some of the utilitarian sciences like medicine and astrology; not least for their predictive and manipulative power. But they did not accept the theory that the sciences of the Greeks were any more than magical manipulations.[55]

The second difference between Islam and its Semitic cousins was Mohammed's clever expropriation of the monotheistic patent first established by the Jews for the Arabs. He showed that they already had the truth that they had previously sought from the religious insights of Christian monks and Jewish rabbis. "Today such expropriations and discoveries take place under the banner of nationalism."[56] This Arab nationalism in a religious idiom was to prove vital in resisting the blandishments of the older civilizations that it sought to conquer, in order to establish one of its own. Whereas Christianity spread through the blood of its martyrs, Islam spread through the blood spilled in conquest by nationalist Arab arms.[57]

This religious nationalism was different from the secular nationalism that eventually led to the rise of nation-states in the West, and eventually as a Western import in the Islamic world. The origins of the West's secular nationalism lay in the purported ethnic differentiation of the Germanic tribes:

Europe had kept its classical culture, its Judaic god and its barbarian invaders conceptually distinct; and it was accordingly in a position to call upon its barbarian ancestors to provide the historical sanction for the plurality of nations within a shared community of truth.... But Islam in contrast had fused its barbarian invaders with both its religion and its culture: on the one hand it sanctioned only one nation, the "umma," and on the other it precluded the manipulation of non-Arab genealogies as legitimate titles to a distinct identity within this "umma." The heterogeneity of the Muslim world was real enough; but it was not till the reception of nationalism from Europe that it became possible to construe this Islamic vice as a western virtue.[58]

The third difference between Islam and Christianity in particular relates to questions of sex and sin. Whereas one of the defining features of Christianity came to be a guilt-based society trying to expiate original

sin,[59] Islam avoided this denouement by a subtle alteration in its adoption
of the Biblical story of the Fall of Man. In its Koranic version

the devil tempts Adam not Eve, to eat of the forbidden tree, with the false promise
that it will lead to eternal life and "to a kingdom that will never decay." We are
not told, as in Genesis, that the forbidden fruit comes from the "Tree of knowledge of Good and Evil," merely that the fruit is forbidden.... This act of disobedience is, however, not dwelt upon. After eating the fruit Adam and Eve
discover their nakedness—to find in sexual activity a pleasurable compensation
for their banishment.[60]

As such the Koranic paradise is a place for luxurious and sensuous living
for the righteous, with each one of the Elect having "seventy houris in
addition to his earthly wives and any other woman he finds attractive."[61]

This Muslim vision of paradise has appeared as a sacrilegious
adolescent's wet dream to the celibate Christian church, which, with its
Manichean dualism, taught of evils of the flesh and of a paradise consisting purely of "spiritual" pleasures.[62] This has meant that whereas the
Christians went on to build a guilt-based process of socialization to expiate original sin, no such sense of guilt underpins Islam. With its celebra-
tion of the Muslim community (the "umma") and the rituals prescribed in
its five pillars to lead a righteous life, Islam's socialization processes, like
those of most of the other non-Christian Eurasian civilizations, depend
upon shame. But to the extent that this sense of shame is tied closely to
the revelatory vision embodied in The Book, Muslims have rightly felt
that questioning it would also undermine the shame-based social cement
of their societies.

The Polity

The Middle East is sandwiched between the two great domains of pas-
toral nomadism in the world. This has colored the nature of its polity. The
great Arab historian Ibn Khaldun's cyclical view[63] of the Islamic polity in
his famous macrohistory of the Islamic polity builds on this material
aspect and has had many subscribers.[64] He saw history as punctuated by
dynastic cycles linked to tribal conquest. His is a world of dynamic interaction between the barbarian nomadic pastoralists and the sedentary civilizations of the cities. The nomadic kinship ties called "asabiyah" every
now and then throw up a tribe with enough warriors to conquer the cities
and towns of the sedentary civilizations and found a dynasty. But, in time,
the luxurious temptations of civilization sap the moral fibre and the

"asabiyah" of the dynasty. With its growing appetite for the fruits of the city, the tribal dynasty bears harder on the sedentary civilization by raising the burden of taxation, and as its members lose their initial fighting vigor, dependent outsiders are introduced to shore up the dynasty. They or some other tribal group eventually take over, making use of the discontent that the increased burden of taxation has caused among the sedentary population.[65]

Perry Anderson[66] has cogently argued that this cyclical view of history applies more to the tribal lands of the Maghreb, from whence Ibn Khaldun came, but cannot explain the relative stability of Muslim society for nearly six hundred years under the Ottoman state. The unique aspect of Islamic polities that allowed such long periods of stability was the induction of slave rulers. These *mamluks* came to form an essential part of the conquest society that Arab arms had created.

This was a conquest society where the conquerors clung to their tribal past. Physically separated from their subjects in the equivalent of modern-day military cantonments, the initial Arab conquerors were faced with the problem of administering and maintaining their newfound empire. The caliphs and sultans who ruled the Islamic state were unable to rely on their tribal clansmen because of both their limited numbers and their lack of aptitude for civilian pursuits. From the beginning of the Arab empire, Islamic rulers turned to an alternative solution to provide themselves with a loyal and trustworthy military and administrative apparatus—a solution that consisted of slaves.

Islam had household slaves, but except for the "plantation economy" in the marshes of southern Iraq created under the Abbasids, it had no tradition of slave labor in production, with its correspondingly lowly social status. From its earliest conquests Islam had acquired slaves by capture. Many of them were converted, manumitted, and placed in military and administrative positions. This had a number of benefits for the rulers. These manumitted slaves were normally aliens who were completely dependent on their master.

The ruler would bring up his foreign slaves as his *children*, and they existed in the Muslim polity only through him. It was this extinction of the soldier's autonomy which made the *mamluk* such a superb instrument of his master's will when it was coupled with personal obedience.... Mamluks were not supposed to think, but to ride horses, they were designed not to be a military elite, but military automata.[67]

Unlike the feudal soldiers of Europe, who were not aliens but members of their own polity, homeborn mamluks who could have acquired a political commitment to Islam were excluded from the army.[68] This mamluk institution spread throughout the Islamic world. The crack troops of settled rulers from the mid-ninth century into modern times consisted of slaves.[69]

But these servile armies needed to be controlled, inasmuch as an uncontrolled mamluk army could lead to the total disintegration of the state.[70] This happened frequently in Islamic history. The great exception were the Ottomans, who in the Islamic tradition relied on the *dervishme*,[71] or dervishes, for their administration and armies. The Ottoman sultans managed to maintain control of the state for a considerable period because of their personal qualities, which were tested in fratricidal wars for succession to be master of the Porte, and which were in the nature of a Darwinian contest for the survival of the fittest. When this system was replaced for humanitarian reasons by the system of the Cage,[72] the quality of the sultans deteriorated, which was partly responsible for the Ottoman decline.

Ibn Khaldun praised the mamluk institution as God's gift to save Islam, but this was because he saw them as institutionalized tribal conquerors. For him the medieval polity consisted of a settled nonpolitical society and a tribal state, either imported or imposed by conquest.[73] Whereas the Chinese in their cyclical view of history looked upon settled rule as the norm and the change of dynasties as resulting from the loss of virtue of an old tired dynasty, the Islamic polity never accepted the notion of settled rule,[74] which Ibn Khaldun considered effeminate. This has been the "black hole" of the Islamic polity from its inception. It has retained the lineaments of a conquest society. The "handing over of power to slaves ... to the more or less complete exclusion of the free males of the community bespeaks a moral gap of such dimensions that within the great civilizations it has been found only in one."[75]

The origins and consequences of this unique phenomenon of the mamluk state are still hotly debated by historians.[76] But, apart from Garcin,[77] most would agree with Cook's[78] judgment that it must have inhibited any form of Promethean intensive growth from occurring in the Middle East from the ninth to the eleventh centuries, when the *mamluks* were prominent. "It is hard to feel confident," writes Cook "that an eighteenth century English society dominated by an imported West African soldiery would have delivered the Industrial Revolution"![79] Muslim armies tend to be despotic, and this quality led to a disjunction between state and society—and between central military power and local economic power.[80] They are, in other words, extreme versions of my predatory state model (outlined in the Appendix). I find Crone and Pipes persuasive in their view that this characteristic goes back to the origins of Islam.

Law, Society, Economy

Neither was the legal system established by Islamic states favorable for development. This is in part due to the importance of the Koran and the *hadith* in Islamic law. Unlike Christianity, Islam is a law-centered religion.[81] By the time of the Abbasids, Islamic law had been codified in the *sharia*. "In reality ... it was both more and less than what is now regarded as law," writes Hourani:

> It was more, because it included private acts which concerned neither a man's neighbor or his ruler: acts of private worship, of social behavior, of what would be called "manners". It was a normative code of all human acts.... It was less than law, because some of its provisions were theoretical only ... and also because it ignored whole fields of action which would be included in other legal codes.[82]

These included contracts and obligations relating to economic activity, but it did not cover criminal law or "constitutional" or administrative law.[83]

The latter is unsurprising. The Islamic state, as a conquest society, had a very simple "constitutional" justification. From its inception, all land was claimed to be the property of the sovereign by right of conquest, and from the Ummayad and Abbasids down to the Ottomans in Turkey and Saffavids in Persia, State monopoly of land became a traditional legal canon of Islamic political systems.[84] A more or less uniform land tax had to be paid irrespective of faith. Nonbelievers had to pay an additional poll tax—the *jizya*—whose substantial contribution to the state treasury made the Islamic state chary of religious conversion. As a result, Islam was much more tolerant of its religious minorities than Christianity.

The sharia's silence on "constitutional" and "administrative" law, combined with its universal claims, led to secular governments' existing in a separate realm. The sovereign had unlimited discretionary power in state matters like war, politics, taxation, and crime to "complete" the sacred law. This inevitably led to a contradiction between a secular polity and a religious community in a civilization that lacked any distinction between church and state. Hence no lucid or precise legal order emerged in Islam, which always had "two justices" at work.[85]

In this respect, as Crone and Hinds[86] note, the Islamic polity had similarities with the Hindu polity. Just as in Islam, in Hindu India a holy law (that of Manu) governed personal lives outside royal control, making the state practically redundant. In both cases, however, rulers had to be obeyed unquestioningly. There was a disjunction between state and society. Dynasties came and went but society did not change.[87]

Although this silence of the sharia on constitutional law gave a license for autocracy, its assumption that each individual was answerable only to God for his actions meant that no group interests other than those based on kinship were publicly recognized. The family came to be the only social structure that enjoyed divine and hence legal recognition.[88]

The sharia also lacked the Roman law concept of legal personality, which prevented the development of the corporate institutions and the group loyalties they embody, and which lay at the heart of Western capitalism.[89] It is difficult to avoid the conclusion that the Islamic legal system was not conducive to development.

The Closing of the Muslim Mind

But at least during the earlier years of Islam, when the sharia was being developed, the process of interpretation and exercise of independent judgment known as *itjihad* allowed some doctrinal flexibility. Sometime between the ninth and eleventh centuries "the gate of *ijitihad*" was closed.[90] This curbed curiosity and innovation—particularly in the educational system, which from then on emphasized rote learning and memorizing instead of problem solving.[91]

This closing of the Muslim mind was all the more surprising given Islam's previous role, under the Abbasids, in being the intermediary between the ideas and techniques of the older civilizations of Greece, China, and India.[92] Thereafter, when Europe began to make its remarkable advances in ideas and technology, the Islamic world showed little interest except in techniques with some military use. The West's intellectual curiosity, by contrast, extended to Islam. Lewis reports that by the end of the eighteenth century ninety-five Arabic, Persian, and Turkish grammars and twenty-one dictionaries had been produced in Europe; "for an Arab, a Persian, or a Turk, not a single grammar or dictionary of any Western language existed either in manuscript or in print. It was not until well into the nineteenth century that we find any attempt to produce grammars and dictionaries of Western languages for non-Western users."[93]

Nor did the scientific efflorescence of the early Islamic period endure. Kuran cites a recent Turkish encyclopedia of "Muslim scientific pioneers" that shows that "of the scientists it lists, 64 percent produced their path-breaking works before 1250, and 36 percent did so between 1250 and 1750; not one lived after 1750."[94]

Crone and Cook[95] attribute this closing of the Muslim mind to the failure of Islam, unlike Christianity, to find a compromise between the conflicting conceptual universes that they both inherited from the Greeks and the Hebrews. From the former they inherited the concept of immutable celestial laws and other doctrines of the Greek philosophers. From the Jews both inherited the notion that God was responsible for all the things to be observed on earth. "Modern science rests on a tense relationship between the mad conclusions of speculative reason which allege that the earth is round, and the common-sense observations of human perception which show that it is obviously flat.... [T]o generate science the laws of heaven and earth have to merge."[96] Christianity, which had never taken the law of heaven as seriously as had Islam, found that it could effect this merger in the form of its Protestant empiricism, whereas Islam could not. After its initial flirtation with the Greeks, the defeat of Islam's rationalist school by the traditionalist ulema meant that only heretics could explore the Greek notion of immutable laws of nature.

There thus seem to be close parallels between the closing of the Muslim mind after the Abbasid efflorescence and that in post-Sung China. In both cases it seems to have been the result of cultural and political factors, which, though different in their specifics, had the same effect in leading to a subsequent period of cultural and technological stagnation—the high-level equilibrium trap that Elvin[97] has identified for China, which could equally be applied to the post-Abbasid Muslim world.

The very success of the Abbasids in creating a prosperous Islamic civilization seems to have bred complacency. The historian Felipe Fernandez-Armesto captures this well, describing the world surveyed by the Syrian geographer al-Muqaddasi at the turn of the first millennium after Christ:

The Islam he beheld was spread like a pavilion under the tent of the sky, erected as if for some great ceremonial occasion, arrayed with great cities in the role of princes; these were attended by chamberlains, lords and foot soldiers, whose parts were played by provincial capitals, towns and villages respectively. The cities were linked not only by the obvious elements of a common culture ... but also by commerce and in many cases reciprocal political obligations. The strict political unity which had once characterized Islam had been shattered in the tenth century ... yet a sense of comity survived, and travellers could feel at home throughout the Dar al-Islam—or to use an image popular with poets—in a garden of Islam, cultivated, walled against the world, yielding for its privileged occupants, shades and tastes of paradise.[98]

The Ottoman economic mind, as delineated by Inalcik,[99] was attuned to maintaining this social stability. To keep their cities prosperous, the sultans developed commercial centers and controlled trade routes. To maintain themselves in power they sought economic stability through price controls, regulated exports, and the establishment of charitable foundations. As with past Islamic states, the countryside bore the burden of taxation through the "cift-hane" system.[100] The Ottomans also resisted organizational change. But their predatory socioeconomic system was productive enough that their empire could continue to expand through conquests for a substantial period of time. Its ideological and institutional sclerosis was revealed only when a resurgent Europe began to assert itself. Though not directly blaming Islam for this increasing sclerosis of the Islamic world, Inalcik observes that Islam legitimized the policies of social stability and thence the status quo.

Islam and the Economy

It is time to sum up Islam's probable role in the economic stagnation of the Islamic world after a brief period of Smithian intensive growth under the Abbasids. This growth was due more to the economic integration of the Mediterranean and Indian ocean regions forged by Muslim arms than to Abbasid ideology.

The trouble with assigning a causal role to Islam in the economic stagnation of Muslim societies is that Islamic texts offer contradictory prescriptions. Thus on the importance of the role of the market, an essential instrument of development,

> some texts in Islamic economics feature long passages on the virtues of the market mechanism which suggest that price movements are vital to the equilibration of supply and demand. These same texts contain other passages that instruct traders to refrain from taking advantage of anticipated shortages through unjust price increases. There is an inconsistency between these two classes of passages, which is that the equilibration lauded in the first is obviated by the principle of the "just price" promoted by the second. Such inconsistencies point to the futility of trying to place Islamic economics squarely in the pro- or anti-market camps.[101]

What is probably more important is that the very flexibility of interpretation that these contradictions allow was closed after the Abbasid renaissance. This closing of the Islamic mind and the poverty of public discourse through the process of "preference falsification" was probably more important than the specific injunctions of Islam vis-à-vis the economy.

The attempts by reformers since Syed Ahmad Khan in nineteenth-
century India to make Islamic teaching conducive to modernization is
instructive in examining whether this medieval Islamic equilibrium of
cosmological beliefs is conducive to economic development. Khan sought
to reinterpret the tradition by using rationalist and historical arguments to
question various Muslim institutions.[102] But he faced the dilemma that
has confronted all reformers trying to reconcile Islam to the modern world:

> The gap between scientific and religious truth could only be bridged by abandon-
> ing literalistic interpretations of the divine texts, or even, in the case of *hadiths*, by
> challenging their authenticity, thus leaving much of the law open to changes
> which, in the circumstances, facilitated western domination and cultural penetra-
> tion. This dilemma persists to this day.[103]

Khomeini's theocratic revolution in Iran was an attempt to solve the
dilemma by a return to the past. It would be fair to say that this has been
both an economic and a political failure.[104] Politically, the Iran-Iraq war
demonstrated that Arab and Persian national identities were proving
more potent in rallying support than Islamic solidarity.[105] Economically
the country has failed to match the growth and industrialization record of
the Shah's regime.[106]

But there are important instances (post-Ataturk Turkey, modern Egypt,
and, most important, major outposts of Islam in Southeast Asia, Malaysia,
and Indonesia) that show that it is not Islamic beliefs in themselves that
have hindered development but dysfunctional étatism and dirigisme,
which, when reversed as in the Muslim parts of Southeast Asia, have
delivered Promethean intensive growth. Even in these countries, however,
where Islam has by and large been confined to the private sphere, there
are signs of an Islamicist backlash. The longstanding Muslim hankering
for the state and church to be conjoined is by no means dead.

But there is hope that as more and more Muslim economies become
integrated with the outside world, and as a sufficient number of Muslims
through their work practices become a part of this emerging global economy, there might be a sufficient weight to shift Muslim public opinion to
the older Abbasid equilibrium that allowed *itjihad* (interpretation) of the
religious traditions and that could remove any doctrinal impediments (for
example, on charging interest) that continue to confuse the Islamic mind.

Another continuing lacuna is political. The traditions of a conquest
society still persist in many Muslim polities.[107] The failure to develop a
civil society and the rule of law will continue to make such Muslim polities
authoritarian and unstable.[108]

Finally, there is one other aspect of Islam—its processes of social-ization—that we need to note. Given its various incoherences "in the dimensions of ethnicity, polity and world view,"[109] it might seem surprising that Islam continues to provide meaning to the lives of so many of its adherents. This, Crone and Cook argue, is because of the central role of the family in the life of Muslims as contrasted with its Semitic cousins. For Christians with their "original sin" and hope of salvation, all family life is "necessarily and radically corrupt," and for the Jews

the religious meaning of the familial present is relativised by the hope of national redemption in the future.... So while the Jews live out the indignity of refugees awaiting repatriation, and Christians engage in their undignified scramble for salvation, Islam can at least make available to the Muslims in their families a resigned and dignified calm.[110]

With no sense of original sin, a guilt-based culture did not develop in Islam; its processes of socialization were shame-based. Islam remained largely communalist, whereas the West turned increasingly individu-alist.[111] This was in part, as we will see, why those institutional reforms that led to the rise of the West did not occur in Muslim countries. But as we argued in the case of China and India, the shame- and family-based processes of socialization need not be a handicap if Muslim societies are able to accept and absorb the technology and commercial institutions of the West. The danger for Islam is that, unlike China and India, its social ethic is supported by a sacred Book. If in the process of secularization that Book comes to be questioned, then it could face the same erosion of its social cement that has affected its Semitic cousin, Christianity.

5   The Rise of the West

I have related these stories about material culture (based on relative factor endowments) and cosmological beliefs (the "ideas" side of culture) which together have influenced the polity and economy to show how the two ancient civilizations of India and China had reached a "high level equilibrium trap" by the Middle Ages. They had probably had periods of intensive growth of the Smithian variety in approaching this equilibrium, which is well documented for the Sung in China but not for the earlier Mauryan period in India. Similarly, Islamic civilization had Smithian intensive growth under the Abbasids. There is no evidence that any of these civilizations was moving toward intensive growth of the Promethean kind. Neither was Japan (see Chapter 8), with its own distinctive mutation of Confucianism, Taoism, and Buddhism, despite evidence of Smithian intensive growth during the Tokugawa period.

Promethean intensive growth remains a European miracle. Its sources have been keenly debated, but there is some convergence in explanations that emphasize both material factors and cosmological beliefs. I will merely summarize the material story very briefly and instead concentrate on the changing cosmological beliefs, contrasting them with those in the other ancient civilizations to see whether they add any explanatory power to the material factors in the rise of the West. This will also allow me to show (in Chapters 6 and 9) that, paradoxically, the very beliefs that engendered Promethean growth may eventually have eroded the cement of society in this civilization. At the end of the millennium, when we again take up the story of the two Asian giants and compare their prospects (and those of Japan and other countries on the East Asian edge) with those of the West, some surprising and no doubt controversial conclusions emerge.

The Materialist Base

The essential features of the material bases of the rise of the West are well known. I can therefore be brief in outlining them. Most economic historians agree that geography was essential to the rise of the trading states around the Mediterranean, which led to the rise of the Greeks and eventually the Romans. In this early stage of Western civilization, the differing factor endowments around this European lake made trade the engine of Smithian intensive growth. But toward the end of the western Roman empire, the land constraint was beginning to take a toll. Diminishing returns, together with the inexorable costs of maintaining imperial armies and bread and circuses for the Roman mob, would have aggravated the problems of the fisc. These worsened from A.D. 180 onward as the empire became subject to mounting attacks and pressures from the barbarians in the north. These increased military requirements and military expenditures were limited by the maximum amount the emperors could squeeze from taxation, compulsory labor, or levies.[1]

The collapse of the western Roman empire led to the political fragmentation of Europe into a number of weak states, with considerable contestability in terms of our model of the predatory state (see Appendix). Hence the revenue available to these states was severely restricted. They, lacking better options, had to rely on a form of subinfeudation for their armies and revenue.

European manorialism developed with the need to tie down what had become a relatively scarce production of factor: labor, as the northern forests were cleared for cultivation and the land area expanded. The decline of population in the Middle Ages—partly due to the spread of diseases from the East, most notably the Black Death—would have worsened labor scarcity. This led to the rise of the distinctive form of European feudalism, whose essential feature was the mutual recognition of quasi-legal rights and obligations, something unknown in the institutions created in China (tenant serfdom) and India (the caste system) to deal with similar problems of labor scarcity in the development of their organic agricultural economies.

Thus, because of differing geographical (ecological) features very different polities developed in the three regions: a unified imperial state in China, unstable predatory states detached from society in India, and a patchwork of competing states in Europe. These Western states were unique in being fiscally bound by quasi-contractual relationships with their constituents. In all three areas of civilization, an overarching set of cosmological beliefs provided cultural unity, even when, as in India and the West, there was no political unity in their geographical space. These ecologically determined institutional differences were to be important sources for the different trajectory that Western Europe took in both its politics and its cosmology.

From the fifteenth century onward,[2] European populations and economies recovered from the breakdown after the fall of the Roman empire. A continuing agricultural revolution and the slowly rolling industrial revolution lessened the need to tie down labor as agricultural labor ceased being scarce. Serfdom disappeared, except in the East.

The major problem for the West remained the threat from Islam. The traditional routes across the Red Sea and the Silk Route had been blocked by the territorial expansion of the new Islamic civilization. The sixteenth century voyages of discovery were impelled in part by the need to find an alternative to the ancient trade routes to the East, where Europeans could obtain the spices essential for preserving meat during the long and lean winters. The voyages of discovery led not only to the extension of the European land frontier through the acquisition of the nearly empty lands—or those that Western arms and disease emptied—in the New World, but also, in time, to the colonization of most of Africa and Asia by the West.

The Industrial Revolution gradually changed the traditional organic agrarian economies—which is all the world had hitherto known—into mineral-based industrial economies, which allowed Promethean intensive growth to become the norm in the West. The linking of the globe through the steamship, as well as the adoption of free trade during the first great golden age in the mid-nineteenth century, then led to the creation of a world economy where foreign trade based on differences in factor endowments led to the integration of various parts of the non-Western world. This led to the Smithian type of intensive growth in many parts of Latin America, Africa, and Southeast Asia.[3] The late nineteenth century also saw the beginnings of the transference of the industrial means of generating Promethean intensive growth to the non-Western world, for example, India and Japan.

The Institutional Base

This materialist interpretation of the rise of the West, in terms of changing factor endowments and technology, however, needs to be supplemented by the important institutional differences between the West and the Rest, which most historians recognize were essential in mediating these materialist forces into the unique outcome—which is the European miracle.

The first is the importance of the city states in creating a hospitable climate for merchants and commerce. They were the main agents in generating the capitalist spirit and the institution of the "market" that was its characteristic form. For, as Gellner has noted, one distinctive feature of a market economy is its instrumental rationality. "What defines the market is not that people exchange things ... but that they do so in the spirit of maximizing economic advantage and above all, that they do it with a complete disregard of other considerations ... what defines a market economy is of course not the presence, but the predominance of such relations."[4] Traders have been par excellence agents of instrumental rationality, but in "most agrarian societies, such activity is ... ritually circumscribed, a small island in a sea of producers of subsistence."[5]

The city states, first of Greece and later of Italy (after the collapse of the western Roman empire), were the progenitors of mercantile societies. As their geography limited their hinterland, they had to depend upon trade for their prosperity and even more for the revenues for the provision of those essential public goods—defense and law and order—which provide the basic justification for the existence of all states. The role of the merchant would necessarily be more important than in the imperial states of India and China. But, as Hicks has emphasized,[6] the real difference would arise if in some of the city states the merchants themselves took over the state as they did in the city states of northern Italy during the Middle Ages.

Second, but equally important for the development of a market economy and the division of labor it entails, is the development of a law of commercial contracts, which allows arm's-length transactions to replace those based on familial links of trust, hitherto the basis for the substantial intranational and international trade in the ancient agrarian empires. The institution of Roman law, including a codification of civil law, was important for this process. There were no similar legal developments in China. But by itself this cannot explain the different fortunes of mercantile capitalism in different parts of Eurasia. For India has had a codification of its civil law, albeit within its casteist framework, in the laws of Manu for millennia. The crucial difference came with the explicit evolution of *commercial* law in the medieval Italian city states. This was impelled as much by "ideology" as by material interests. We will take up its genesis later.

The third essential feature was the recognition of private property rights by the state. Here again Europe's evolution was unique. With the consolidation of the weak and fragmented polities of the Middle Ages into the absolutist nation states of Renaissance Europe, the relative security of property rights that the medieval lords had secured was not extinguished, as in the absolutist states of the ancient civilizations. As Perry Anderson rightly notes:

the term "absolutism" [is] in fact ... technically a misnomer ... [for] one basic characteristic ... divided the absolute monarchies of Europe from all the myriad of other types of despotic, arbitrary or tyrannical rule, incarnated or controlled by a personal sovereign, which prevailed elsewhere in the world. *The increase in the political sway of the royal state was accompanied, not by a decrease in the economic security of noble ownership, but by a corresponding increase in the general rights of private property.* The age in which "absolutist" public authority was imposed was also simultaneously the age in which "absolute" private property was progressively consolidated. It was this momentous social difference which separated the Bourbon, Habsburg, Tudor or Vasa monarchies from any Sultanate, Empire or Shogunate outside Europe.[7]

North and Thomas have presented an account of the rise of the West in terms of the securing of these rights of private property. This, essentially meant, tying the hands of predatory governments through devices such as "no taxation without representation."

The final and, for some, decisive element in the rise of the West was the routinization of "the inquisitive Greek spirit" into science. This takes us decisively into the realm of ideas, and it is to its history we turn to see what were the crucial ones which affected the polity and the economy, and if and to what extent they were impelled by material interests.

The Greek Legacy

The ancient Greek legacy is important to this story for three reasons. First, for essentially ecological reasons the Greeks were able to create democratic states that left the West an important institutional political legacy. As in the ancient Indian republics in the Himalayan foothills, the light soils and thence relatively low labor intensity of agriculture in the Greek hinterland did not require the degree of social control and stratification needed by more labor-intensive types of agriculture that provided the economic base for the ancient agrarian civilizations. Combined with the physical compactness dictated by geography, of the ancient Greek states before Alexander, democracy arose. It was based on the

ancient tribal assemblies that were common among the nomadic pas-
toralist ancestors of both the ancient Greeks and Hindus. However, whereas the polities of tribal societies were based on associations of related
lineages, the Greeks went a stage further and invented the *polis*, the self-
governing city state. Its central organizing principle—the supremacy of
citizenship over all other forms of human association—was unique, as
witness its absence in either ancient India or China. It has profoundly
affected the political development of the West.

Second, the ecologically determined permissiveness in the degree of
social control that was required for the coordination of economic activity
in ancient Greece also allowed a greater consciousness of the multiplicity
of answers to the ultimate questions about life, death, and salvation,
which fostered the inquisitive Greek spirit. McNeill[8] tells us that Greek
religion was compounded of two distinct elements. The first was the pan-
theism that the Indo-Europeans brought from the north, which resembled
what the Aryans brought to India. The second were the fertility myths
associated with the ancient goddesses who had been worshipped in the
land before the arrival of the Greeks. It was not easy to reconcile the contradictions of these two incompatible traditions. The resulting logical dis-
array allowed speculation about the relationship between man and nature,
and philosophy was born.[9] And it was a novel philosophy. It was in Ionia
that the first philosophers

finding conflicting and unsupported stories about the gods to be unsatisfactory ...
took the drastic step of omitting gods entirely, and boldly substituted *natural law*
instead as the ruling force of the universe.... The Ionian concept of a universe
ruled not by the whim of some divine personality but by an impersonal and
unchangeable law has never since been forgotten. Throughout the subsequent history of European and Middle Eastern thought, this distinctively Greek view of the
nature of things stood in persistent and fruitful tension with the older, Middle
Eastern theistic explanation of the universe.[10]

This was the origin of Western science. McNeill speculates that

the Ionians hit upon the notion of natural law by simply projecting the tight little
world of the *polis* upon the universe. For it was a fact that the *polis* was regulated
by law, not by the personal will or whim of a ruler. If such invisible abstractions
could govern human behavior and confine it to certain roughly predictable paths
of action, why could not similar laws control the natural world? To such a question, it appears the Ionians gave an affirmative answer, and, in doing so gave a
distinctive cast to all subsequent Greek and European thought.[11]

Third, in their processes of socialization and thus in their ethical beliefs,
the ancient Greeks were closer to their cousins in the Indian and Chinese

civilizations. As Bernard Williams has shown in a briiliant book, *Shame and Necessity*, ancient Greek society was a shame society. It was not based on guilt. Thus, Moses Finley notes,

what was lacking [among the Greeks] was a sense of sin. A Greek or Roman could offend his God easily enough, and at times though not often, we meet notions that come close to the idea of sin. Basically, however, their wrong acts were external, so to speak, and therefore amends were made by ritual purification, or they were intellectualized, as in the Socratic doctrine that no man does evil knowingly.[12]

Nor did the individualism that many see as the hallmark of Western civilization arise with the Greeks. As the sociologist of "Homo Hierarchicus" in India, Louis Dumont has noted, the individualism espoused by the Greek Stoics was similar to that of the Hindu renouncer of the world. It was an "other-worldly" individualism. The rise of that distinctly "this worldly"—or in-worldly—individualism of the West had to await its acceptance of a new religion from the desert, Christianity. This ultimately provided the West with a very different basis of socialization and morality than was common to the Greek, Hindu, Islamic, and Sinic civilizations—guilt rather than shame. We turn to the contribution of this Semitic religion to the rise of the West.

The Rise of Christian Europe and Individualism

But first we must define "individualism"—the personality trait that so many have seen as unique to the West, and an important element in its material success. The anthropologist Alan Macfarlane's definition will be sufficient for my purpose. He describes it as "the view that society is constituted of autonomous, equal units, namely separate individuals and that such individuals are more important, ultimately, than any larger constituent group. It is reflected in the concept of individual property, in the political and legal liberty of the individual, in the idea of the individual's direct communication with God."[13]

Basing his view on English local records, legal textbooks, and autobiographical documents going back to A.D. 1200, MacFarlane argues that since the thirteenth century England "has been a country where the individual has been more important than the group and the hierarchy of ranks has not been closed."[14] The present English family system is the same as it was in 1250 and is not the result of the Industrial Revolution of the eighteenth and nineteenth centuries. Because the Pilgrims took the system to America, it has also been the family system in the United States from its inception. This "modern 'individualistic' system, with its stress on the nuclear family ... and romantic love," is in stark contrast with the "traditional, extended household, arranged-marriage, kinship-based" system found in "peasant type" societies.[15] More controversially, Macfarlane argues (without providing any evidence) that this "individualism" was unique to England and not to be found in the rest of Europe. As to its origins, he is unable to fix these except to speculate with Montesquieu that it arose in the German woods![16]

Be that as it may, there is little doubt that by the thirteenth century "individualism" was in place in at least a part of Western Europe. Moreover, it embodied a notion of the "person" unique in human history.[17] To understand why, we need to trace the rise of this singular aspect of its cosmological beliefs within the general framework that has conditioned Western minds: Christianity.

Christianity arose in the eastern part of the Roman empire when paganism ruled. There were a multiplicity of cults, and Christianity at first was one among many. However, with its Jewish descent, it differed from the pagan religions in its monotheism. Like the Jews, but unlike the pagan cults, it was also a religion of the Book—the Bible.[18] The Book facilitated the conversion of people who were scattered thinly over the whole of the Mediterranean littoral and not in constant contact with other fellow worshipers.

The Jews remained an ethnically exclusive group, with their jealous God who had anointed them as his chosen people. For Judaism was not universalistic; Jews were born, not made, and they did not proselytize. Christianity's great innovation was to combine the monotheism of Judaism with a new claim to universalism. By prosleytizing and gaining converts who believed in the Book, it could conquer the world. The Hindus and Chinese resembled the Jews, in the nonprosleytizing religions of their people. Their gods could not become everyone's. The Christian God could.

In the subsequent competition between religious cults in the Near East, Christianity eventually triumphed with the conversion of Constantine, which "to us, as to contemporaries," writes Robin Lane-Fox "remains an entirely unexpected event."[19] His exhaustive survey of recent research based on archaeological discoveries and interpretations basically endorses Gibbon's

five causes of the Christian's ... missionary success: an "intolerant zeal," derived from the Jews but purged of their "narrow and unsocial spirit"; the "menace of eternal tortures"; the miracles and "awful ceremony" of exorcism; the "serious and sequestered life", whose "faults, or rather errors, were derived from an excess of virtue"; the government of the Church, with its scope for ambition and authority.[20]

The Idealist Account

But was this new religion individualistic? Louis Dumont argues persuasively that it was not, in the sense *individualism* has come to mean in the modern world, of individuals in the world—the *in-worldly* individual rather than the *out-worldly* individual who is to be found in both the Hindu renouncer and the Greek Stoic. "The renouncer is self-sufficient, concerned only with himself. His thought is similar to that of the modern individual, but for one basic difference: we live in the social world, he lives outside it."[21] "There is no doubt," claims Dumont, echoing Troeltsch, "about the fundamental conception of man that flowed from the teaching of Christ: ... man is an *individual in-relation-to God*; for our purpose this means that man is in essence an outwardly individual."[22] He continues:

Sociologically speaking, the emancipation of the individual through a personal transcendence, and the union of outwardly individuals in a community that treads on earth but has its heart in heaven, may constitute a passable formula for Christianity.... When Christ teaches "render unto Caesar the things that are Caesar's, but unto God the things that are God's" ... it is for the sake of God that we must comply with the legitimate claims of Caesar. In a sense the distance thus stated is greater than if the claims of Caesar were simply denied. The worldly order is relativized, as subordinated to absolute values. There is an ordered dichotomy: "outwardly individualism" encompasses recognition of and obedience to the powers of the world.[23]

This "hierarchical complementarity," as Dumont labels it, is similar to that in Vedic India, where the priests were subject to the king but considered themselves to be religiously or absolutely superior.[24] And we know that in-worldly philosophical individualism did not develop in India. So how did it emerge from Christianity in the West? Dumont gives a two-part answer. One is in the realm of ideas, the other in politics.

It is important, as Ernst Troeltsch stressed, to note the borrowings of the early Christian fathers of the idea of natural law from the Stoics. "Its leading idea is the idea of God as the universal, spiritual [and] physical Law of Nature, which rules uniformly over everything and as universal law of the world orders nature, produces the different positions of the individual in nature and in society, and becomes in man the law of reason which acknowledges God and is therefore one with him."[25] This leads on to a hierarchical relativization of values.

While the sage remains indifferent to external things and actions, he is nevertheless able to distinguish among them according to their greater or lesser conformity to nature, or reason: some actions are by themselves relatively commendable against others. The world is relatativized as it should be, and yet values, *relative values*, maybe attached to it. Here is the relative law of nature that will be extensively used by the Church. To these two levels of the Law correspond two pictures of mankind, in its ideal and in its real state. The former is the state of nature ... which the Christians identified with the condition of man before the fall.[26]

This, of course, still yields the hierarchical complementarity of church and state.

It was Saint Augustine who restricted the field of application of natural law while extending that of providence or the divine will. More radical in political matters, he substitutes the absolute submission of the state to church for the previous endorsement of sacral kingship, analogous to the Hindus. It is only within this new framework that Natural Law retains a limited value.[27] Augustine demands that the state be judged from the church's transcending viewpoint of man's relation to God. This is a step toward imposing outwardly values on in-worldly conditions. Augustine thus presages the main developments of the following centuries. In the words of Gregory the Great, "Let the terrestrial kingdom serve—or be the slave of—the celestial."[28]

The primacy of the church over the state allowed it to acquire temporal power in the West in the eighth century, when the popes cut their ties with Byzantium. This claim to an inherent right to political power changed the relation between the secular and the divine. With the divine now claiming to rule the world through the church, the church becomes in-worldly.[29] This was the crucial step in transforming the out-worldly into an in-worldly individual, a process completed by Calvin.[30]

It is important to note that Dumont dates the rise of Western individualism to St. Augustine in the fifth century.[31] If it is identified, as in Max Weber's famous thesis, with Protestantism, then its role in generating capitalism is open to the fatal objection about its dating made, for one, by Hicks. For an essential element in the rise of capitalism was the "appearance of banking, as a regular activity.... This began to happen ... long before the Reformation; in so far as the 'Protestant Ethic' had anything to do with it, it was practice that made the Ethic, not the other way round."[32] If, however, on the basis of Dumont's argument we recognize that "in-worldly" individualism began with "Augustine's mutation" (as we may call it) then this temporal contradiction disappears.

This growing individualism also allowed the early shoots of the Renaissance to appear from 1300 onward in the city states of northern and central Italy. They

became the seat of a conscious renaissance of classical antiquity, meaning, in practice, the Roman rather than the Greek past. Many educated Italians discovered that the study of the pagan Latin poets and of Cicero offered not only models of literary excellence but fresh and valuable insights into the question of how men should live and conduct themselves. Humanists, as men who cultivated these concerns were proud to call themselves, seldom broke explicitly with Christianity.[33]

Except for Machiavelli, who based his model of the republican city state on Livy and developed a practical science of politics divorced from not only Christianity but also any private morality. Its rationale was to subserve the political principle, the *raison d'état*. The subsequent political practice of the absolutist states of Europe based on this principle was only possible because the church had earlier developed a similar principle, and because in medieval Italy the real end of political action seemed as Machiavelli had seen so clearly and coldly—the pursuit of power.[34]

This essentially "idealist" account of the rise of Western individualism, which is the feature which above all distinguishes the cosmological beliefs of the West from the Rest, needs to be qualified in a number of "materialist" ways. But some of the elements of these materialist accounts are, I will argue, debatable.

The Materialist Account

We begin with the post-Roman world of the early Middle Ages. Eric Jones has emphasized the importance of the European state system that developed in Europe after the fall of the Roman Empire, helped by geography "and ancient ethnic and linguistic apartheid dating from early folk movements and settlement history [which] helped to maintain the individuality of political units."[35] Europe was also a continent with a diversified portfolio of resources. The smaller political units that rose on the ruins of the Roman empire had to allow trade and commerce, in particular the bulk transport of basic commodities (grain, meat, fruit, wine, and so on), by taxing rather than pillaging them. Because of these ecological constraints, European states could not be as predatory as the imperial states of Eurasia. This allowed intensive growth, which Jones believes is

just waiting to bubble forth but for the restraints imposed by the predatory state.[36]

But Michael Mann is surely right in pointing to the illegitimacy of the
implicit assumption underlying this argument. "Why is Europe," he writes

to be regarded as a continent in the first place? This is not an ecological but a social
fact. It had not been a continent hitherto. It was now created by the fusion of Germanic barbarians with the northwestern parts of the Roman empire, and it was
bounded by the blocking presence of Islam to the south and east. Its continental
identity was primarily Christian. It was known as Christendom rather than Europe.[37]

This is crucial.

The rise of the West is really, as the title of a famous book by Trevor-
Roper is called, *The Rise of Christian Europe* and even more narrowly, as
Southern[38] has emphasized, the Latin rather than the Greek part of the
post-Roman Christian world. That dynamic, which led to that unique
form of Promethean growth in the West, was part of "the identification of
the Church with the whole of organized society ... the fundamental feature which distinguishes the Middle Ages from earlier and later periods of
history. At its widest limit it is a feature of European history from the
fourth to the eighteenth century—from Constantine to Voltaire."[39] The
church thus provided cultural unity to a politically divided continent.

But this raises another puzzle. For this cultural unity amid political dis-
unity was not unique to Europe but has been true of the Indian subcontinent for millennia. Imperial unity has been rare, but Hinduism and its
social expression—the caste system—have provided a cultural unity,
much like Christianity did for the Middle Ages in the state system in
Europe. So why did individualism and its descendants, the instruments of
Promethean growth, develop in Europe rather than in India? It could not
have been, as Jones maintains, because of the political decentralization of
the Continent under the states system, as something similar also existed
in the subcontinent. It is more plausible to look for differences in the
"ideological" systems that underwrote their respective cultural unities.

An important clue is provided by Mann's observation that there were
two parallel diagonal lines creating a corridor to the heart of the medieval
trading world:

One line gathered the produce of Scandinavia and the North to the mouth of the
Rhine, moving it up the Rhine to Switzerland and thence to northern, especially
northeastern Italy, receiving Mediterranean and eastern produce in return. The
other line began in Flanders, gathering North Sea produce, then moving mostly
by land transport through northern and eastern France to the Loire and thence to
the Mediterranean and Northwestern Italy.[40]

The major "powers" along this trading network were ecclesiastical "states." They provided the trading dynamic of the medieval European world. Control by the Christian church of these trading "states" essentially distinguishes them from Hindu India. What explains the difference?

The most important of these differences, as our discussion of Dumont has noted, is that between cosmologies of "homo hierarchicus" and "individualism." I have showed[41] that the cosmological beliefs relating to the former were formed as part of the development of a social system serving "material" interests. Is a similar explanation available for the diametrically different development of individualism from Christianity, despite the striking parallels between the "other-worldliness" of the individual and the "hierarchical complementarity" between the sacred and secular in both Hinduism and Christianity in its earlier phases?

The crucial difference arises with the second of the two factors in Dumont's explanation for the rise of individualism. This, as Southern, Trevor-Roper, and Berman have emphasized, was the papal revolution of 1075, when Pope Gregory VII "declared the political and legal supremacy of the papacy over the entire church and the independence of the clergy from secular control. Gregory also asserted the ultimate supremacy of the Pope in secular matters, including the authority to depose emperors and kings."[42]

Most historians now date the beginnings of the so-called European dynamic from about A.D. 800.[43] But, as Southern notes, "that moment of self generating expansion, for which economists now look so anxiously in underdeveloped countries, came to Western Europe in the late eleventh century. There was no single outstanding technical innovation behind this expansive movement, but a combination of many circumstances: growing accumulation of capital, rising population, the return of the Mediterranean to western control, the political decline of the Greek and Moslem empires, all helped to open up ever-enlarging prospects of the West."[44].

The papal revolution provided the institutional infrastructure for this Western economic dynamic. Berman has shown how the whole Western legal tradition really derives from the development of both canon and secular law during the eleventh to thirteenth centuries under the aegis of the church.[45] The most important for the economy was the development of the "law of the merchant"—the *lex mercatoria*—in which

the various rights and obligations associated with commercial relations came to be consciously interpreted as constituent parts of [this] whole body of law.... Many diverse commercial legal institutions created at that time, such as negotiable instruments, secured credit, and joint ventures, together with many older legal institutions that were then refashioned, were all seen as forming a distinct and coherent system.[46]

Berman lists many of the features that we currently associate as being the modern institutional infrastructure for trade and commerce, as having arisen in these three centuries of the high Middle Ages. They include

the invention of the negotiability of bills of exchange and promissory notes; the invention of the mortgage of movables (chattel mortgage); the development of a bankruptcy law which took into account the existence of a sophisticated system of commercial credit; the development of the bill of lading and other transportation documents; ... the invention of the bottomry loan ... ; the replacement of the more individualistic Graeco-Roman concept of partnership (societas) by a more collectivistic concept in which there was joint ownership, the property was at the disposition of the partnership as a unit, and the rights and obligations of one part- ner survived the death of the other; the development of the joint venture (com- menda) as a kind of joint-stock company, with the liability of each investor limited to the amount of his investment; the invention of trademarks and patents; the floating of public loans secured by bonds and other securities; the development of deposit banking.[47]

In short, all the essential legal infrastructure for a modern commercial and industrial economy![48]

It was also during this time that the Roman Church formed itself into a church-state,[49] a law-state, that also "developed the governmental institu- tions and the bureaucratic apparatus needed to make this legal system work: a professional judiciary, a treasury, a chancery. This was the first modern Western system of government and law. It was eventually emu- lated by the secular polities that took form in the succeeding genera- tions."[50] This was the great divide between the path taken by the two otherwise similar ancient religions—Hinduism and Christianity—situated in (prima facie) similar political and ecological environments.

To understand the reasons for Pope Gregory VII's papal revolution of 1075, it is necessary to go back to the centuries after the collapse of the western Roman empire and the gradual expansion of the Western church through conversions in the northern and northwestern barbaric Germanic lands. These conversions of the Germanic peoples and their tribal chiefs were successful for two complementary reasons.

The first was Christianity's disenchantment of Nature, which allowed the expansion of agriculture into the northern forests.[51] The role of Christian monastics particularly of the Cistercians, was crucial in this.[52] The second was that it transformed "the ruler from a tribal chief (dux) into a king (rex). Once converted to Christianity, the king no longer represented only the deities of his tribe: he represented, in addition, a universal deity whose authority extended to all tribes, or at least to many tribes. He became, in effect, the head of an empire."[53]

It is interesting to note that, as I argue in *The Hindu Equilibrium*, a similar dual function was also performed by the Hindu Brahmins in the expansion of Hinduism in southern India. In both these cases the religious carriers of these secular gifts themselves became enriched through land grants.[54] But in both cases the priests upheld the primacy of sacral kingship in matters that were secular. It was the uniqueness of the papal revolution that it upset this dualistic system and set the church above the state not only in matters concerning the world hereafter, but also in this world.[55]

Jack Goody's brilliant book *The Development of the Family and Marriage in Europe* provides the clues to answering the question of why Pope Gregory VII launched "the first of the great revolutions of Western history ... [which was] against [the] domination of the clergy by emperors, kings, and lords and for the establishment of the Church of Rome as an independent, corporate, political and legal entity, under the papacy."[56]

Goody, citing the venerable Bede, "tells of some problems involved in converting the pagan English." He explains how after "Augustine, the first archbishop of Canterbury, arrived in 597, he sent messengers back to Pope Gregory [I] at Rome seeking advice on certain current questions, including ones relating to marriage.... Four of the nine questions on which Augustine asked advice from the Pope had to do with sex and marriage."[57] Gregory's answers, Goody shows, overturned the traditional Mediterranean and Middle Eastern patterns of legal and customary practices in the domestic domain. This traditional system "permitted, indeed encouraged, the practices of firstly, marriage to close kin; secondly, marriage to close affines or the widows of close kin (possibly by inheritance, of which the levirate was the extreme form); thirdly, the transfer of children by adoption; and, finally, concubinage, a form of secondary union."[58]

The pope forbade all four practices in his reply. This papal response, Goody argues, owes little to Scripture, Roman law, or the existing customs in the old or new areas colonized by the Christian church. Combined with the Christian injunction against divorce, which goes back to the words of Christ (Matthew 19:3–9), all the rejected practices had one common aspect. They concerned "strategies of heirship": inheritance of familial property, the provision of an heir, and maintaining status in an advanced stratified agricultural society.[59]

Thus, argues Goody,

marriage between kin serves to reinforce "family" ties. These particular forms also prevent female heiresses from removing property from the "family," and thus combat the problem of the absence of sons. They do nothing to eliminate the dangers of heirlessness in general. Any "direct" system of inheritance (one in which children are the primary beneficiaries of parental wealth and status) has to contend with the fact that approximately 20 percent of couples will have only girls and a further 20 percent will have no children at all[60]; the figures will be higher if there are high rates of sterility, homosexuality or contraception. These forms of close marriages would take care of the absence of sons; other strategies, adoption, polygyny, divorce and remarriage can be used to provide a solution to childlessness. But prohibit close marriage, discourage adoption, condemn polygyny, concubinage, divorce and remarriage, and 40 percent of families will be left with no immediate male heirs.[61]

These sixth-century papal injunctions therefore inhibited a family from retaining its property and promoted its alienation.[62] This is, of course, what the church wanted, for, from its inception, it had grown and become a rich landlord through gifts and donations.

Robin Lane-Fox, summarizing the composition of the church at the middle of the third century, notes,

The Christians were a small minority, hardly known in the Latin West or the underbelly of northern Europe, on which so much of the military effort of third-century Emperors was to be expended. They were not only concentrated in the bigger cities, but they were prominent in towns of varying rank and degree; ... their center of gravity lay with the humbler free classes, not with the slaves, whom they did little to evangelize.... Women of all ranks were conspicuous and there was a notable presence in some churches of women of high status.[63]

The last point is crucial. "One of the major demographic contrasts between an ancient and a modern population," writes Lane-Fox,

lies in the ancient's higher proportion of young widows. Because the age of girls at marriage was frequently very low, as low as thirteen, older husbands were likely to die first, leaving their wives to the second marriages which secular laws encouraged: under Augustus's rules, widows were penalized if they did not remarry within two years. In the churches, however, widowhood was an honored status and remarriage was often seen as a concession to the weak.... Christian teaching thus tended to keep widows as unattached women, and their presence became significant.... The rules of female inheritance in most of these women's home cities would allow them to control or inherit a proportion of their husband's property. The Church, in turn, was a natural candidate for their bequests.... Nor did the churches profit only from widows. They exalted virginity, and their young female membership actually practiced it.... Again, these women grew up without any family, yet they were heiresses to parts of their fathers' and mothers' property.

Bequests were antiquity's swiftest route to social advancement and the increase of personal capital. By idealizing virginity and frowning on second marriage, the Church was to become a force without equal in the race for inheritance.[64]

Pope Gregory's reply to Augustine was thus clearly in line with a self-interested trend in the church's behavior from its earliest inception.[65] And the church's accumulation was phenomenal. "It has been estimated," writes Goody, "that one third of the productive land in France was in ecclesiastical hands by the end of the seventh century.[66] In the two following centuries the growth was again rapid. 'In German lands, in Northern France, and in Italy the Church owns twice as much land in the ninth century as in the eighth. In Southern France, too, between the first and second quarter of the ninth century, Church property increases from 21 to 40 percent'."[67,68]

But from the tenth century onward this enormous accumulation of property by the church attracted both external and internal enemies. Considerable depredation of church land began. The great secularization of the tenth century led to attacks on ecclesiastical lands, especially on those of the monasteries, "partly by the State, partly by freebooters such as Normans, and partly by reprobate clerics who used the Church property for their own ends."[69]

The papal revolution was the answer. It was aimed at recovering the church's pillaged patrimony.[70] "The reforms instigated at this time included the enforcement of celibacy of the clergy and the wide extension of the prohibitions on marriage, the latter tending to weaken the control of property by kin, the former helping to retain in Church hands what had already been secured."[71] By creating the church-state, and the administrative and legal system associated with it that we have charted, the church was—we must accept with Goody—protecting its material self-interests!

But how could a "power" without arms enforce its will on the secular power over which it had proclaimed its supremacy? It was through the threat of excommunication. Having successfully sold its cosmological beliefs about purgatory and salvation to both kings and their people, the church could coerce obedience by threatening eternal damnation. It could use its power in the next to redress its weakness in this world. For rulers, the threat of excommunication threatened not only their souls but also their estates, as it legitimized rebellions by their Christian subjects in the name of God. There were some spectacular instances of the seeming efficacy of this power: "Henry IV of Germany at Canossa, Henry II of England in his shirt at Canterbury, King John a vassal of the Pope, the family of Fredrick II destroyed, a Papal nominee on the throne of Sicily."[72] But, as Southern notes, in the long run this "power over princes could only be effective by being over-effective. It was impossible for [the Pope] to pluck out and destroy an individual without bringing about a general political, and sometimes an ecclesiastical collapse."[73] It took only a few centuries for Henry VIII in England, caught in the web of domestic problems that Pope Gregory I's answers about marriage to Archbishop Augustine's questions had created for him, to take the step no medieval king had thought of taking: "And that was to cast off the authority of Rome, to keep the churches open on his own authority, and to accept papal excommunication as a permanent condition."[74] Once that happened, the church-state was dead and the nation-state was born.

But the two revolutions of Pope Gregory I on the family and Pope Gregory VII in the creation of modern legal institutions have had lasting effects on the West, besides being the crucible for its central cosmological belief—individualism. The effects of Pope Gregory VII's legal revolution on the economy are well known, but we need to look further at the consequences of Pope Gregory I's family revolution.

The Nuclear Family and the Rise of the West

The role of the Western type of family in the rise of the West has gone through a curious metamorphosis in recent years as a result of the researches of various historians, sociologists, and demographers. The older view adumbrated, for instance, by Marx and Engels, saw preindustrial societies dominated by extended families, with their non-Western cousins further distinguished by being polygynous.[75] The Industrial Revolution was supposed to have led to the replacement of the extended by the nuclear family, and modernization theorists believed that as they industrialized non-Western societies would also converge to this modern norm.[76]

Two different research programs have overturned these presumptions. The first is the result of the detailed demographic data that has been collected and analyzed by the Cambridge Group for the History of Population and Social structure.[77] The second is the work of anthropologists also based at Cambridge who have gone beyond the more statistically secure studies of the demographers to show that the unique pattern of household formation they discovered from the sixteenth century for northwestern Europe went much further back in time, possibly to the sixth century in the case of Britain.[78] We have already seen how, according to Goody's account, the role of the church was central in overturning the Eurasian marriage and inheritance systems in Western Europe.

If this account is true it led to the distinctive form of household formation—the "Northwest European" kind as characterized by Hajnal[79]—many centuries before the Industrial Revolution of the late eighteenth and early nineteenth centuries. It is now being claimed that rather than being the consequence, this exceptional household and family pattern was a cause of the Industrial Revolution.

The three distinctive features of this system, as contrasted with India, China, Russia, and to some extent southern Europe, are late marriages, the employment of the unmarried outside rather than within households, and the fission of households on marriage.[80] These characteristics allowed fertility to be controlled, essentially by alterations in the age at marriage, according to varying economic circumstances through the "living-in" system.[81] Northwestern Europe thus escaped the Malthusian immiserization that followed unchanged breeding in the rest of Eurasia.[82] The "living-in" system was crucial as it allowed variations in the numbers remaining unmarried and in the age of marriage, whereas in the "joint household systems" an increase in population "led to the underemployment of married adults rather than a temporary or permanent delay in marriage itself."[83] This variable fertility allowed the West uniquely to have some economic surplus available for investment, however small, which was not eaten up by population growth. Thus, slowly, its growth trajectory was changed from that of the rest of the world.

But Goody was surely right in arguing that this argument "that Europe was capable of controlling its population when others were not seems to lack substance.... In Asia, people resorted to female infanticide, to less fertile forms of early marriage, to coitus reservatus, while delays in marriage were potentially just as possible when the young stayed in the household as when they moved outside.[84] The great expansion of population in China and India took place in the context of highly productive economies."[85] He pointedly adds, "many of the fundamental contributions to mercantile capitalism were made in Italy where the alternative system prevailed. Nor would it be correct to underplay the important contributions to mercantile capitalism in India made by the 'Hindu undivided family'. As to contemporary development, it is the area of 'joint household' regimes in the East that seems now to be making much of the running."[86]

This recent historical and demographic research has rightly destroyed the older view that the Western nuclear family was the product of the

Industrial Revolution, but its claim that instead it was its cause is equally unsustainable. Hence, too, are both corollaries drawn from the history of the family for the rest of the world: industrialization does not necessarily have to lead to the spread of "Western" families as the convergence thesis argued on the basis of the older view, nor are "joint household" systems likely to inhibit development as the revisionists imply.

The consequences of the "Western family system" initiated by Gregory I have nevertheless had momentous indirect economic effects through promoting individualism, which came about through its support for the independence of the young in choosing marriage partners, in setting up their own households, and in entering into contractual rather than affective relationships of care for the old.

Two related features of the Western nuclear family are worth noting in this respect, and they too go back to the twelfth century—and perhaps earlier in England[87]: retirement contracts and public provision for the poor.[88] Both concern aspects of insuring against the inevitable vagaries of life. This insurance function was and continues to be provided by and large through the family in non-Western Eurasian civilizations. In joint households where adult children stayed with their parents they could work the land when there parents became infirm and looked after them in their old age. But in the Western nuclear family system, where the children moved out when they were adults, there had to be some way of passing on the productive resources of the aged as well as to provide the old some of the output of the working population. This was done partly through inheritance contracts, and partly through the aged leasing out their land or living off past savings. Finally, the church, the guilds, and the manor took on the responsibility for destitutes of all ages. "This non-familistic provision we also know stretches back into the thirteenth century and earlier."[89] Unlike the other Eurasian systems, this Western system did not depend on the responsibility of children to their parents or vice versa. "Parents could disinherit children, while children could, in a sense, disinherit their parents, by refusing to maintain them"[90] The cold-hearted attitude to the old, which has struck many non-western observers of the West,[91] was thus set very early on. The resulting loneliness Macfarlane notes, "is a price that is paid for economic and political individualism."[92] As is the substitution of public for private safety nets to deal with the problems of destitution and conjunctural poverty.

In both respects the West had deviated from the other Eurasian civilizations long before the Industrial Revolution. The Rest continue to rely mainly on the family as the major means of social insurance,[93] and the fear (or hope) of some that these familial mechanisms will necessarily be undermined by industrialization is as fallacious as the older view which held that the Western nuclear family was the consequence of the Industrial Revolution. The cosmological beliefs of the West led to its unique family structure. If many of its features are currently being bemoaned in the "debate on the family" it is worth noting that it was the self-interested agenda of the medieval church to undermine kinship and the inheritance systems based on it which were the basis of the "extended" families of most other civilizations, which led to the early undermining of this domestic form in the West. As Goody notes,

The Church's insistence on consent and affection, as well as on the freedom of testament, meant taking "a stand against the power of heads of households in matters of marriage, against the lay conception of misalliance, and, indeed, against male supremacy, for it asserted the equality of the sexes in concluding the marriage pact and in the accomplishments of the duties thereby implied."[94] Duby describes these effects as "unintentional." The result was to encourage the love match rather than the arranged marriage, the freedom of the testator rather than inheritance between kin. But these features, sometimes seen as definitive of the Western family ... are surely intrinsic to the whole process whereby the Church established its position as a power in the land, a spiritual power certainly, but also a worldly one, the owner of property, the largest landowner, a position it obtained by gaining control of the system of marriage, gift and inheritance. Such factors are associated with the guidelines supposedly laid down by Pope Gregory I. ... In essence they owe little to the later transformations of feudalism, mercantile capitalism, industrial society, Hollywood or the Germanic tradition.[95]

Love, Sex, Sin, and Guilt

Many have also seen the monogamous conjugal relationship based on romantic love as unique to the West, the feature that distinguishes it from all the other systems of marriage in Eurasia. On the last there is little disagreement. Even in the culture closest in its origins to the west, Islam, as Crone and Cook note, "the emotional repertoire of Islamic culture was a decidedly unromantic one."[96] The ditty "love and marriage go together like a horse and carriage" describes a Western characteristic not shared by most other civilizations.

Romantic passion is not, however, a uniquely Western cultural trait developed during the Middle Ages by troubadours and court society, as many historians have claimed.[97] Anthropologists Jankowiak and Fischer[98] found in their cross-cultural study of 166 cultures that romantic passion could be documented in 89 per cent of them.[99] The universality and biological basis of this emotion is confirmed by Liebowitz's[100] psychological research, which has shown that there are distinct biochemicals associated with this emotion. The stage of infatuation when "in love" is clearly associated with increased levels of phenylethylamine, an amphetamine-related compound. After a period of attachment, Liebowitz conjectures,[101] the brain's receptor sites for the essential neurochemicals become desensitized or overloaded and the infatuation ends, setting up both the body and brain for separation and divorce. This period of infatuation lasts, as Tennov and Money[102] have shown, for about three years. Moreover, Fisher's cross-cultural study[103] of divorce patterns in sixty-two societies between 1947 and 1989 found that divorces tend to occur around the fourth year of marriage; most divorce in their twenties when they are at the height of their reproductive years; marriages most often break down when they are childless or with only a single child; most divorcees of reproductive age remarry; and "the longer a mateship lasts, the older the spouses get, and/or the more children they bear, the more likely they are to stay together."[104]

Given a universal emotion with a biological basis, sociobiologists have tried to provide an explanation of how it arose.[105] In the primordial environment it was vital that males and females were attracted to each other to have sex and reproduce and also that the males were attached enough to the females to stay around and raise the young until they were old enough to move into a peer group and be raised by the band. The traditional period between successive human births is four years,[106] which is also the modal period for those marriages that end in divorce today. Darwin strikes again! The biochemistry of love, it seems, evolved as an "inclusive fitness" strategy of our species.[107] The capacity to love would thus seem to be universal, but its public expression is culturally controlled.

For though romantic passion may be a universal human emotion, it is, as everyone's personal experience will attest, an explosive one. Particularly given its relatively rapid decay, once settled agriculture was established the evolved instincts for mates to stay together for about four years and then to move on to new, fitter partners to conceive and rear new young would have been dysfunctional. Settled agriculture requires settled households. Hunter-gatherer bands wandering over a vast expanse can accommodate changing households, but settled agriculture requires particular households to settle on particular parcels of land. If households are in permanent flux, changing every four years, agriculture could not be settled. It is not surprising, therefore, that most civilizations would tend to curb the explosive primordial emotion that would have destroyed their way of making a living. Cultural constraints would be devised to rein in these socially destructive emotions:

Most societies have realized that romantic love and marriage make tricky partners; they develop intricate ways of curbing this dangerous hominid tendency and rely on arranged marriages, infant betrothal and the like, restricting passion to relationships outside wedlock. It is a paradox that, while 99 percent of societies recognize the dangerous nature of this biological universal in undermining the social order and the family, we in the West have used it as one of the bastions of marriage.[108]

If Goody's argument is correct, it was the church's greed that overthrew the Eurasian system of marriage, which kept this passion under control. Friar Lawrence's egging on the young lovers in *Romeo and Juliet* on their doomed path to true love, against the wishes of their families, is emblematic of the change the Church wrought. But it also provided other means for curtailing the social chaos that would have ensued if this passion had been allowed to run its course.

First, it separated love and sex. Then, by creating a guilt culture based on original sin, it provided a powerful means of enforcing its morality, including its injunctions against divorce. We consider both in turn.

In considering the church's separation between love and sex, it maybe useful to denote the biological instinct we have so far discussed as romantic passion and distinguish it from what we are about discuss— Christian love.[109] Clearly romantic passion and sex are closely entwined. But this is not so with the Christian notion of love, which is not self-interested but, as Lindholm notes, is an experience of transcendence.[110] "Its heritage," he writes,

includes the Jewish concept of *nomos* transformed into Christian notions of God's unconditional, unreserved, and undeserved love for humanity (*agape*), as expressed in the sacrifice of Jesus. This notion of God's boundless love of humanity made love itself a value in Western culture while simultaneously devaluing sexuality. Love was further humanized in the cult of Mary, and ... afterward was secularized in the courtly love that bound the courtier to his lady.[111] Thereafter "the Christian could hold not only that God is Love but also that Love is God."[112]

This desexualising of love was accompanied by the creation of a guilt culture built on original sin. The French Annales historian Jean Delumeau[113] has provided a detailed account of how a guilt culture emerged in the West, which led to a religion of anxiety as contrasted with the religions of "tranquility" of the East.[114]

Unlike Islam, which ... did not incline towards the macabre, Christian civilization placed the Fall at the center of its preoccupations and construed it as a catastrophe initiating all history. Although the story of Adam and Eve's crime appears in the first book of the Old Testament, ancient Judaism did not focus its theology on the first sin. Only during the earliest Christian era did certain non-canonical Jewish writings date the penalties that weigh upon humanity back to Adam.[115]

It was Augustine who definitively elaborated and probably invented the expression "original sin."[116] In doing so he was drawing on the body of doctrines developed by the early Christian ascetics—the origin of various *contemptus mundi*—with their scorn for the world and contempt for mankind and "a lasting nostalgia for a primitive, asexual man-angel, 'spiritualized' and dedicated to pure contemplation."[117] Augustine "clearly asserted that we are all guilty in Adam because 'we all were this unique man'.[118] Hence ensues our misery: We are born guilty, and not only that, but the concupiscence released by the first sin lures us into committing more and more sins."[119]

From the fourteenth to the seventeenth centuries, argues Delumeau, building on this Augustinian notion of original sin and humankind's continuing and primordial guilt, all over Christendom there was the growth of "'scruple sickness' ... the fear of one's self."[120] Christians had to free themselves from their evil instincts to rise above their base nature. Sexuality was in particular ferociously attacked. Augustine had said that sexual relations in the Garden of Eden were bereft of lust, but since the Fall, humanity "has become like the beasts and engenders like them."[121] By the time of the *De Contemptus Mundi* of the future Pope Innocent III, the church taught that "sexual desire and its fulfillment are contaminating. Marriage is filth (*sordes*) from which only the blood of martyrdom washed St. Peter.... Marriage is tolerable only in view of procreation, the pains of childbirth constituting a justified penalty for sinful pleasures.... Consequently, chastity is always preferable to the religious virtues."[122]

This pervasive Christian teaching against sex based on its notions of original sin and the unavoidable guilt this engendered was the necessary antidote to the "animal passions" that would otherwise have been unleashed by the church's self-interested overthrowing of the traditional Eurasian system of marriage. But as the deadly sins encompassed more than mere concupiscence, the guilt associated with being the sinful Adam was also a very powerful means of maintaining social control.[123] The obsessive preoccupation with death in early modern Europe[124] (with the "Danse Macabre" as its emblem) was fed by the chronological progression that defined the goals of life: "death, judgment, Hell (or Paradise)."[125] It led to the conviction that the moment of death is the decisive point on which all the rest of eternity hinges—a conviction maintained throughout the age of humanism. Hence the importance of a good death, and of the father-confessor, who by absolving the sinner of his sins at the moment of death might allow him to attain salvation on the Day of Judgment. Thus also the importance of the priest in absolving the laity of all the deadly sins that mortal flesh was heir to and the guilt associated with them through suitable penances and indulgences.

The Reformation strengthened the hold of this guilt culture.[126] "Man was but 'dung' and 'filth'—no wonder the result was despair. Yet it was exactly this despair that was destined to save those who, miserable and naked, abandoned themselves entirely to God."[127] It was not until the Enlightenment that the religious roots of this collective guilt culture were to be questioned. But the importance of conscience, or as Arapura calls it "conscience about conscience," was to continue with the secular ethical thinkers such as Kant. For although conscience as "a notion and fact of general morality ... is universal," in the Christian notion taken over by secular Western philosophers of "the conscience about conscience ... the association with guilt is very deep-rooted": *pace* Kant's notion of the categorical imperative.[128] This is very different from other cultures. In Hinduism, for instance, conscience plays a role in

providing the impulsion to practice [the precepts of moral conduct, but it] ... plays no further role and certainly not that of an accusing, judging and condemning power towards those who fail to obey these noble precepts.... By contrast, the problem of disobedience of the [moral] law, strangely enough unavoidable—not in spite but because of freedom—is lodged in the very heart of the Christian version of conscience.... On account of this it is clear that only in Christianity does conscience have its source in guilt which is not true of the Eastern religions—or any other for that matter.[129]

Why did this guilt culture arise and intensify from the twelfth century onward in Western Christendom? Deulmieu writes,

The answer would seem to lie in a coincidence, which might otherwise not have occurred, between a pessimistic brand of preaching that was rapidly widening its appeal and a series of vast collective disasters that besieged Europe from the Black Death to the end of the Wars of Religion. The preachers seemed to have good reason to say that mankind was guilty and to foretell punishment in both this world and the next. In the eighteenth century and after, the alleviation of serious threats to daily life encouraged challenging the validity of these dire pronouncement.[130]

But in addition, in my view, the usefulness of this guilt culture in undoing some of the harm that the church's greed had done in undermining the ancient Eurasian family system cannot be gainsaid. This seems particularly important given the dating of the intensification of this guilt culture from the twelfth century onward, that is, soon after the papal revolution of the eleventh century, which completed the formalization of the church's role as the arbiter in both the personal and Caesar's realms, which itself was the culmination of a process to preserve the Church's newfound wealth.

The power of this guilt culture in maintaining social control in the West cannot be underestimated. It still exercises a powerful influence on the minds of those brought up in this culture even if they have repudiated its theology. Here, for instance, is the contemporary British novelist Angela Palmer describing her experience in Japan. She notes that all the Japanese she knew had read the same books, listened to the same music, and seen the same movies, so that

their intellectual experience will have been very similar to mine. And then what you come up against is the jarring fact—for instance, I was standing somewhere once and I saw this young girl running down a flight of steps, and clear as anything, I thought, She never realized that Christ died for her sins.... Not only does she not know, she wouldn't care if you told her. Yes, because he never did. I mean, he didn't for mine either but for twenty years an awful lot of people told me he did.... What I mean is that the Judaeo-Christian tradition was built into me at some point. I've consciously rejected it, but I've obviously retained some of it on an unconscious level. And it isn't in them! And I think this makes an immense difference.[131]

We will return to this contrast in later chapters. But at this stage all we need to note is that in the individualistic society launched by Gregory I's family revolution, social control was still maintained through church-mediated mechanisms of guilt and the fear of purgatory. This has led to paradoxical consequences, as we will see in Chapter 9.

By contrast, the legal institutions resulting from the same self-interested papal revolution of Gregory VII, but underwritten by the Book, have ultimately led to the European miracle. As Berman reminds us, "without the fear of purgatory and the hope of the Last Judgment, the Western legal tradition could not have come into existence."[132]

Thus there is a complex interaction between ideas—the cosmological beliefs of culture as we defined them—institutions, and material interests. No one single cause can explain "the cunning of history" that led to the rise of the West.

The Greek Orthodox Church and Russia

It remains to outline the fate of the other half of Christianity—the Greek Orthodox—after the schism from its Latin parent in 1054. This is of some importance because it underlines a major argument of this chapter, that it was not the Christianity preached by Jesus but the Augustinian mutation in Christian theology and the twin revolutions of the two Popes Gregory concerning the family and the law that lie behind the unique rise of the West.

The major difference between the Greek and Latin branches of Christianity is that whereas with the papal revolution the Latin church was seeking to render the things that were both God's and Caesar's unto God, its Greek cousin came to accept that both the things that were Caesar's and God's should be rendered unto Caesar. The basic ideology of the Byzantine system were formulated by the court prelate Eusebius in the 330s at the court of the first Christian emperor Constantine I. "The Eusebian theory can be summed up in the phrase 'As in heaven, so on earth'. The emperor is to be seen as the living icon of Christ, God's viceregent on earth. The terrestrial rule of the emperor reproduces God's rule in heaven....Just as God regulates the cosmic order, so the emperor regulates the social order."[133] This doctrine, which promoted what many historians have called "Caesaropapism," was completely different from Augustine's political theory of the two cities: a city of God that is radically distinct from any human city or society in the world after the Fall. Augustine provided the argument for placing the human city in the hands of the city of God.[134]

What Justinian labeled the "'happy concord' between priesthood (*sacredotium*) and kingship (*imperium*)"[135] proved particularly attractive to Vladimir, who ruled the young Kievian state from 980 to 1015, and which was the precursor of the future Russian empire, when he was shopping around for a religion. The legendary account is that the Russians selected their religion "spurning Islam because it prohibited alcohol—for 'drink is the joy of the Russians'—and Judaism because it expressed the beliefs of a defeated people without a state,"[136] and chose the Byzantine liturgy and faith instead, which has underwritten the autocratic Russian state ever since. With the fall of Constantinople in 1453, Ivan III laid claim to the inheritance of the Kievian state with the assumption of the title of Sovereign of Russia. Having declared its independence from the Mongol's golden horde, Moscow became the Third Rome. It took over from Byzantium as the center of the Greek Christian civilization. This "meant

that Russia remained outside the Roman Catholic Church, and this in turn
not only deprived Russia of what that church itself had to offer, but also
contributed to the relative isolation of Russia from the rest of Europe and
its Latin civilization. It helped notably to inspire Russian suspicion of the
West."[137]

But orthodox Christianity did give Eastern Europe a cultural continuity
despite the lack of political continuity given its geography. "Cut into and
crossed by invaders' corridors, its open, flat expanses and its good communications and dispersed populations contribute to an environment in
which states can form with ease, survive with struggle, and thrive with
rarity. It favors vast and fragile empires, vulnerable to external attack and
internal rebellion."[138] Despite this, in the fifteenth century Muscovy's rate
of expansion exceeded that of any Western state: "During Europe's 'great
age of expansion' in the early modern era, while westerners were founding the conspicuous, remote, and ultimately doomed maritime empires all
over the globe, the Russians created ... one of the largest and longest-
lived of all the European's extra-European empires in Siberia."[139]

The thinly spread population of this growing Russian empire meant
that it was faced with a scarcity of labor relative to land, as in the other
agrarian civilizations, a scarcity aggravated by the growing military needs
of Moscow as it confronted various enemies, the Swedes and Poland-
Lithuania to the north and west and the Tatars in the south, from the
second half of the fifteenth century. By the middle of the seventeenth
century the peasants had been enserfed.[140]

Eastern feudalism differed from that in the West in having repartitional
tenure. Periodically, village land was reapportioned among the households in the village in proportion to the labor power of each household.
The purpose was to maintain family labor based farms, much as in the
"cift-hane" under the Ottomans in the Middle East.[141] This meant that,
unlike in the West, the peasants did not acquire any property rights in the
land. The system was finally abolished with the emancipation of the serfs
in 1861.[142] But there was never the development of the contractual ties
that developed between vassals and their sovereign in the west. Russia
remained a "tribute collecting hierarchy"[143] where the noble landowners
had total authority over their peasant serfs and the tsar had unchallenged
and complete authority over them.

With its divorce from Latin Christendom, the East was soon left behind
in the changes in cosmology and technologies that led to the rise of the
West. This has led to a recurrent "pattern in Russia's relations with the
[west]. . . . There has been the effort to 'catch up' and more or less play a

major role in the world, followed by periods of relative decline."[144] The first period of catchup was during the reign of Peter the Great in the first quarter of the eighteenth century. The second was during the second half of the nineteenth century following the abolition of serfdom by Alexander II. The third was under Stalin in the 1930s. The first two "pushes" sought to emulate the fruits of the "individualism" that had led to the growing ascendancy of the West. The third was also based on a Western import: the collectivist body of Marxist thought that had risen during the late nineteenth century. Russia is again turning to the more individualistic and liberal traditions of the West. But as with the previous non-Communist attempts at catchup, the old debate is again joined between the Westernizers, who argue that the only way for Muscovy to regain its position in the world is to modernize, and the Slavophiles, who argue that the only salvation lies in cleansing Mother Russia of corrupting western influences. Andrei Sakharov and Aleksandr Solzhenitsyn are representative of these two positions, respectively. How this debate will be resolved remains to be seen.

But this brief excursus into the history of the third Rome does emphasize two points. First, Christianity per se did not deliver Promethean growth. The cosmological mutation wrought by Augustine and the conjunctural revolutions of the two Popes Gregory concerning the law and the family created the institutional conditions for the European miracle. Second, the course of individualism in the West that began in the Middle Ages has not been steady. As the Western imports of the period of catchup under Stalin shows, the West for a time gave up on its earlier liberal beliefs and has only recently recovered them. This story of the puzzling course of individualism—its rise, fall, and rise—is instructive in many ways for my purposes and is the subject of the next chapter.

6   The Course of
       Individualism

If individualism is the unique value of the West whose origins go back to the high Middle Ages, its subsequent course in Western thought has not been a smooth one. Though in time, unlike its other Eurasian contemporaries, this unique Western value delivered the scientific and industrial revolutions, it remained in creative tension with the more traditional forms of communalism, as we will see. The Christian cosmology formulated in the main part by Saint Augustine also continued to haunt Western minds.

The Reformation shattered the ideological unity of Western Christendom. This had profound effects on political thought and action. It provided fertile ground for questioning political legitimacy by raising the question of who had the right to make laws, in a new way not found elsewhere in Eurasia. Until then both rulers and ruled were bound by the Common Law of Christendom; because it was God's law there could be no question of disobedience.[1] But after the Reformation, who represented God's law, the Catholics or the Protestants? Whose law should you obey if you were a Catholic in a Protestant kingdom or vice versa? The notion of the social contract was born.

The ancient Greeks and Romans had looked upon the state as a unified corporate structure, like a body.[2] Christianity, with its separation and demotion of politics to the maintenance of peace and justice in the temporal world and its emphasis on the care of the individual soul as the basic purpose of life, had shaken this ancient conception of civil harmony. On Aristotle's classical view, man was a political animal. By the thirteenth century Aquinas had distinguished man as being both a political and *social* animal. But it was not till the seventeenth century that the distinction between state and society became a dominant part of Western thought, with social-contract theorists distinguishing between the beginning of society—now seen as an autonomous mode of association—and the construction of a state.

Further associations were subsequently abstracted from the state. First
was the economy—as the growth of European commerce and industry
showed that humans were also associated with another distinctive set of
associations as producers, consumers, and distributors of commodities.
Unlike the set of social and political relationships, which seemed to be
ruled by unpredictable human decisions, economic relationships seemed
closer to the impersonal relationships of nature that were then being
uncovered by the new physical sciences. These economic relationships
could be seen to be governed—as Adam Smith was the first to show—
by abstract laws resembling the laws of nature. Second, with the Romantic revolt against the Enlightenment, people also began to see themselves
as bearers of a distinctive culture, based on speaking a particular language
or dialect, with their own customs, artistic heritage, and cuisines. This
separation of culture from society was to lead to nationalism.

Thus modernity in the West came to distinguish between different
forms of human associations. If society was *sui generis*, the three others,
the polity, the economy, and the culture—which are also the three triads
of the subject matter of these lectures—have come to be seen in Western
thought as equally important but differing forms of association between
human beings. But most important, as Minogue has stressed, these "self-
conscious associations set the scene for the dramas of modern political
conflict."[3]

But there was a more far reaching development following from the
Protestant claim of the sinfulness of the hierarchy of the Catholic church.
If the traditional interpreters of God's will appointed by the pope were
sinful, where were the true interpreters of his word to be found? "If not
the Church, then only the congregations."[4] These became self-governing,
choosing and dismissing their pastors. But if the church is to be governed
by its members, why not the state? Thus were the seeds for the rise of
Demos sown.

The Reformation also brought to an end the commonly accepted view
from Aristotle to Aquinas that there was general agreement within communities about the ends of the good society, which politics was concerned with establishing.[5] There was now radical disagreement among
communities about the ends of life, with Catholics and Protestants, hitherto parts of the same Western Christian community, willing to send each
other to the stake for heresy. The ensuing bloody internecine ideological
conflicts within Western civilization over the succeeding centuries have
no parallel in the histories of other non-Semitic Eurasian civilizations. It
also gives the lie to any claim of universality for a particular Western

cosmological belief, as each one has been contested—often with blood—by a countervailing belief within the same corpus of Western thought.

To see that this cosmological turmoil had important temporal consequences, we can do no better than pick up the story briefly summarized at the beginning of the last chapter concerning the rise of the West till the end of the third quarter of the nineteenth century: the Industrial Revolution spreading slowly to Europe and the United States, the integration of the world economy wrought by Pax Britannia, and the spread of Smithian intensive growth in much of the Third World during the first great age of reform with the creation of a liberal international economic order (LIEO), involving free movements of goods, capital, and labor. Since then the world has seen a horrendous century in which Europe's deadly disputes have drawn in the rest of mankind.

The economic pillars of the LIEO—free trade and laissez faire—gradually began to be undermined by nationalism and collectivism. The two sets of ideas supported each other, not least in the economic nationalism sown by the ideas of Hamilton and List concerning the need for infant industry protection in "late developers," ideas adopted by protectionist political coalitions in the United States and Germany. This began the process of creeping protectionism that was finally to destroy this LIEO. The political nationalism that began with the wars of liberation in the Americas and then spread through various mutations throughout Europe led to a nationalist battle for empire: "the carving up of the Chinese melon," the scramble for Africa, the substitution of rule by the Crown for rule by the East India Company in India, were all part of a process whereby the virus of nationalism spread worldwide. It was accompanied by a growing collectivism[6] that repudiated the economic individualism that had provided the intellectual energy behind the institutional processes that had delivered the Industrial Revolution.

World War I was the watershed. It was a completely unnecessary war inasmuch as no one was being threatened. It was born, writes Skidelsky, "in the imagination of rulers; once started, it enlisted the forces of nationalism on its behalf, and could not be stopped."[7] It led to that road to serfdom so eloquently denounced by Hayek. The classical liberalism of the high Victorian era was at an end. "Before the war there were collectivist dreams; after it collectivist projects, which turned into collectivist nightmares."[8]

For the next three quarters of a century the world it seemed had gone mad: two world wars, a Great Depression, a prolonged Cold War, and the initial victory and eventual defeat of two totalitarian creeds—Fascism and Communism—marked the period. The idea of progress, which had seemed so natural to the high Victorians, looked Polyannaish to anyone surveying the unprecedented carnage, pillage, murder, and sheer human misery these disasters of our century have wrought.

Most surprising was the wide acceptance of collectivist ideas. Cassandras like Hayek were initially hailed as if they were drawing on some individualist spring in the West's collective memory, forgotten for three decades. But gradually in the West and more suddenly in the Second and parts of the Third World, this collectivist nightmare came to an end, with 1989 being emblematic of the return to sanity. It was as if a great tidal wave had gathered force from about the 1870s, grown and smashed the nineteenth-century world, and then, its force spent, had left a world that in many economic respects looked surprisingly like that of 1870. There have, of course, been breathtaking technological advances, and there can be no compensation in heaven or earth for the millions of lives destroyed or blighted by the insane collectivist experiments and their fallouts during the intervening century. But essentially the world economy is again knit tightly as in the high noon of the first LIEO through relatively free flows of goods and money—but not of labor. The empires built by the maritime European powers ended soon after the second war, and in 1989 the last empire, the land-based empire of Muscovy, also saw its demise.

In the world of Western ideas, the major change has been the completion of the project of secularization inaugurated by the Enlightenment. The death of God announced by Nietzsche in 1881[9] is now apparent in the lives if not the words of most people in the West. This, as we shall see, has had enormous consequences for the major socializing force— guilt—that the Church had used to check the individualist passions its greed had unleashed. The resulting spiritual void is filled by new "religions" such as Freudianism and environmentalism. The wholesomeness of the individual self or nature, not God, is increasingly the object of worship of Western men and women.

Politically, the major change has been the virtual victory of Demos in the West. One of its major effects has been on the other social cement— shame—which (as we will see) was based on the systems of deference common in anciens regimes. The erosion of this second socializing force, reining in the passions, is also a theme we will take up later. The ending of guilt and shame has also led to what Laslett[10] called the Grand Cliametric for the Western family in the 1950s and 1960s associated with the sexual revolution, the growth of feminism, and a general skepticism for any rules—be they God's or humankind's—in the domestic domain.

With Pax Americana now secure, it would be natural to expect a glorious age of peace and prosperity in the coming millennium. Yet, a fin de siècle pessimism reminiscent of the last century seems to be infecting the West. It is based on a sense of growing rottenness in their own societies, succinctly expressed by the title of Robert Bork's recent book, *Slouching Towards Gomorrah*. Why has this come to pass?

A whirlwind tour of changing Western ideas, since the Reformation relating to ethics, epistemology, and political economy will hopefully provide some answers.

The Course of Augustine's *City of God*

The "*Philosophes*" and After

It is banal to say that the *Enlightenment* is the hinge of modernity in the West. What needs to be emphasized however is that the *philosophes* were still haunted by Augustine's medieval philosophical system set out in his *City of God*, with its emphasis on original sin. As Carl Becker showed in a gem of a book written more than sixty years ago, "there is more of Christian philosophy in the writings of the *Philosophes* than has yet been dreamt of in our histories."[11] He shows that they "demolished the Heavenly City of St. Augustine only to rebuild it with more up-to-date materials."[12]

The Garden of Eden was displaced by classical Greece and Rome, and God became an abstract First Cause—the Divine Watchmaker—and instead of Holy Writ, God's laws were recorded in the Great Book of Nature that the scientific revolutions of the nineteenth century had begun to decipher. "Having denatured God," the *philosophes* "deified nature."[13] There was no need for Christian revelations. These were a fraud and an illusion; God expressed his purpose through the laws of nature. Moreover, Locke had showed in his *Essay Concerning Human Understanding* that the mind of a newborn child was a tabula rasa and that there were no innate ideas. This allowed an escape from the Christian doctrine of original sin. For Locke's psychology had destroyed "the Christian doctrine of total depravity, a black, spreading cloud which for centuries had depressed the human spirit."[14] If man and his mind were shaped by God's laws of nature, men could "by the use of their natural faculties"[15] make their conduct, ideas, and institutions in harmony with the universal natural order.

But there was a fly in this ointment, as Hume acutely noticed in his *Dialogues Concerning Natural Religion,* which concerned the nature of evil in the world. The old Christian notion of sin provided one explanation, but if in the view of the enlightened all was good in God's sight, they would also have to deny that there was any evil in the world of nature or of man. Hume put it succinctly: "Epicurus's old questions are yet unanswered. Is he [God] willing to prevent evil, but not able? Then he is impotent. Is he able, but not willing? Then he is malevolent. Is he both able and willing? Whence then is evil?"[16]

Not willing to embrace the two choices out of the conundrum—atheism or a return to Christian beliefs—Hume locked up his manuscript, and it was published posthumously. The *philosophes,* sensing the same problem, sought to finesse Hume's conundrum by searching for a general human nature through comparative history. Individual men may be evil but "Man in general," was not. The *philosophes* began a search for qualities of humankind, in order to judge which ideas, customs, and institutions were out of harmony with the natural order. Just as Augustine had created a "new" history in his *City of God,* the enlightened began writing *their* "new" history, because, as Hume again put it pithily, "Mankind are so much the same, in all times and places, that history informs us of nothing new or strange in this particular. Its chief use is only to discover the constant and universal principles of human nature."[17]

The voyages of discovery brought other exotic cultures within their ken. Along with the golden age of Pericles and Augustus, the "'wise Chinese', the 'noble Indian', the 'good savages'—. . . could now be happily turned against the Christian centuries to refute and confound them."[18] With the Dark Ages of medieval Christianity, their superstitions were now the "fall and expulsion, the unfruitful probationary centuries when mankind, corrupted and degraded by error, wandered blindly under the yoke of oppression."[19] But redemption was at hand with the dawning of the Age of Reason. A new golden age was in the offing:

Posterity would complete what the past and present had begun.... Thus, the Philosophers called in posterity to exercise the double illusion of the Christian paradise and the golden age of antiquity. For the love of God they substitute the love of humanity; for the vicarious atonement the perfectibility of man through his own efforts; and for the hope of immortality in another world the hope of living in the memory of future generations.[20]

As Diderot put it, "Posterity is for the Philosopher what the other world is for the religious." The eighteenth-century philosophers had replaced

Augustine's City of God with their own heavenly city, one ruled by an abstract first cause.

But with Hegel this beneficent author of the universe faded away "into a diaphanous Transcendent Idea, and with Darwin the Transcendent Idea disappeared altogether."[21] The answer to Hume's question whether we were "living in a world ruled by a beneficent mind, or in a world ruled by an indifferent force"[22] was now clear in the Darwinian world of the blind watchmaker.[23] "God and all the substitutes for that conception, could be ignored since nature was conceived not as a finished machine but as an unfinished process, a mechanistic process, indeed, but one generating its own power."[24]

The eighteenth-century philosophers of the Enlightenment thought they had been able to salvage a basis for morality and social order in the world of the divine watchmaker. But once he was seen to be blind, as Nietzsche proclaimed from the housetops at the end of the nineteenth century, God was dead, and the moral foundations of the West were thereafter in ruins.

Kant, in his *Critique of Practical Reason*, had tried to find a rational basis for morality. His two major insights were the recognition that human freedom was intrinsic to morality, as adumbrated in his famous principle "ought implies can"; and the principle of universality flowing from the categorical imperative, which gave logical content to the Biblical injunction, "Therefore all things whatsoever ye would that men should do to you, do ye even so to them: for this is the law and the prophets."[25] This universal *Language of Morals*, as a famous contemporary book of ethics by the Kantian moral philosopher Richard Hare has it, is, however, empty of content, as Hegel noted. Kant's view merely tells us about a principle of logical consistency. It does not tell us about our specific moral duties.[26]

Hegel's second objection was that Kant's view offers no solution to the conflict between morality and self-interest. Hegel claims that "any desire can be put into a universal form, and hence once the introduction of particular desires is allowed, the requirement of universal form is powerless to prevent us justifying whatever immoral conduct takes our fancy."[27]

The subsequent attempts to found a morality based on reason are open to Nietzsche's fatal objection in his aphorism about utilitarianism: "Moral sensibilities are nowadays at such cross purposes that to one man a morality is proved by its utility, while to another its utility refutes it."[27] Nietzsche's greatness lies in clearly seeing the moral abyss that the death of God had caused for the West. It is worth quoting him, as it is an essential part of the argument of these lectures. In *Twilight of the Idols* he writes,

When one gives up the Christian faith, one pulls the right to Christian morality from under one's feet. This morality is by no means self-evident: this point has to be exhibited again and again, despite the English flatheads. Christianity is a system, a *whole* view of things thought out together. By breaking one main concept out of it, the faith in God, one breaks the whole: nothing remains in one's hands. Christianity presupposes that man does not know, *cannot* know, what is good for him, what evil: he believes in God, who alone knows it. Christianity is a command; its origin is transcendent; it is beyond all criticism, all right to criticism; it has truth only if God is the truth—it stands and falls with faith in God.[29]

I do not believe there has been an adequate answer to the problem Nietzsche posed, and the West has been morally adrift since the death of its God. Hume perhaps foresaw the likely implications of his *Dialogues on Religion* for morality. For, unlike the other *philosophes*, he did not try and ground morality either in a belief in God or Reason but on Tradition. He notes that "moral good and evil are certainly distinguish'd by our *sentiments*, not by *reason*"[30] and "that the sense of justice and injustice is not deriv'd from nature, but arises artificially, tho' necessarily from education, and human conventions."[31] He grounds the origins of these conventions in self-interest when humans have to cooperate to achieve their ends. Once they are in place "a *sympathy* with public interest is the source of the *moral approbation*, which attends that virtue [justice]."[32] This leads parents "to inculcate in their children, from their earliest infancy, the principles of probity, and teach them to regard the observance of those rules, by which society is maintain'd as worthy and honorable, and their violation as base and infamous."[33] Hume clearly sees the role of morality in maintaining the social cement of society and in turn being dependent on a society's traditions and forms of socialization. Neither God nor Reason needs to be evoked (or can be) to justify these conditioned and necessary habits. This is very much the view about ethics taken by the older Eurasian civilizations based on shame.[34]

The death of the Christian God did not, however, end variations on the theme of Augustine's City. The idea of the "heavenly city" and the Christian narrative with a Garden of Eden, the Fall with its unavoidable taint of original sin, and a millennial redemption was to go through two further mutations in the form of Marxism and Freudianism, and a more recent and bizarre mutation in the form of Ecofundamentalism. We briefly examine each in turn.

Marxism, like the old faith, looks to the past and the future. There is a Garden of Eden—before "property" relations corrupted "natural man." Then the Fall as "commodification" leads to class societies and a continuing but impersonal conflict of material forces, which leads in turn to the

Day of Judgment with the Revolution and the millennial Paradise of Communism. This movement toward earthly salvation is mediated, not as the Enlightenment sages had claimed through enlightenment and the preaching of good will, but by the inexorable forces of historical materialism. A secular City of God has been created.

Becker notes the fundamental similarities between the French and Russian revolutions—the political fallouts from these two post-Augustinian secular mutations of the Christian narrative:

> The Russian is most of all like the French Revolution in this, that its leaders, having received the tablets of eternal law, regard the "revolution" not merely as an instrument of political and social reform but much more as the realization of a philosophy of life which being universally valid because it is in harmony with science and history must prevail.[35]

It is fitting that this particular secular mutation of Augustine's City of God should have come to an end in 1989, two hundred years after the events of 1789 tried to create the heavenly city of the philosophers on earth.

But there was to be yet another mutation of Augustine's "city," incorporating the Christian narrative: the theories of *Freudianism*. This provided the *coup de grace* to the processes of "civilizing" Natural Man built on guilt in the West. As Gellner has noted in a brilliant book, *The Psychoanalytic Movement: The Cunning of Unreason*, Freud created a new faith with traditional Judeo-Christian roots[36] but which answered Nietzsche's question in an original way. It was also ideally suited to deal with the new fears emerging in the West, once nature had been demystified. That Freudianism is a religion is shown by a number of features it shares with Christianity. "The Unconscious is a new version of Original Sin";[37] the analysts form a new priesthood, offering personal salvation to the faithful through the confessional of the analyst's couch; the priesthood is controlled by a guild of acolytes, who preach a doctrine that though clothed in the mantle of science is, like any religion, a closed system that is unfalsifiable.

Its great popularity in the West, particularly in its most individualist outpost, the United States, is due to the new fears it helps to quell in a world where each man and woman is increasingly "an island unto itself." Christianity had spread in the Dark Ages by becalming the terrors that nature held for pagans. With the taming of nature by the scientific revolution, and with the ancient fears about obtaining the necessities of life quelled by the power of Promethean growth, the fears of the individual in the modern West switched to concerns about personal relationships. "His fulfillment and contentment, and his self-respect, are at the mercy of other people: of his spouse, other close kin, and work colleagues and superiors."[38] With God's death the Christian Hell had been dismantled. Now, in Sartre's words, "Hell is other people."[39]

Freud had peered with Nietzsche into the deep abyss of nihilism: what values should Western humankind live by in a naturalized world in which God was dead? If reason cannot guide us and nature is mute, where are we to derive our values? Nietzsche gave the vague and incomprehensible answer: in a general "transvaluation of values." Freud found the solution at a practical level in the relationship between the analyst and the "patient," in which an individual solution for intermediating between the id and the superego is worked out for the special circumstances of each individual. "This ethical revelation is, in all its details, adjustable and adjusted to the requirements of each customer, and presumably each individual salesman.... The transvaluation of values, virtually unmarketable when Nietzsche first launched it upon the world in an impersonal and general form, is now made to measure for individual customers. Analysis is the bespoke transvaluation of values."[40]

This has led to the individualization of ethics, and psychologists preach an unrestrained permissiveness and display an animosity against any authority. Hayek cites the Canadian psychologist G. B. Chisholm, the first secretary general of the World Health Organization, who saw that the task of pyschiatrists was "to free the human race from 'the crippling burden of good and evil' and the 'perverse concepts of right and wrong' and thereby to decide its immediate future."[41] This led to "child centered" education and other aspects of the "progressive" socialization process in the West. Though Freud in his later *Civilization and its Discontents* seems to have become disturbed by what he had done, Hayek is surely right in arguing that "through his profound effects on education, Sigmund Freud has probably become the greatest destroyer of culture.... [H]is basic aim of undoing the culturally acquired repressions and freeing the natural drives, has opened the most fatal attack on all civilization."[42]

The latest of these secular mutations of Augustine's City of God is what I call *Ecofundamentalism*. It carries the Christian notion of *contemptus mundi* to its logical conclusion. Humankind is evil and only by living in harmony with a deified Nature can it be saved.

The environmental movement (at least in its "deep" version) is now a secular religion in many parts of the West. It has great similarities with the religious fundamentalisms sweeping the world, which implicitly are the source of Huntington's cultural fault lines. For though it may appear that the environmental movement is "scientific" and hence "modern" whereas the religious fundamentalists are "non-scientific" and "pre-modern," they both share a fear and contempt of the modernity whose central features are rightly seen to be an instrumental rationality that undermines humankind's traditional relationship with God or Nature. The sense of loss with modernity's "disenchantment of the world" of the ecologists is paralleled by the fundamentalists' fear of losing cherished traditional lifestyles. Both are also premodern in that they "claim to have a privileged, uncontested view of the nature of reality, which brooks no discussion, a claim which still flies counter to the work of science, as it did in the great historical disputes."[43]

The ecological movement—though religious in one sense—arose in part as a reaction to the death of God in the West with the Enlightenment. The historian of the ecological movement Anna Bramwell notes that in the past Western humankind was

able to see the earth as man's unique domain precisely because of God's existence. Before, both religious and natural theology were impregnated with the idea of a God-centered world. When science took over the role of religion in the nineteenth century, the belief that God made the world with a purpose in which man was paramount declined. But if there was no purpose, how was man to live on the earth? The hedonistic answer, to enjoy it as long as possible, was not acceptable. If Man had become God, then he had become the shepherd of the earth, the guardian, responsible for the oekonomie of the earth.[44]

And their beliefs? Bramwell sums them up as follows:

Ecologists believe in the essential harmony of nature. But it is a harmony to which man may have to be sacrificed. Ecologists are not man-centered or anthropocentric in their loyalties. Therefore they do not have to see nature's harmony as especially protective towards or favoring mankind. Ecologists believe in an absolute responsibility for one's actions, and for the world in general. There is no God the Shepherd; so man becomes the shepherd. There is a conflict between the desire to accept nature's harmonious order, and a need to avert catastrophe because ecologists are apocalyptical, but know that man has caused the impending apocalypse by his actions. Ecologists are the saved.[45]

The stronghold of the ecological movement since the late nineteenth century, as Bramwell emphasizes, has been the Protestant north of Europe (mainly Britain and Germany) and the United States. There has been a scientific root in Britain, drawing on Darwin and Malthus, and an atavistic romantic stream stemming from Matthew Arnold.[46] Bramwell identifies the distinctive qualities of ecologism as consisting of two distinct strands.

"One was an anti-mechanistic, holistic approach to biology deriving from the German zoologist Ernst Haeckel. The second strand was a new approach to economics called energy economics. This focused on the problem of scarce and nonrenewable resources. These two strands fused together in the 1970s."[47]

The religious nature of the movement is further supported by its failure ever to admit that its predictions have been wrong, and to continue making the same assertions based on its world view despite evidence to the contrary. Thus, take the Malthusian roots of the movement, which have led it to predict cataclysmic effects from an exploding population, mainly in the developing world. Yet one of the most firmly established stylized facts of modern demography is the so-called demographic transition.[48] The rise in Third World populations was primarily due to a fall in death rates because of better sanitation and public-health measures such as vaccinations. If parents are aiming for a particular completed family size, the number of live births they aim for will depend upon how many children are likely to survive to maturity. It is only after a lag that parents will begin to recognize that something systemic has changed in the falling death rates, particularly for infants. They will then lower the number of live births they seek because fewer are required to attain the required family size. Thus, as has been observed in numerous developing countries, population growth rates rise with the fall in death rates and then fall back as fertility rates adjust. This demographic transition is aided by falling infant mortality, better female education and health, and above all by rising incomes, which, by raising the value of time of the parents, lead to a substitution of quality for quantity in children.

The spiritual and moral void created by the death of God is, thus, increasingly being filled in the secular Western world by the worship of nature. In a final irony, those haunted natural spirits that the medieval church sought to exorcise so that the West could conquer its forests, are now being glorified and being placed above Man. The surrealist and anti-human nature of this contrast between ecomorality and what humankind has sought through its religions in the past is perfectly captured by Douglas and Widavsky, who write, "the sacred places of the world are crowded with pilgrims and worshippers. Mecca is crowded, Jerusalem is crowded. In most religions, people occupy the foreground of the thinking. The Sierra Nevada are vacant places, loved explicitly because they are vacant. So the environment has come to take first place."[49] The guilt evinced against sinning against God has been replaced by that of sinning against nature. Saving Spaceship Earth has replaced the saving of souls![50]

There are other stories in terms of the history of Western ideas that we need to take up. They concern politics and epistemology. Fortunately we have excellent guides who can guide us through this vast complex jungle.

The Rise and Fall and Rise of Economic Liberalism

Our guide to the story of political thought is Michael Oakeshott, and to the related political economy story from the Renaissance to the present, Bertil Ohlin's famous colleague and eminent economic historian Eli Heckscher. The story of the rise of nationalism is due to Benedict Anderson and the rise and fall of certainty to Stephen Toulmin.

Oakeshott's Story

Oakeshott[51] makes a crucial distinction between two major strands of Western thought on the state: the state viewed as a *civil* association, or alternatively as an *enterprise* association. Oakeshott notes that the view of the state as a civil association goes back to ancient Greece. The state is seen as the custodian of laws that do not seek to impose any preferred pattern of ends (including abstractions such as the general (social) welfare, or fundamental rights), but which merely facilitates individuals to pursue their own ends. This view has been challenged by the rival conception of the state as an enterprise association—a view that has its roots in the Judeo-Christian tradition. The state is now seen as the manager of an enterprise seeking to use the law for its own substantive purposes, and in particular for the legislation of morality. The classical liberalism of Smith and Hume entails the former, whereas the major secular embodiment of society viewed as an enterprise association is socialism, with its moral aim of using the state to equalize people.

Oakeshott[52] notes that as in many other preindustrial societies, modern Europe inherited a "morality of communal ties" from the Middle Ages. This was gradually superseded from the sixteenth century by a morality of individuality, whereby individuals came to value making their own choices "concerning activities, occupations, beliefs, opinions, duties and responsibilities" and also came to approve of this "self-determined conduct" in others. This individualist morality was fostered by the gradual breakdown of the medieval order which allowed a growing number of people to escape from the "corporate and communal organization" of medieval life.

But this dissolution of communal ties also bred what Oakeshott terms the "anti-individual," who was unwilling or unable to make his own choices. Some were resigned to their fate, but in others it provoked "envy, jealousy and resentment. And in these emotions a new disposition was generated: the impulse to escape from the predicament by imposing it upon all mankind."[53] This the anti-individual sought to do through two means. The first was to look to the government to "protect him from the necessity of being an individual."[54] A large number of government activities epitomized by the Elizabethan Poor Law were devoted from the sixteenth century onward "to the protection of those who, by circumstance or temperament, were unable to look after themselves in this world of crumbling communal ties."[55]

The anti-individual, second, sought to escape his "feeling of guilt and inadequacy which his inability to embrace the morality of individuality provoked"[56] by calling forth a "morality of collectivism," where "'security' is preferred to 'liberty', 'solidarity' to 'enterprise' and 'equality' to 'self-determination'."[57] Both the individualist and collectivist moralities were different modifications of the earlier communal morality, but with the collectivist morality in addition being a reaction against the morality of individualism.

This collectivist morality inevitably supported the view of the state as an enterprise association. Although this view dates back to antiquity, few if any premodern states were able to be "enterprising," as their resources were barely sufficient to undertake the basic tasks of government—law and order and external defense. This changed with the creation of centralized "nation-states" by the Renaissance princes and the subsequent Administrative Revolution, as Hicks[58] has labeled the gradual expansion of the tax base and thus the span of control of the government over its subjects' lives. Governments now had the power to look upon their activities as an enterprise.

Oakeshott identifies three versions of the collectivist morality such an enterprise association has since sought to enforce. Since the truce declared in the eighteenth century in the European wars of religion, the major substantive purposes sought by states seen as enterprise associations are "nation-building" and "the promotion of some form of egalitarianism." These correspond to what Oakeshott calls the *productivist* and *distributionist* versions of the modern embodiments of the enterprise association, whose *religious* version was epitomized by Calvinist Geneva, and in our own times is provided by Khomeini's Iran. Each of these collective forms conjures up some notion of perfection, believed to be "the common good."[59]

This Oakeshottian taxonomy is sufficient in my view to think clearly about the links between ethics, economics and politics. The fog created by distinctions such as negative and positive liberty and continuing attempts to reconcile these irreconcilable[60] can be readily dispelled by keeping Oakeshott's distinction between these two visions of the state in mind. The state seen as a civil association does not seek to legislate morality, as an enterprise association does. But this does not mean that the "order" promoted by the former is immoral. The sages of the Scottish Enlightenment were clear headed on this.

The "Morality" of the Market

Both Smith (in *The Moral Sentiments*) and Hume recognized benevolence as the primary moral virtue. But they also recognized its scarcity. However, fortunately, as Adam Smith was at pains to show in *The Wealth of Nations*, a market economy that promotes a country's "opulence" does not have to depend upon this moral virtue for its functioning. A market order merely requires a vast number of people to deal and live together, even if they have no personal relationships, as long as they do not violate the "laws of justice." The resulting commercial society does promote some moral virtues—hard work, prudence, thrift, and self-reliance. But inasmuch as these benefit the agent rather than others, they are inferior to the primary virtue, altruism. Nevertheless, as these lower-order virtues promote general prosperity, they do unintentionally help others. Hence the market economy is neither immoral or amoral. A good government in this classical liberal view is one that promotes "opulence" through a policy of promoting natural liberty by establishing laws of justice that guarantee free exchange and peaceful competition, the improvement of morality being left to nongovernmental institutions. It would be counterproductive for the state to legislate morality. On what *form* of government will best promote *good* governance these classical liberals were agnostics.

I think this is as good and as spare an outline of the case for the state viewed as a civil association as we need. But given its merits, is there some inevitable evolutionary process (as Hayek at times seems to argue) that will ensure that it will drive out the alternative vision of the state as an enterprise association? I can see none, and a thumbnail sketch of the rise and fall and rise of economic liberalism over the last two hundred years shows why.

Heckscher, Nation-Building, and Mercantilism

The mercantilist system, which provided the foil for Adam Smith's great work, arose, as Eli Heckscher has showed in his monumental study *Mercantilism*, from the desire of the Renaissance princes of Europe to consolidate their power by incorporating various feuding and seemingly disorderly groups, which constituted the relatively weak states they inherited from the ruins of the Roman empire, into a "nation." This was a "productivist" enterprise in Oakeshott's terms. The same nationalist motive also underlay the very similar system of mercantilist industrial and trade controls that were established in much of the postwar Third World.[61]

In the Third World the jealousy, envy, and resentment that bred the European anti-individualist was based not merely on the dissolution of the previous communal ties that industrialization and modern economic growth entail, but also because in these postcolonial societies, such emotions were strengthened by a feeling among the native elites of a shared exclusion from positions of power during the period of foreign domination. It is not surprising, therefore, that the dominant ideology of the Third World came to be a form of nationalism associated with some combination of the productivist and distributivist versions of the state viewed as an enterprise association. Historically, both these secular collectivist versions have led to dirigisme and the suppression or control of the market.

In both cases of "nation-building" (in post-Renaissance Europe and the modern Third and Second Worlds) the unintended consequences of the similar system of mercantilist controls instituted to establish "order" was to breed "disorder." As economic controls became onerous, people attempted to escape them through various forms of evasion and avoidance. As in eighteenth-century Europe, in the postwar Third World dirigisme bred corruption, rent-seeking, tax evasion, and illegal activities in underground economies. The most serious consequence for the state was an erosion of its fiscal base and the accompanying prospect of the unMarxian withering away of the state. In both cases economic liberalization was undertaken to restore the fiscal base, and thence government control over what had become ungovernable economies. In some cases the changeover could only occur through revolution—most notably in France.[62]

But the ensuing period of economic liberalism during the nineteenth century's great Age of Reform was short-lived, in part due to the rise of

another substantive purpose that most European states came to adopt—
the egalitarian ideal promulgated by the Enlightenment. Governments in
many developing countries also came to espouse this ideal of socialism.
The apotheosis of this version of the state viewed as an enterprise association were the communist countries seeking to legislate the socialist ideal
of equalizing people. The collapse of their economies under similar but
even more severe strains than those that beset less collectivist, neo-
mercantilist Third World economies is now history, though I cannot help
remarking on the irony that it took two hundred years for 1989 to undo
what 1789 had wrought!

Political Nationalism and the Rise of the Demos

There is yet another story we need to take up if we are to explain the
events of the last century. This concerns the rise of political nationalism
and of "the people" (demos). Benedict Anderson[63] has cogently argued
that there are four waves of political nationalism which can be distinguished.

The first are the "creole" wars of liberation in the Americas, starting
with the American War of Independence in 1776 and the liberation
movement headed by Simón Bolívar in South America in the early part
of the nineteenth century. Unlike the subsequent nationalisms where the
"imagined communities" of the nation were created by the newly acquired
status of vernacular languages and their speakers, the creole revolts were
led by people who were part of the same cultural and linguistic world as
their metropoles. These revolts were partly prompted by the policy of the
European powers of barring the entry of the creole elite to higher official
and political office in the metropole, even as "penisulars" had access to
high positions in both the colonies and the metropole. This led to resentment amongst the creole elites. The accident of birth in the Americas
seemed to condemn the "creole" to an inferior status, even though in
every other respect—language, descent, customs, religion, manners—he
was indistinguishable from the "peninsular." "There was nothing to be
done about it: he was *irremediably* a creole. Yet how irrational his exclusion must have seemed! Nonetheless, hidden inside the irrationality was
this logic: born in the Americas, he could not be a true Spaniard; *ergo,*
born in Spain, the *peninsular* could not be a true American."[64]

But if independence was to be declared in the name of a "nation" whose
inhabitants were distinguished by being born in the New World, it would
have to include all the people in the territorial area formerly controlled by

the metropolitan power. Recognizing this, Bolívar's fellow-liberator, San Martín decreed that "in the future the aborigines shall not be called Indians or natives; they are children and *citizens* of Peru and they shall be known as Peruvians."[65] The ideas of the Enlightenment, which had spread from the metropole, also meant that these new "nations" were opposed to dynastic rule, and were pervaded by republicanism. The nation-serving Demos, which has been a defining characteristic of the modern age, was born.

The French revolution brought these principles into fruition in Europe, carried across it by Napoleon's armies. This in turn gave rise to a second wave of nationalism. Its origins lay partly in a reaction against the "French cultural domination of the Western world," the Romantic reaction against the "disenchantment of the world" flowing from the scientific revolution and the Enlightenment; but most important, it was a result of the spread of a "vernacular" nationalism, engendered by the comparative study of languages that in turn had been promoted by the project of comparative history initiated by the Enlightenment, and the systematic study of the ancient civilizations that the age of discovery had unearthed. Out of this came the study of philology.

The world of Christendom had a common language—Latin—but this was the lingua franca of administration, diplomacy, theology, and scholarship. In the localities there was a multiplicity of tongues. The vernacular languages that most people spoke acquired an importance once a mass market arose for the printed word with the spread of the printing press. This made it commercially profitable to produce books in the vernacular, which in turn gradually raised the literary status of these languages. Some of these vernacular languages, such as French and early English, had become competitors of Latin as "languages of power" by the sixteenth century.[66] In England, the vernacular had become the legal language in 1362; in France, this occurred in 1539.[67] But in many other parts of Christendom, Latin survived as the official language for much longer. With the growth of bureaucracies following the post-Renaissance Administrative Revolution, the expanding bureaus had to extend their recruitment to people of lower social origins, who became clients of the printing press. The emergence, though uneven, of a commercial bourgeoisie also expanded the demand for the products of the vernacular presses.

This expansion of the ruling groups from their original narrow aristocratic base also unraveled the feeling of solidarity among Europe's ruling classes that had defined a common European community and identity.

Given their small size, the traditional aristocracies were linked to each other fairly closely, despite differences in their vernacular languages and cultures, by "the personalization of political relations implied by sexual intercourse and inheritance." Their community was concrete and not imagined. By contrast, the rising middle classes, once incorporated into the polity, knew each other not through such personal relations but as visualized through the medium of print. "Thus" writes Anderson "bourgeoisies were the first classes to achieve solidarity on an essentially imagined basis."[68] But because by the nineteenth century the vernacular languages had replaced Latin as the print language for more than two centuries, the "imagined community" of the rising bourgeoisie could not extend beyond the vernacular boundaries, as had the political community in the age of aristocracy. For, as Anderson puts it, "one can sleep with anyone, but one can only read some people's words."[69]

Thus began the second phase of vernacular nationalism demanding a vernacular language of state. Because this demand then required a definition of who comprised the relevant group that in turn comprised the nation-state, it was identified with the territorial boundaries containing the speakers of that language. Aided by the examples of the French and American revolutions, a "model" of the nation-state had, appeared by the second decade of the nineteenth century: "republican institutions, common citizenships, popular sovereignty, national flags and anthems ... and the liquidation of their conceptual opposites: dynastic empires, monarchical institutions, absolutisms, subjecthoods, inherited nobilities, serfdoms, ghettoes."[70]

The threat that this vernacular nationalism posed to the dynasts of Europe led to the third wave of nationalism: "official" nationalism,[71] whereby the dynasts sought to identify themselves with the newfound vernacular "nation." For this new identification "shored up legitimacies which, in an age of capitalism, skepticism, and science, could less and less safely rest on putative sacrality and sheer antiquity."[72] The russification of Muscovy by the Romanovs represents one spectacular example of this welding together of nation and dynasty, which is of the essence of this phase of nationalism, and which was a reaction to the vernacular nationalisms of the 1820s. The spread of this official nationalism was in turn to lead to the scramble for empire and to World War I.

The final phase of nationalism is that evoked in the areas of the world where, directly or indirectly, the spread of Western imperialism had damaged the amour propre of indigenous high-status groups. The earliest case was of Japan after its opening by Commodore Perry, when the Meiji reformers adopted a type of "official nationalism" modeled on Hohenzollern Prussia-Germany. But the more typical cases were the nation-states that arose when the Treaty of Versailles at the end of World War I buried the dynastic age, and the nation-state became the international norm.

The old colonial empires were now threatened by a variant of creole nationalism, which their own policies of "russification" had engendered. With the growing need of local collaborators and interpreters between their new subjects and the metropole, in varying degrees they had adopted the policy of creating a bilingual native elite on the lines set out in Macaulay's famous "Minute on Education" in British India, whereby he sought to create a completely English educational system which would create a bilingual middle class "who may be interpreters between us and the millions whom we govern; a class of persons, Indian in blood and color, but English in taste, in opinions, in morals, and in intellect."[73] But these "brown sahibs"—Gandhi and Nehru being prominent examples—were to be the undoing of the Raj for two reasons. The first was the policy of the Raj (as of the European empires in the Americas) of not allowing the creoles any say in the government or politics of the metropole, whereas the peninsulars' life choices were not similarly circumscribed, inasmuch as they included job prospects both at "home" and in the "colony." This bred a sense of injustice and outrage among the brown sahibs, as it had in the American creole elites. Second, their Western education provided them with access to the cosmological beliefs of the West and the model of the nation-state that had become its political norm. They could and did use the spiritual weapons forged in the West to challenge the legitimacy of its control over the Rest, by pointing to the contradiction between its ethical beliefs and political practice. With the end of World War II the colonial nationalists had won. The Age of Empire came to an end and the Age of Nationalism was in full flower.

The ex-colonial, new nation-states of Africa and Asia did not, however, follow the practice of vernacular nationalists in basing their nationhood on a particular vernacular "nation." This was in large part because these Third world nationalists inherited states that had been created by imperial powers whose territorial borders were determined more by *realpolitik* and the fortunes of war than by any coherence in terms of ethnic or linguistic homogeneity. These "artificial" boundaries were deemed to be sacrosanct by the succeeding nationalist elites, who then faced the problem the Austro-Hungarian empire confronted during its period of official nationalism: what official language should it adopt? If the language of any group in a multilingual state is adopted as the official language, native speakers are immediately put at an advantage, one that will be fiercely resisted by other groups. To allay these discords, like the Austro-Hungarians, the colonial nationalists kept the old imperial lingua franca as the official language. But this then gives rise to the problem of forging a sense of nationhood out of their multilingual polyglot inheritance, similar to that faced by the absolute rulers of Renaissance Europe. As we have seen, this led to similar forms of mercantilism, and similar denouements.

The Rise and Fall of Certainty

This story of the rise of nations and demos is paralleled by a story about the rise and fall of certainty. This has been outlined by Stephen Toulmin. This story, arising from the West's individualistic cosmological beliefs, concerns the search for certainty launched by Descartes, and the ensuing project of modernity with all its implications for epistemology, ethics, and politics.

Toulmin argues that there were two strands to modernity: the skeptical humanism of the late Renaissance epitomized by Montaigne, Erasmus, and Shakespeare, and the rationalism of the late sixteenth century epitomized by Descartes's search for certainty, which underpinned the triumphs of the scientific revolution as well as the methods of mechanistic Newtonian physics as the exemplary form of rationality. Toulmin's most original insight is that the rationalist project was prompted by the Thirty Years War, which followed the assassination of Henry IV of France in 1610. Henry's attempt to create a religiously tolerant secular state with equal rights for Catholics and Protestants mirrored the skeptical humanism of Montaigne. Henry's assassination was taken as a sign of the failure of this tolerant Renaissance skepticism. With the carnage that followed the religious wars in support of different dogmas, Descartes set himself the project of overcoming Montaigne's skepticism by defining a decontextualized certainty.

This rationalist project, which created the scientific revolution, found resonance, argues Toulmin, in the coterminous development of the system of sovereign nation-states following the Peace of Westphalia. The ascendancy of these two "systems" continued in tandem until World War I. But chinks were appearing in the armor of the rationalist Cartesian project with its separation of human from physical nature with the developments in the late nineteenth century associated with Darwin and

Freud. Despite the replacement of Newtonian physics by the less mechanistic physics of Einstein and his successors, the political disorder of the
1930s led, as in the 1630s, to a search for certainty, and the "logical posi-
tivist" movement was born.

The final dismantling of the scaffolding of the rationalist project begun
with the Peace of Westphalia, according to Toulmin, occurred in the
1960s, with Kennedy's assassination being as emblematic as Henry IV's.
Many hoped that Kennedy was about to launch a period ending the Age
of Nations and begin one of transnational cooperation through transnational institutions. There was also hope of reinventing the humanism of
the Renaissance, which had been sidelined by the rationalist Cartesian
project of the sixteenth century. As Toulmin writes, "By the 1950s there
were already the best of reasons, intellectual and practical for restoring
the unities dichotomized in the 17th century: humanity vs. nature, mental
activity vs its material correlates, human rationality vs. emotional springs
of action and so on." He then goes on to argue that the postwar generation was the first to respond "because they had strong personal stakes
in the then current political situation." The Vietnam War

shocked them into rethinking the claims of the nation, and above all its claim to
unqualified sovereignty. Rachel Carson had shown them that nature and humanity
are ecologically interdependent, Freud's successors had shown them a better grasp
of their emotional lives, and now disquieting images on the television news called
the moral wisdom of their rulers in doubt. In this situation, one must be incorri-
gibly obtuse or morally insensible to fail to see the point. This point did not relate
particularly to Vietnam: rather what was apparent was the superannuation of the
modern world view that was accepted as the intellectual warrant for "nationhood"
in or around 1700.[74]

There are various more complex reasons—which we cannot go into here
—why the moral authority of the center in many Western states has been
undermined. This has given rise to sources of moral authority outside the
hierarchical structure of the nation-state, which echoes a return to premodern Western medieval forms. As Toulmin notes,

One notable feature of the system of European Powers established by the Peace of
Westphalia ... was the untrammeled sovereignty it conferred on the European
Powers. Before the Reformation, the established rulers ... exercised their political
power under the moral supervision of the Church. As Henry II of England found
after the murder of Thomas a Becket, the Church might even oblige a King to
accept a humiliating penance as the price of its continued support.[75]

With the undermining of the moral authority of Western nation states,
Toulmin notes that this moral authority is increasingly being taken over

by nongovernmental organizations (NGOs) such as Amnesty International, and in many cases by the environmental NGOs.

Douglas and Wildavsky make a similar point about the cultural and political characteristics of the environmental movement. They define a hierarchical center, which has been characteristic of the nation-state, much as Toulmin does. Opposing this have been what they call "border" organizations. They comprise "secular and religious protest movements and sects and communes of all kinds."[76] They argue that

the border is self-defined by its opposition to encompassing larger social systems. It is composed of small units and it sees no disaster in reduction of the scale of organization. It warns the center that its cherished social systems will wither because the center does not listen to warnings of cataclysm. The border is worried about God or nature, two arbiters external to the large-scale social systems of the center. Either God will punish or nature will punish; the jeremiad is the same and the sins are the same: worldly ambition, lust after material things, large organization.[77]

Like Toulmin, they see the Vietnam War and Watergate as having undermined support for the center in the United States, giving greater legitimacy to the border—particularly to the segment that emphasizes nature.

Globalization and Tying Governments to the Mast

This process of weakening the powers of the nation state has been accelerated by the process of globalization in the last few decades. This is the last of the stories we need to note in the rise and fall and rise of economic liberalism. One important consequence of World War I, which promoted the collectivism of the next near century, was the novel way in which it was financed: deficit finance funded by the central banks that most European countries had established in the nineteenth century, following Britain's lead in establishing the Bank of England in 1694. Governments had discovered their ability to deal with their perennial problem of a shortage of money by raising revenue through the (implicit) inflation tax.

Two great economists, Schumpeter and Keynes, noted this momentous change but drew different implications. Schumpeter[78] realized that now governments, including his relatively backward Austria-Hungary, had the power, partly through taxation but mainly through borrowing, to mobilize the entire liquid wealth of the country. Whereas in the past the limited ability of governments to tax and borrow had made inflation self-limiting, now the only safeguard against inflation was political self-discipline, and Schumpeter was not very sanguine about politicians' capacity for this. Keynes, too, saw that money and credit had become important instruments in the hands of governments after World War I. But he thought this would allow the "economist-king" to reign. They now had a magic wand that would allow countries to achieve social justice, economic progress, and, they hoped, stability. Schumpeter was more skeptical. He saw it as pure hubris that the "economist king" would rule; it would instead be politicians and generals who would use the economists for their own purposes. And so it came to pass in the post–World War II Keynesian age of deficit financing that ended with the stagflation of the 1970s.

But it was not until the growing integration of world capital markets that followed that the hands of national governments were tied in their pursuit of various forms of "enterprise." In the new LIEO, full-blooded Keynesianism is dead. As is increasingly accepted by many governments around the world, unemployment is normally of the classical variety, as Pigou and Robertson maintained, and the NAIRU (non-accelerating inflation rate of unemployment) can be reduced only by removing impediments (mainly created by public policy) in the efficient functioning of the labor market.

But the hankering after some form of Keynesian tinkering is likely to persist—as Hayek clearly saw late in his life[79]—as long as there is a government monopoly of money in a world unable or unwilling to accept the rigors of the nineteenth-century gold standard. He saw that ending the political management of national monies must form an essential element of a refurbished classical liberalism. For, unlike many economists who continue to assume that the state is benevolent, Hayek, like the classical political economists and contemporary public-choice theorists, recognized that it was more likely to be predatory—especially in its modern democratic form.[80] Hence his proposal for abolishing the government's monopoly of money.[81] The global integration of capital markets, aided and abetted by the revolution in communications brought about by the computer and its accessories, is in effect bringing about this denationalization of money.[82]

There are striking parallels between the nineteenth-century and post–World War II golden ages. However, unlike the first golden age, the second was (until recently) marked by capital and exchange controls. It was the destruction of the world capital market as a result of the troubles of the interwar years and the continuance of capital and exchange controls (in the United Kingdom until 1979) that allowed predatory democratic states to squeeze "capital" in the interests of "labor" in the Keynesian decades after World War II. The removal of these controls and the integration of capital markets in the 1980s has destroyed this option. When even Sweden has to abandon its "middle way" because Swedish companies fight shy of holding their country's debt instruments, the public-borrowing route to financing government activism is closed. The near-universal tax revolt in OECD countries means that this route, too, has become perilous.

Finally, with currencies floating against each other, their relative value determined as much by capital than trade flows, there is in effect already competition among national monies, which limits any single government's ability to act as the currency monopolist of yore. In effect, money has become denationalized. The bond market—not any money supply or nominal expenditure target—increasingly informs the principal authorities whether national money supplies should be loosened or tightened. Any hint of the danger of the future inflationary financing of public borrowing is reflected in raising the current and future costs of servicing government debt. The recent trend toward Gladstonian rectitude in managing the public finances is no longer a matter of choice but necessity. With massive global flows of capital triggered at the press of a button, governments are now faced with an instantaneous international referendum on their fiscal and monetary policies. Thus, as classical liberals have always sought, governments are now tied to the mast against the siren voices of their predatory instincts. The Central Bank (or Treasury) proposes, but the money market disposes!

The Present Situation

So at the end of its second millennium, the West has come to a strange pass. Its unique and distinctive cosmological belief, individualism, which has led to its great material prosperity has finally triumphed in the material sphere. The globalization of the economy has meant that the whole world now seeks to adopt those "market-friendly" institutions on which Western material prosperity is now clearly seen to be based. This in turn means that "nation-states," which economically are increasingly becoming mere regions in an integrated world economy, are gradually losing their autonomy in the economic sphere on which their past predatoriness depended. This is the blessing that individualism has wrought. It also promises to abolish that mass structural poverty that has been mankind's lot at least since the great agrarian civilizations arose.

However, the death of certainty—an extreme version of the "individualistic" project—instead of leading to the humanism of the Renaissance is leading to a slow disintegration of the "center" and a return to the "border," reminiscent of the Middle Ages in the West.[83] For those not committed to a unilinear or evolutionary advance in human affairs, and who note the "restlessness" and the creativity of those times, this may not be a mere retrogression.

Some other important conclusions emerge at the end of this chapter on the course of individualism begun with the twin papal revolutions of the Popes Gregory in the Middle Ages. The first is the importance and persistence of a particular set of cosmological beliefs in the West. Crudely, this can be put as the Christian narrative about human nature, sin, and salvation as put together in Augustine's *City of God*. Through the Enlightenment to Marxism, Freudianism, and Ecofundamentalism, the same story has been refurbished to appeal to contemporary tastes.

Second, although the individualism Augustine's mutation engendered, buttressed by the legal and institutional Papal Revolution of Gregory VII, has allowed the West to take a distinctive trajectory to Promethean intensive growth, it has also, through the Scientific Revolution, the Enlightenment, and the rise of Demos, undermined the guilt- and shame-based social cement of these "Christian" societies. The Nietzcheian nihilism provoked by the death of God has been followed by a bespoke individualized ethics and the deification of Nature.

Third, contrary to much current liberal thought but in consonance with the views of the sages of the Scottish Enlightenment, there is no necessary connection between economic and political individualism nor with the individualistic libertarianism in personal beliefs that the death of certainty and the latest versions of Augustine's mutation have wrought. The market, as I have been at pains to show, does not depend upon a certain set of moral beliefs nor political arrangements, even though there were specific contingent associations in the rise of the West outlined in the last chapter. Democracy, particularly in its majoritarian form, is a relatively recent form of government in the West. Hereditary monarchy has been the most common form of government around the world, and it delivered the Industrial Revolution in a Western outpost of Eurasia because of a host of contingent factors we have already outlined.

Finally, an account that combines changes in cosmological and material beliefs can provide a spare and persuasive explanation of the destruction and restoration of the LIEO over the last century.

But what of the other great civilizations, which have had to cope with these great disturbances in their lives flowing from the products of Western individualism? We need to examine how they have dealt with the disruption of their ancient equilibrium by the West, most often under the pressure of superior arms.

7 India and China in Modern Times

We next examine how the two most ancient contemporary civilizations—India and China—have responded to the rise of the West. Having been "opened up" by Western arms, these proud civilizations have since been trying to rectify the hurt to their *amour propre* while attempting to acquire a parity of military power to prevent any future humiliations. There are remarkable similarities, despite appearances, in their economic policies since independence and in the outcomes.[1]

Dirigisme

Historical Cultural Stability and Economic Stagnation

Both countries were marked at "independence" in the 1940s by centuries of cultural stability and economic stagnation, as I outlined in Chapter 3. There was, as we have seen, *extensive* growth, but there were no obvious signs of Promethean *intensive* growth. This in turn was due in large part to both countries having made near perfect adaptations to the environments in which their respective "organic" economies had been placed.

Both had succeeded, by the Middle Ages, in creating economies that maintained what Elvin calls a "high equilibrium trap,"[2] with an average level of living that was the envy of the contemporary world. But the forms of cultural stability and political organization differed, reflecting in part the differing ethnic compositions of the two countries, China's remarkable ethnic homogeneity[3] contrasting with India's long history of maintaining a multiethnic society. Second, whereas political instability has been the norm in India, China has shown a remarkable political unity under centralized imperial rule for millennia.

These differences did not, however, prevent the emergence of relatively stable revenue economies[4] and what I call predatory states[5] in both

countries. The main cultural and political differences were the decentralized form of social control as embodied in the Indian caste system and the
relatively autarkic village communities, in a polity that has usually been
regionally fragmented and only rarely encompassed the subcontinent
under imperial rule[6]; compared with the more centralized social control in
an absolutist state—in a relatively integrated national market—run by
Confucian mandarins in China, which, except for brief periods when the
Mandate of Heaven switched between regimes, has been politically united
from Sung to modern times.[7]

Rowe sums up the enduring characteristics of late imperial China as

an ethos that stressed harmony, social order, continuity, and community service,
all prompted by the State via that unparalleled vehicle of elite indoctrination, the
civil service examination system; a fairly successful state monopolization of the
approved channels of upward mobility; an emphasis on merit; a customary law of
partible inheritance, which made downward mobility over generations an ever
present possibility for the elite; and an orthodoxy that to a greater or lesser extent
viewed commerce with suspicion and disdain. Perhaps paradoxically, the late
imperial Chinese economy was marked by the existence of comparatively strong
property rights and based on these rights, an agrarian system emphasizing free
alienation of land, household-scale proprietorship, and an elaborate and flexible
system of mortgaging and leasing.[8]

Thus, unlike India, where the land market was created by the Raj, the
Chinese have had a dynamic land market for centuries. The Chinese
meritocratic acquisition of status through education contrasts with the
ascription of status in the Indian caste system. This has led to a greater
emphasis on mass education in China than in India. In fact, in India, as
Weiner has argued,[9] when education and status became correlated after
independence, the upper castes, controlling the state apparatus, thwarted
the lower castes' desire for education by soft-pedaling the constitutional
commitment for the provision of universal elementary education.

Both countries had social systems that accorded merchants and traders
a lowly status, and their wealth was not translated into political influence.
Both needed to escape from the "high equilibrium trap" of their "organic"
economies by promoting Promethean growth.

Development Strategy

In both China and India the "modern" ideologies under which they sought
to foster intensive growth after their "independence"—Communism in
China, Fabian socialism in India—did nothing to undermine their tradi-

tional attitudes to trade and commerce. Both countries were opened up to the modern world through the force of Western arms in aid of its commerce. The nationalism this provoked has sought to adopt the West's technology, particularly military, without adopting its soul. Xenophobia and a suspicion of foreigners is endemic in both countries. Both promoted heavy industries through dirigiste means, because of the political imperative to provide the material means for resisting future military threats to their independence rather than any desire to promote economic welfare.

Both, thus, found the Soviet model resonant in their drive for industrialization—though in India, in the softer tones associated with a democracy. The resulting development strategy was also, by and large, similar insofar as both countries followed hothouse industrialization through the promotion of heavy industry under the aegis of state enterprises. Both followed relatively autarkic trade policies accompanied by a battery of trade and exchange controls, which progressively cut any link between domestic and world relative prices. This had well-known deleterious effects on the economy's efficiency and thence productivity.

Both also systematically discriminated against agriculture by taxing it directly or indirectly. But this policy went much further in China during the Maoist Great Leap Forward and the establishment of communes. This disaster led to one of the worst famines in human history and set back Chinese agricultural productivity for a decade.[10] The policy was completely reversed by the establishment of the "household responsibility system" in the late 1970s. By contrast, India switched in the late 1960s to various policies to promote agriculture, which led—in ecologically suitable parts of the country—to what is termed the Green Revolution.

From the late 1970s onward, moreover, both countries have been gradually trying to escape from the dirigiste system of controls of foreign trade and industry that they had previously set up. We need to outline the consequences of this dirigisme, which might provide reasons for this move to liberalization, which is discussed in the next section.

Relative Performance

A comparison of the relative performance of the two giant Asian economies is bedeviled by statistical problems relating to estimates of Chinese GDP and population. By contrast, Indian national income figures and population data are much more secure.[11] So what can we conclude on relative performance? It would appear that until the late 1970s China grew faster than India. This was largely due to differences in the rates of growth of industry. The rate of growth of agricultural output was about the same. In China between 1952 and 1978, before the introduction of the household responsibility system, it was 2.9 percent; in India between 1950 and 1986 it was 2.6 percent. Grain output grew at 2.4 percent in China and 2.6 percent in India.[12] But the performance of both was well below that of the Asian newly industrialized countries in terms of industrialization and other developing countries (e.g., Kenya, Indonesia, and Pakistan) in terms of agricultural growth.

Reported social indicators appear to be better in China than India, but the overall level of inequality, particularly in rural areas, was about the same (the Gini coefficient was 0.31 in 1979 for rural China and 0.34 in rural India in 1973–76).[13] "Though the same sources report a somewhat higher inequality in urban income distribution in India, because of the large weight of rural areas in both countries overall income distribution was roughly similar."[14] Despite different political systems, the overall performance of the two economies in their dirigiste post-independence phases was thus not too dissimilar, and well below their respective potentials.

Reform

The damage that this dirigisme had done to economic performance gradually came to be recognized in both countries, and slowly they have sought to liberalize their economies.[15] It is useful to distinguish between the policy-induced distortions created by irrational dirigisme in commodity and factor markets. These were much more severe in China, particularly in factor markets, which had been virtually extinguished. In both countries the liberalization of commodity markets started with partial trade liberalization in the early 1970s, and has followed a tortuous route since then. Despite considerable liberalization of its near autarkic trade regime, China probably has a less liberal trade regime today than India's and a less open economy. In the factor markets, even though the Indian capital market is inefficient, it is still way ahead of the Chinese, who are just beginning the process of setting up an efficient banking system and stock markets. The land market has been virtually free in India, whereas its extinction in China led to a collapse in agricultural output, which provided the major impetus for the reforms under Deng. But, unlike in India, the delineation of property rights and their legal enforcement is still limited—partly for ideological reasons.

In both countries major distortions remain in the labor market, particularly in the public sector. Instead of dealing directly with the inefficiencies of the public sector, both countries are hoping to circumvent the problem by concentrating on promoting the buoyant private economy and thence through the reduced share of the state sector to mitigate its deleterious effects on the growth of the economy. But in both countries, the resulting hemorrhaging of the fisc has led to problems of macroeconomic stability. It was a macroeconomic crisis that led to India's latest attempt at reform.[16] In both countries, their atavistic and nationalist objections to foreign capital are being overcome. Both have used the capital of their diaspora, but the Chinese have been able to obtain stable flows in the form of direct investment, whereas the Indians have to rely on short-term inflows in the form of bank deposits. Their reversal triggered the Indian macroeconomic crisis of the late 1980s.

Given these similarities in the course of liberalization and the roadblocks in its continuation, as well as in the pre-reform "initial" conditions, similar effects—in terms of some boost in productivity and growth rates—as reform progresses[17] are only to be expected.

Future

What of the future of reform in the two countries? Appearances can be deceptive. The current euphoria in the media and financial circles about China, in contrast with the growing despondency about an India beset by various ethnic and religious conflicts, might suggest that the course of reform is assured in the first country but not the second. The impediments in the path of reform are essentially political in both cases, inasmuch as the next stage in their reform must involve the dismantling of systems of unviable entitlements, in particular to organized labor and the bureaucracy. It might appear that a dictatorship committed to reform would find it easier to do so than a democracy. This commitment is in question in both countries.

Recently *The Economist* summarized the necessary conditions for successful liberalization that have emerged from the Latin American experience in the catchphrase, "commitment, competence and consensus." This, it argued, in Latin America involved "(1) people at the top committed to it, (2) other people technically qualified to implement it, (3) a national trauma, such as hyperinflation, that lives on in the memory of voters as a horror to which they never wish to return."[18] Of these conditions the second seems to be met, insofar as there are undoubtedly competent technical teams in both countries capable of implementing reform. Doubts about the first and third conditions give one pause in both countries.

In India, it is now apparent that past reforms are secure. The loose coalition of thirteen parties that in 1996 succeeded the reforming Congress
government of Narasimha Rao and his finance minister, Manmohan Singh,
has not reversed any of their reforms. But given its fragility, the coalition
government has put further reforms on hold. This is largely because of
the long ideological shadow that has been termed Nehruvianism—a variant of Fabianism—still casts on the minds of the political and intellectual
classes. The comments by both ministers and many (but by no means all)
press commentators were hostile to many of the eminently sensible suggestions for a wholesale bonfire of controls and subsidies, in the July 1993
Bhagwati-Srinivasan report commissioned by the minister of finance. Old
shibboleths were on display—maintaining some form of socialism to help
the poor, for which the public distribution of food to low-income urban
consumers, as well as parts of the public sector, and a continuing ban on
consumer-goods imports are deemed essential.[19] The long-standing and
atavistic brahminical disdain for commerce and trade was also apparent, as
was the continuance of a prickly nationalism as some took umbrage at an
official report written by NRI (non-resident Indian) economists.

This nationalism, however, provides some hope for the future. One of
the important themes of the Lal-Myint comparative study is the role of
nation-building in explaining both the rise of dirigisme and its demise.
Dirigisme, invoked to foster "order" by nationalism, leads over time to
the unintended consequence of breeding disorder, as economic agents seek
increasingly to escape the official net. Liberalization is then undertaken by
nationalists to restore order in what seem to have become ungovernable
economies. Heckscher's historical work on mercantilism (discussed in
Chapter 6) provides an almost exact parallel in this cycle of dirigisme and
disorder, namely liberalization in post-Renaissance Europe. The Indian
case fits this thesis. Hence, if nationalism is still alive and well in India, it
may lead its adherents to see that further liberalization is essential to
acquire the economic strength without which the nation will not be safe
from disorder from within or without. The media hype about China has
helped in this context.

Moreover, there has been a remarkable alteration in the climate of
public opinion, where the empowerment of the common people against
the many tyrannies of the Permit Raj promised by the reformers gladdens
many middle-class hearts hankering after Western style consumerism. The
relatively shrinking rewards from public service, as compared with those in
the private sector, are persuading many of their children to seek commer-

cial careers. This should help to undermine the long-standing Brahminical attitudes against Banias (merchants). These cultural attitudes, which in the past favored seemingly selfless mandarins over selfish markets, have also been undermined by the contempt in which nearly all politicians and many bureaucrats are increasingly held by the public. If both mandarins and markets are now seen as equally corrupt (in the Augustan sense),[20] the ethical preference for the former is undermined, and the efficacy of the two alternatives in promoting "opulence" becomes the paramount consideration. Even the partial liberalization that has so far taken place may have helped to strengthen this shift in attitudes toward the market.[21]

Against these hopeful signs are more dire ones. The major potential losers from the reform are businesses in previously protected sectors and the bureaucracy. The interlocking interests of the politicians, industrialists, and bureaucrats in perpetuating the rents generated by the Permit Raj, which financed a corrupt politics, are well known. An alternative source of electoral finance is still not in place; without it, the continuing commitment of Indian politicians to economic liberalization must remain questionable. The potential losers are grouping together and lobbying for more gradual reforms and for various concessions to allow them to compete on an equal playing field with foreign investors. These potential losers have implicitly threatened to finance the Hindu Nationalist party (BJP), which has played the populist anti-foreign card and argued for internal liberalization with little or no liberalization of foreign trade and direct foreign investment. Interestingly, though, the newer business groups[22] have lobbied for a faster process of liberalization as they, unlike their older brethren, feel they can compete in global markets.

Bureaucrats form the most recalcitrant group. Production workers in public-sector enterprises are less of a problem insofar as they can be pensioned off through the National Renewal fund or some other severance scheme.[23]. But white-collar bureaucrats, numbering in the millions, seek the job security, and perquisites of the All India civil services. They seek also to enlarge the base of their respective job pyramids so that there are more lucrative jobs on top. In the traditional Indian casteist framework they want to protect not merely their incomes but their status. They include not only the officers but also the *karamchari* (clerical workers') unions in nationalized banks, para-statals, and the central and state governments. No government has tackled the thorny issue that a large number of them will have to be made redundant in the interests of both economic efficiency and the fisc. The example of the DGTD (Directorate

General of Technical Development), whose functions became redundant with the ending of industrial licensing, does not augur well for the future. Evidently, even though redundant, officers of the DGTD still show up even when there is no work for them, and they continue to draw their pay and perquisites.

Finally, until recently, the conversion of the state governments to economic liberalization was less evident than of the center. Because the states control agriculture, irrigation, power, road transport, health, and education—amounting together for over half of the GDP—this matters. But more recently, prompted by their own fiscal crises, the states seem to be reforming[24] at a time when, with the easing of the fiscal and foreign exchange crisis, the center seems to be cooling its heels.

There are clearly many rocks ahead in the path of Indian economic reforms. The technical competence is there, and there appears to be a general consensus in the country for reform, but the commitment of the politicians and hence the credibility of the reforms must still remain in doubt.

What of China? Here I can do no more than speculate on the basis of what little we know of the inner workings of the Chinese government.[25] As long as Deng Xiaoping was alive it seemed that those committed to reform in the Chinese polity would remain on top, purely because Deng had repeatedly proclaimed his continuing support for reform. With his demise this may have changed.

This raises the question of why Deng supported liberalization and how if at all he envisaged it to proceed. A few clues are provided in a recent biography of Deng by a former British ambassador to China,[26] in which three themes emerge: Deng as a passionate nationalist, as a man keen on preserving the Communist party and the morale of its members, and as a true believer for whom socialism "was associated with prosperity ... [and who] was ready to try a wide variety of means in the quest for prosperity."[27] He did not have any particular economic theory to guide him. Evans, the biographer, reports Deng as saying, "I am a layman in the field of economics. I have made a few remarks on the subject, but all from a political point of view. For example I proposed China's economic policy of opening to the outside world, but as for the details or specifics of how to implement it, I know nothing."[28] We also learn from Evans that during one of his periods of disgrace Deng turned to reading Chinese history, and his speeches thereafter reflected his studies. It is pure speculation, but if he did read the history of the Sung, could that not have provided him with the vision of a vigorous China ruled by mandarins under an imperial dynasty that nevertheless tolerated a market economy and the prosperity it begat? It would reconcile "the contradictions many outside China have seen between Deng's readiness to experiment boldly in the economic sphere and his political conservatism. Far from seeing political liberalization as a necessary condition for economic liberalization, he has seen it as a serious potential threat to social and political stability and therefore to development."[29]

If Deng's commitment to reforms (as long as they were controlled by the party) was assured, that could not be said of the rest of the party. The debates between those who want to return to planning and those who want to go further in economic liberalization still continue. Given the past history of the turns in the roulette wheel in intraparty disputes, it would be foolhardy to predict what the outcome will be of Deng's meeting Marx.[30]

As in India, there are conflicting tendencies. First, the sapping away of both administrative and fiscal authority from the center has made the regions and their officials more powerful in determining China's future.[31] Those in the south have benefited personally from all forms of effectively privatized enterprise in which they and their relatives have become partners.[32] Second, the People's Liberation Army is deeply involved in joint ventures and commerce with foreign investors.[33] These constitute important groups whose self-interest must now lie in continuing reform. This effective cooptation of apparatchiks and the army in the reform process, in stark contrast with India, makes the commitment of the political elite to reform much more credible.

It may seem redundant to discuss any popular consensus about reform in a dictatorship, but Chinese history is replete with examples where, although authoritarian dynastic rule has been the norm, a dynasty could see another replace it if in the eyes of the people it lost the Mandate of Heaven. Here, as in India, the dirigiste system established by the Communists did conform with atavistic cultural attitudes. It is impossible to judge how far the current dynasty and in particular the reformers have been tarred with the visible signs of the blatant "rent-seeking" and corruption that has accompanied economic liberalization and the spread of "crony capitalism."[34]

Finally, the Chinese suffer from having lost a whole generation of youth to miseducation during the Cultural Revolution. The only technically sound economists are very young, and although there are enough of them now around the world, it is difficult to judge whether they can be put together into a team and given their head, as India has been able to do so spectacularly.

Thus, for slightly differing reasons, but ultimately because of problems concerned with politics and culture, the reforms in both China and India remain insecure. As ever, the potential of the two Asian giants remains immense if only they could be unshackled from dirigisme, It is not yet certain that this potential will be realized.

8   The Far East

As India and China seem to be slowly awakening, a number of Far Eastern economies—the Four Little Dragons and Japan—have already (or nearly) achieved developed-country status. Are cultural factors responsible for their spectacular economic transformation? Is their Confucian or neo-Confucian culture responsible for this "miracle"?

The East Asian "Miracle" Economies

The Materialist Base

The so-called miracles of the neo-Confucian societies of the East Asian edge—Korea, Hong Kong, Taiwan, and Singapore[1]—are not really miraculous, as Alwyn Young[2] and Ian Little have recently showed. These miracles can instead be explained in conventional economic terms as being due to very high rates of savings and investment efficiently deployed, most importantly by making use of the possibilities of the international division of labor through international trade.

Similarly, the argument propounded by the so-called market governance school, which I have examined in detail elsewhere,[3] that enlightened dirigisme led to their success cannot be sustained. As the World Bank's *Miracle* study[4] shows, through the convoluted use of total factor productivity (TFP) accounting in the "miracle" economies it studied—Hong Kong, Singapore, Indonesia, Malaysia, Thailand, Korea, Taiwan, and Japan—there was little evidence that the pattern of sectoral growth at the two-digit International Standard Industrial Classification (ISIC) level was any different from what the standard Heckscher-Ohlin model would have predicted. It also found that in these economies the least selective intervention—the commitment to manufactured exports—was the most successful.

Moreover, the revisionists need to show that industrial dirigisme yielded social rates of return equal to or above the social discount rate in the industries that were to be promoted. They do not provide such evidence. Ian Little has done so for the Korean case for 1963–82. Not surprisingly, he finds that social rates of return improved in the early part of the period, when Korean policy moved toward openness, and fell (from 31 percent to 19 percent) in the second half (1974–79), when dirigiste policies were adopted.

Finally, I have argued elsewhere that the explanation for the undoubted dirigisme to be found in, for example, Korea and Taiwan is to be explained by the problem of "agency," which a country faces when it moves up the ladder of comparative advantage into more capital-intensive lines of production. In these there are likely to be indivisibilities in investment. In the absence of private concentrations of wealth, there is then likely to be a separation of ownership and control in these industries, leading to an agency problem, as the interests of the managers who control the day-to-day operation of a firm and the owners who are concerned with maximizing the return to their "shares" diverge.[5] The problem is one of maintaining beneficial control over resources when there are economies of scale and scope in a firm. This control is in turn related to the amount of private wealth that is required to reduce the degree to which ownership is separated from control of the relevant resources. Inequalities in private wealth may therefore be productive in allowing fewer people to own firms and thus exercise greater control over the managers than would be true if wealth and "shares" in the firm were more dispersed.

Various alternative routes are available to overcome this agency problem, which becomes important once a country moves to the more capital-intensive rungs of its ladder of comparative advantage. For at the lower rungs, given the small concentrations of capital required to set up enterprises, they can be owner-managed. The Koreans overcame the agency problem by promoting the *chaebol* through credit subsidies and a ruthless winnowing of winners and losers through export targets, which were a good measure of the relative efficiencies of the industrialists being promoted. Singapore relied on direct foreign investment to overcome the agency problem, Taiwan on the public sector with predictable inefficiencies. Hong Kong alone allowed its industrial structure to evolve naturally. The economic performance of Hong Kong, judged by the productivity of investment, was the best in this group.[6] In Korea the artificial promotion of a concentration of wealth and industrial assets had predictable political effects when the polity came to find this unacceptable. It led to the usual rent-seeking and corruption, as has become clear from the recent admission by ex-president Roh Tae Woo, that from the time of Chung Hee Park, Korean presidents have created huge slush funds from "donations" from the businessmen they were promoting. Surely this is not the sort of "crony capitalism" that the "market governance" school would commend for the rest of the Third World?

Cosmologies

The role of cultural factors in the success of these countries of the East Aaian edge is open to question. As regards the success of the overseas Chinese and these purportedly neo-Confucian societies, Jenner is surely right in stating that their success has little to do with China's past but with "European economics, commercial law, science and technology."[7] The interaction of these Western institutions with some inherited Asian values brought about successful development.[8] In the absence of the

dynamic, alien, Western institutions and forms of economic organization ... that have transformed these other countries the familistic values [of the mainland] are more likely to impede than to support change and development. In particular, China is still under the rule of a thinly disguised, pre-modern imperial bureaucracy, unlike those former colonies.[9]

A similar explanation and prognosis for different parts of the Chinese world is provided by Pye.[10] Morishima[11] also argues that deviations from Japan's Confucian past in large part explain its extraordinary economic success.

Finally, Vogel's argument[12] that the meritocratic tradition of China has been an important contributor to East Asia's success can be countered by two counterexamples. India and the United Kingdom established modern meritocratic bureaucracies with considerable social cachet in the late nineteenth century. They compare favorably on every dimension with those of East Asia. Nevertheless, these mandarins have not been able to improve the economic prospects of their respective countries.

The most heated debates surround the role of the Chinese family as the agent of a distinctive and productive familial capitalism in the Sinic world. As Whyte[13] notes in an excellent survey of the literature on the role of the Chinese family, there has been a virtual 180-degree shift in views. The traditional view associated with Weber and various modernization theorists was that the Chinese family was a major brake on economic progress because its nepotism, initiative-sapping patriarchy, and personal rather than universalistic value system would make enterprises based on it inefficient. Now, by contrast, the same Chinese family is being hailed as the engine of growth in the Sinitic world, based on the undoubted success of the family-based businesses of Hong Kong and Taiwan and the growth of family-based industry in the non-state sector in China.[14] Many of these arguments in favor of familialism—for instance, that the form of cronyism called *guanxi* is efficient—are just not persuasive, particularly in a broad comparative framework.[15] The argument that Chinese families have always been entrepreneurial but have been "cabin'd cribb'd and confin'd" by predatory states has more merit. The most important reason for taking the optimistic view about the role of the Chinese family in development is the undoubted success of the family "mode of production" in the Sinic world. This needs an explanation.

Whyte argues that as the Chinese family has changed over the last century, many aspects—for example the strict patriarchy—have altered. At the same time, there has been a change in the nature of production relationships in the world economy, which has made particular features of the Chinese family economically valuable in this emerging world division of labor. This particular advantage is the flexibility in switching seamlessly from one activity to another, which small-scale, family-based enterprise offers.

His argument can be put in a wider perspective. Hicks[16] characterized the major feature of the Industrial Revolution as the substitution of fixed for circulating capital, epitomized by, for example, the replacement of the "putting out system" by the "factory system." The "putting out system" was of course largely based on household enterprises. What we are witnessing today is a substitution of human for fixed capital in many aspects of industrial production.

Unlike heavy industry, much of industry supplying consumer goods seems to be going "bespoke." This means that instead of mass-produced consumer goods relying on large production lines—called Fordism by some in recognition of the revolution in standardized mass production of consumer durable goods achieved by Henry Ford—the current tendency is to produce differentiated versions of the same good more closely tailored to differing individual tastes. Variety, not standardization, is the name of the game in this "designer" world of commodities in the affluent West. Shifts in its variegated tastes are increasingly reflected in changes in differentiated products to meet this volatile demand. This has created the need for highly flexible production enterprises that can quickly shift from producing one type or variety of good to another. Scale economies are of less importance in these "designer" goods than in the old standbys of Fordist consumerism, so that small-scale enterprises that can react flexibly to shifts in tastes (designs) are not only not at a disadvantage, but are also likely to have a comparative advantage over more traditional and bureaucratically organized firms.

It is this emerging niche that the Sinic family-based enterprises in both mainland China and its smaller outposts in Southeast Asia have filled. It is a modern version of the "putting out" system, where the "design" capacity, which is human-capital intensive, is located in "rich" countries. They then have "virtual factories," with their production bases spread across the world, which, using modern telecommunications, convert these "designs" into the differentiated "bespoke" consumer goods increasingly demanded by consumers in the West.[17] These "design centers" are not a monopoly of the West, as witness the transformation of Hong Kong from a manufacturing to a service economy that mediates this fickle, affluent consumer economy between the "designers" in the West and the flexible production lines based on family-type enterprises in southern China. This is an ideal environment to unleash the family-based entrepreneurship of the familial business, and the Sinic family has taken advantage of it in a spectacular manner. But without modern communications and legal and commercial codes, it would come to nought.

The importance of Hong Kong for the development of southern China lies in its colonial institutional and legal system, which has allowed this late twentieth-century division of labor to be affected than in its traditional role as an entrepôt and financial center. Thus, as Whyte rightly emphasized, particular circumstances at the end of the millennium, rather than any essentialist Confucian attributes of the Chinese family, have made it an engine of growth today, as it was not in the past.

Where cultural factors may have played a part is in the processes of socialization resulting from the notions of "shame" associated with Sinic cosmological beliefs. These have provided the cement of their societies, and to the extent that they are based on the ancient veneration of the family in Chinese culture, they can also explain the widespread prevalence of that "delayed gratification" that has led to unbelievably high rates of savings (and thus investment) in these countries. The more dynastic family interests govern individual choices, the lower is likely to be the private rate of time preference and hence the higher the savings rate. But equally, the same argument should apply to the "joint family"-based society— India. But as we have seen, its savings rates have been about half of its Far Eastern neighbors. More important perhaps is the fact that, as Lee Kwan

Yew has rightly noted, these "family"-based societies can still rely on the social safety nets of the family rather than having to create welfare states like the West, which, as we will see, have paradoxically been both a symptom and indirect cause for the growing erosion of the cement of societies in the West.[18]

Japan

The Materialistic Record

Finally, we come to the other clear non-Western case where there is evidence of intensive growth of the Smithian type before the premodern period, and which *par excellence* succeeded in generating intensive growth of the Promethean kind in this century—so much so that it is now challenging the West's supremacy in many areas.

Surprisingly, unlike the cases of Smithian intensive growth that we have so far observed in the ancient Mediterranean world and in Sung China, which were based on policies of what nowadays would be called "openness," the intensive growth that occurred during the Tokugawa shogunate (1600–1868) was during a period when Japan turned inward. It occurred after the shoguns promulgated the policy of *sakoku*, by which the economy was closed from foreign contacts for security reasons.[19] Part of the growth was, as in the past, of the extensive variety. Thus "throughout the Middle Ages the population had been rising, from 5 million in the 11th century to almost 10 million by 1300 and 18 million by about 1600."[20] This increase was based not only on a rise in paddy acreage[21] but also on an increase in agricultural productivity.

This period saw the growth of nonagricultural groups—clerics, traders, and warriors. The emergence of these groups, which were to provide the entrepreneurial drive for Japanese growth, can be traced to the practice of primogeniture, which the Japanese had adopted in contrast to that of partible inheritance found in China. These differences in turn were most likely due to the different polities that had emerged in Japan and China.

As Morishima traces them, these differences go back to the Taika reforms, and the enactment of the Seventeen Article Constitution in 604. This in effect created a constitutional monarchy where the emperor was the de facto ruler for only a brief period since. For most of the historical era in Japan there was dual, and at times triple, government, when political power lay with shoguns (military chiefs), or prime ministers or chief advisers backed by military power.[22] This system of dual government is in marked contrast to the unified bureaucratic imperial state that has governed China for much of its history. It has meant that whereas the predatory state in China is chiefly contested by various barbarians from the north and south (as long as the net revenue maximizing tax rate—in the predatory state model of the Appendix—is not exceeded), in Japan the state has been internally more contestable, and this has limited its powers of predation.

But the very continuity of the divine emperor has fueled "a defensive nationalism" in Japan, very unlike China. Thus, whereas in China even established dynasties that had unified the mainland did not last as long as two hundred years, Japan maintained "a long line of Emperors unbroken for ages eternal" through the political neutralization of the emperor while making him sacred and inviolable.[23] This unbroken, divine imperial house provided the focus for Japanese loyalties and nationalism, which continues to our day.

The politically fragmented system of the Middle Ages, when the gradual process of intensive growth was fructifying, led to a decentralized politics where armed resistance could prevent predation by would-be national leaders. The Tokugawa unification should have changed this.[24] So how did the Smithian growth under the Tokugawa occur, given its policy of *sakoku* and given its ostensible ending of competitive manorial politics with the unification it had wrought?

That it did occur seems incontrovertible. "Between 1600 and 1850 agricultural output almost doubled. Since population rose only by about 45%, a considerable increase in output per head must have occurred. This was the result of an expansion of the arable acreage [noted earlier] but also of the diffusion of technical innovations, individually small but linked and cumulatively impressive."[25] These included the introduction of American crops—part of the "Columbian exchange"—that had been imported into Japan via Portuguese traders before foreign trade was prohibited by the shogunate.

The policy of the Tokugawa—reminiscent of Louis XIV's—of forcing the *daimyos* (rural lords) to live half the year and spend a large part of their revenues in their palaces in Edo, helped the growth of the urban market. Other aspects of Tokugawa policy, which had features of a police state, as well as the policy of "inwardness" should have stifled growth. But it did not. Jones claims that the reason is that "growth emerged because behind its stern exterior the absolutism of the regime proved surprisingly weak. Internally pacified, much of the initial impetus spent, Tokugawa Japan sat back. By 1732, 60% of the daimyo supporters of the shogunate had managed to settle permanently on lands they were to hold until at least 1868. Effective lordly power rose, notwithstanding the rigidity of form and show of stability in high politics."[26]

The central governments and local *daimyo* also took various measures to remove internal trade barriers—abolishing tolls, breaking guild monopolies—and were active in the provision of public goods—flood control, fire prevention, sanitary arrangements, judicial and policing bodies.

What emerged, claims Jones, is a peculiar balancing act as far as the effects on the polity were concerned:

The results of rising productivity flowed sufficiently to the Japanese producer to reinforce change. The benefits of this were clear enough to the local lords for them not to stifle the process. Here we have political fine-tuning able to bring into being a system in which individually centralized *hans* retained their economic autonomy but were nevertheless linked in a national market not unlike the grander linking of the nation-states in the European states-system. Perhaps convincing explanations of Japanese and European growth have eluded us because of balancing acts like these. What were being balanced were sets of incentives and disincentives of a largely institutional nature, with interacting effects that are hard to describe and almost impossible to quantify.[27]

Here, we seem to have a not very convincing political-economy "explanation" for this period of intensive growth. What is more certain is that Pax Tokugawa would in itself have created a larger market fueling Smithian intensive growth, with the distinctive Japanese polity and the underlying logic of thrift, productivity, and enterprise further propeling this growth. No distinct cultural explanations in terms of the Confucian ethic and the like are needed.

But would this period of Smithian intensive growth have led to Promethean growth? Clearly not, as the Meiji reformers clearly saw when Commodore Perry's warships appeared across the horizon, and sought to adopt Western technology and institutions as rapidly as possible.

The difference in the responses of Japan and China to the appearance of the "foreign devils," Morishima argues, was due to the differing nature of their elites. The Chinese bureaucracy was learned in the Chinese classics and skilled at poetry and literature. By contrast, Japan's warrior bureaucracy was interested in weaponry and thence in science and technology. Though both countries were Confucian, China's bureaucrats were stolidly opposed to Western science. Japan's, from the Tokugawa Bakufu to the Meiji reformers, were enthusiastic about acquiring Western science.[28] Within a short period they were able to demonstrate that they could thereby generate phenomenal Promethean growth based on Western technology and their own unique form of capitalism while maintaining their souls.

Cosmological Beliefs

It is undeniable that the Japanese have uniquely been able to garner the benefits of Western materialism without its social consequences. Why is a question I will come to eventually. But before that we need to know something more about this Japanese "soul"—the set of cosmological beliefs, as I have labeled them.

Morishima has sought to identify the mutations in Confucian doctrine that took place as the doctrine came to Japan via Korea. Citing the Imperial Rescript to Soldiers and Sailors in 1882, he notes:

In this document five of the Confucian virtues were emphasized—loyalty, ceremony, bravery, faith and frugality.... [By contrast] in Chiang Kai-shek's army the major elements required for a soldiery spirit were wisdom, faith, benevolence, bravery and strictness; in the ancient Silla dynasty of Korea the qualities stipulated for soldiers ... were loyalty, filial piety, faith, benevolence and bravery. Only faith and bravery are virtues common to all three countries. Benevolence is common to both China and Korea, but there is no mention of it in the case of Japan. Loyalty is common to both Japan and Korea but does not appear on China's list of virtues.... In Japan it was loyalty rather than benevolence which came to be considered the most important virtue ... loyalty in conjunction with filial piety and duty to one's seniors, formed a trinity of values which regulated within society the hierarchic relationships based on authority, blood ties and age respectively.[29]

Thus, whereas "Chinese Confucianism is ... humanistic, Japanese Confucianism is remarkably nationalistic." As was the case, mutatis mutandis, of non-French Continental Europe,[30] it was in part a reaction against the cultural and for long periods military superiority of China vis-à-vis Japan. This defensive Japanese nationalism marked the Japanese response to the West.

The second influence on Japan was the mystical Chinese religion of Taoism. This, argues Morishima, formed the basis of Shintoism, the religion of the court, while Buddhism, in various forms, became the religion of the people. But this has not led to any great religious feeling among the people. Moreover, as we saw in the case of India, Buddhism has been the religion of the merchants. The religiousness of the Japanese people thus turned to materialism, and being nationalistic, "they had no hesitation in working together for the material prosperity of Japan as a nation."[31] There was a further marriage of Confucianism and Shintoism:

the former justifying a constitutional-monarchic but bureaucratically run state, the latter promoting nationalism. "It is therefore not surprising to find that Japanese capitalism was—and still is—nationalistic, paternalistic and anti-individualistic."[32]

Karel van Wolferen makes much the same point as Eisenstadt's in a massive comparative study of Japanese civilization.[33] One of the aims of the Meiji reformers was to inoculate curious Japanese minds against potentially subversive foreign ideas such as individualism, liberalism, and democracy. A "national identity" was invented that allowed power to be explained and justified in new ways and enabled new methods of control to be introduced.[34] This ideology of the "family state," set out in the Imperial Rescript of Soldiers and Sailors of 1882, was spread through military conscription and indoctrination in the national educational system.

At the same time, the Meiji oligarchs created a political system in which there was no single focus of effective political power. This reflected their reluctance to write a constitution in which power could be concentrated in the hands of a leader legitimized by the emperor, inasmuch as this would have threatened the positions of some of them, and the oligarchy would have disintegrated.[35] Thus "an uncertain sharing of responsibility was preferred, so that no one person could be pointed out as bearing the ultimate responsibility for decisions. It is obvious that it had the danger of developing into a colossal system of irresponsibility,"[36] as was shown in the events leading to and during World War II.

The Meiji oligarchs' propaganda that all politicians were unpatriotic, concerned with narrow party and personal self-interest, meant that politicians could not exercise power, and another group had to be found to manage the country. This was the meritocratic bureaucracy created in the early days of the Meiji revolution. One of the oligarchs, Yamagata Aritomo, made it immune to political meddling by obtaining "a personal communication from the emperor—as distinct from a formal Imperial edict—[which] could never be overruled," and which made the Privy Council the guardian of edicts drafted by Aritomo "relating to examinations, appointments, discipline, dismissal and rankings of the bureaucrats."[37] Since then bureaucrats, largely recruited from the Law Department of Tokyo University (Toadi), have in effect governed Japan.[38]

This, however, did not lead to the creation of an "administrative state" as in France.[39] This was because the bureaucracy was riven with internal strife, essentially with each intra- or interministerial bureau trying to preserve or expand its turf. With no political overlord to settle or adjudicate these bureaucratic disputes, decisions could only be made by "consensus"—which in many cases was just a polite word for paralysis.

The Japanese "Miracle"

This political system, and in particular the bureaucrats, survived the post-war purges and the imposition of an American-drafted constitution.[40] The system the Meiji bureaucrats dreamed of has been gradually reconstructed. But given, as van Wolferen himself grants, its effective lack of a political center to adjudicate disputes, could it have provided the centralized dirigiste system of planning that he, along with many of his fellow travellers in the "market governance" school, believe is responsible for the Japanese "miracle"?

Clearly not, as the magisterial Brookings study edited by Hugh Patrich and Henry Rosovsky[41] showed for the supposedly "miraculous" period until 1973. As a more recent account by Bill Emmott[42] also emphasizes, the laws of economics have not been abrogated in Japan. It could not and did not succeed by "getting the prices wrong"! Even in Japan speculative bubbles burst, as has so distressingly been demonstrated in the 1990s, and corporatism has its costs in terms of the knock on effects on the banking system of its speculative loans—particularly in housing—to its partners.[43] Emmott is surely right that Japan is different from the West, but not in ways "relevant to its trade and economic behavior."[44]

Moreover, as Scott's detailed comparative historical analysis of growth rates in OECD countries based on his "new" growth model shows, there was no Japanese "miracle." Until 1973 (after which the Japanese GDP growth rate fell from 9.2 percent in 1960–73 to 3.8 percent in 1973–85),[45] nearly all of Japan's growth can be explained by the investment rate, the growth in the quality adjusted labor force, and a catchup variable.

Thus, it is arguable whether the bureaucracy has been directly responsible for Japan's economic success as the "market governance" school claims. As other recent surveys of the evidence show,[46] Japan's success is in spite rather than because of MITI. The fierce competition between the *keiretsu* and the continuing battle for export markets have determined the efficiency of the considerable savings the Japanese have been able to make. Nothing beyond standard economics would seem to be needed to explain the Japanese "miracle"—though, as we have seen, its form has in part been determined by cosmological beliefs and the polity these have created.[47]

What is incontrovertible is that Japan has belied the predictions of the materialists. Substantial aspects of social life—the very cement of society—have not been effected by material prosperity in the same way as in the West. The process of socialization in Japan, as Ruth Benedict[48] argued in a famous book, still depends upon shame—as has been true of most of the existing civilizations. There is no sign that this process has been altered.[49]

Dramatic confirmation of this is provided in a study done by social psychologists Ekman and Friesen[50] on the facial expression of emotions. As we saw in Chapter 1, the emotions are likely to be universal, but their expression is culturally conditioned. Ekman and Friesen conducted an experiment in which American and Japanese subjects viewed identical intense stress-inducing pictures, while their facial expressions were secretly videotaped. There were no differences in the expression of the same emotions evinced by the same pictures in the two groups. Next, the same experiment was repeated, but this time in the presence of a high-status experimenter—an older male dressed in a suit, tie, and lab coat. The secret videorecording showed no differences among the Americans from their previous responses, but the Japanese now differed from the Americans and from their previously unmonitored responses. "In every instance the Americans showed negative emotions, the Japanese either showed no emotions or smiled."[51] Cultural conditioning had clearly changed the expression of the basic emotions.

Other cross-cultural evidence[52] also supports these cultural differences, which in turn are linked to different patterns of child socialization and preschooling, with the Americans emphasizing individualism and the Japanese communalism.[53] The latter seems to consist of "loyalties" to concentric ingroups from the family to the firm and the nation. Behavior within ingroups is based on status differentials and the proper deference that is entailed. Shame is the emotion evinced by the social maladroitness of "losing face."[54] But the distinction made between ingroups and outgroups by the Japanese means that competition between ingroups can be fierce, and behavior to outgroups can be quite brutal, as witness the pushing and shoving so common on Japanese subways. The negative emotions suppressed within ingroups are openly expressed toward outgroups, which are only tempered if there is a possibility of future harmonious relationships. Hence the apocryphal story of how someone pushing and shoving a fellow passenger to get into the subway stopped dead in his tracks when the passenger being shoved turned and looked at his attacker and said "I know you."[55]

Convergent Cosmologies?

Some sociologists, however, maintain that there will be a convergence in cosmological beliefs between Japan and the West because of the common spread of consumerism. MacIntyre provides a suitable antidote. He first notes that this view, which is based on the simple contrast between social and individual aspects of morality, is misleading. He then notes that the Japanese have a unified sense of the self, whereas in the West, particularly in the United States, that sense of self is fractured and incoherent.

The Western notion of self, he argues, has three contradictory elements. The first derives from the Enlightenment and views the self as being able to stand apart from social influences, allowing individuals to mold themselves in accordance with their own true preferences.[56] The second component of the Western self concerns others' evaluation of oneself. Here the standards are increasingly those of acquisitive and competitive success in a bureaucratized and individualist market economy.[57] The third element of the Western self derives from its remaining religious and moral norms and is open to various "invocations of values as various as those which inform the public rhetoric of politics on the one hand and the success of *Habits of the Heart* on the other."[58] This aspect of the self harks back to the conception of the soul, whose transcendental salvation depended on being inworldly after what we have called Augustine's mutation.

These three elements comprising the Western conception of self are not only mutually incompatabile but also incommensurable, and they lead to incoherence inasmuch as there are no shared standards by which the inevitable conflicts between them can be resolved. "So rights-based claims, utility-based claims, contractarian claims, and claims based upon this or that ideal conception of the good will be advanced in different contexts, with relatively little discomfort at the incoherence involved. For unacknowledged incoherence is the hallmark of this contemporary developing American self, a self whose public voice oscillates between phases not merely of toleration, but admiration for ruthlessly self-serving behavior and phases of high moral dudgeon and indignation at exactly the same behavior."[59]

The Japanese do not share in this incoherence. They have never had any place for the soul. For them an individual manifests facial expressions and spoken words and actions often conventionally ordered and at the same time has unspoken thoughts and feelings:

The former is not only what is socially presented, it is what in and through its conventional orderings constitutes social life. There is not the individual with inner and outer aspects and then, independent of these in some way, the institutionalized social order. The outer aspects of the individual *are* the social order.[60]

Thus the Japanese conception of self excludes both the soul of Western theology and modern individualism.

The Japanese have stuck to this conception of self despite the various transformations their economy and society have seen. Thus the Japanese have adapted the Western notion of rights, which fits in with an older Western tradition, whereby in Roman law they were the norms governing social relationships. But in the later Middle Ages the concept came to apply to those rights adhering to individuals in a state of nature, that is, before they joined society. "Rights became primarily rights *against* others."[61] The Japanese have never accepted this notion of Western rights, and instead have understood them as "secondary aspects of more fundamental norms and relationships, belonging therefore not to individuals qua individual, but to the roles and relationships through which individuals realize and constitute themselves."[62]

These relationships are still ordered hierarchically, with deference based on social distinctions being ubiquitous. But unlike other hierarchical societies and its own past, hierarchical status is no longer ascribed or inherited but acquired, largely through the fierce meritocratic contest for educational attainment. Thus the Japanese have been able to adjust to the needs of modernization without westernizing their selves.[63]

Though many aspects of social life will be affected by changing material factors accompanying this modernization—for instance, the increasing participation of women in the labor force, the increasing value of time, and so on—it is not obvious, at least so far, that many others, described crudely as "the decline of the family" in the West, will follow the rising material prosperity and its inevitable concomitant, the spread of a market economy. One crude index of this is figure 8.1, taken from Becker's *Treatise on the Family.* As he notes, divorce rates have inexplicably increased much less in Japan than in other rich countries, even though other changes in the variables emphasized by the new "household economics" have changed as predicted. But, he goes on, "still, the main message of these data, and those for other developed countries, is not diversity but uniformity: the family has changed in a similar revolutionary manner in essentially all economically advanced countries during the last several decades." This is hardly surprising, inasmuch as most of these countries, besides Japan, belong to the West and its individualist cosmology, which,

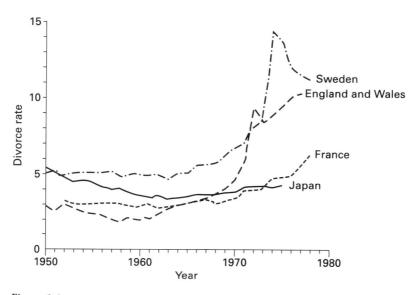

Figure 8.1
Divorce rates per 1,000 married women in England and Wales, France, Japan, and Sweden, 1950–1978

as we saw in chapter 5, was determined by the church's self-interested promotion in the Middle Ages of a breakdown of the traditional form of extended family—to gain bequests. Having acquired the technological basis of the West's prosperity, the Japanese have not yet adopted this peculiar Western form of individualism.

Glazer notes that there had been startling changes in the Japanese family partly promoted by the legal norms based on Western customs enforced by the American hegemons after World War II. Household size began to decline, the number of "nuclear" families (based on the "household" criterion) began to rise, as did the proportion of single-parent families, while the birth rate fell. But despite these changes there were signs of substantial stability, particularly as compared with the United States, in terms of the divorce rate, the numbers receiving public assistance (which fell between 1962 and 1971 from 1.7 to 1.3 million, only about 1 percent of the population as compared with a figure of 7 percent in 1972 in the United States), the smaller percentage of single-mother families on welfare, the smaller percentage of the aged in nursing homes as compared with those living with their children or in their own homes, and the relatively lower rates of juvenile delinquency and crime in general.[64] Thus, he concludes, "the Japanese family is undoubtedly changing: but for a developed country it still maintains a remarkable stability, which underlies the stability of the value pattern and ... contributes to the pattern of achievement in school and work"[65].

That is why the Japanese case is of such importance. Is Japan likely to become like the West in its family and social mores? Is this also the fate of the other ancient civilizations, as they, however slowly and grudgingly, embrace market capitalism and the material prosperity that it brings? We turn to these questions in the next chapter.

There are some universal and permanent needs of mankind on which moral laws are based; if they are broken all men everywhere at all times have connected notions of guilt and shame with the breach.

(De Tocqueville, vol. 2, Pt. II, Ch. 18, pp. 798–9)

Two major differences have emerged in our historical survey of the West and the Rest. The first is in the cement of their societies. The second is in the unique importance of individualism of the inner-worldly kind in the cosmological beliefs of the West, which have engendered its scientific and material triumphs. This individualism has, however, until recently been conjoined with religious beliefs based on guilt, which has provided the personal ethics underpinning their social fabric.

By contrast, non-Western societies have neither been individualistic (except of the "otherworldly" kind) nor based their processes of social-ization on guilt. They have instead relied on shame. To that extent, their social fabric is unlikely to be undermined by the death of God, resulting from the rationalism bred by Western individualism. This has some im-portant implications, which I will come to. But before that we must note that at least in Europe—until recently—the process of socialization was also aided as much by manners as by morality.

Manners, Shame, and Guilt

Norbert Elias, in his two-volume work *The Civilizing Process*,[1] shows how the rise of the absolutist state in post-Renaissance Europe was accom-panied by the rise of court society and the evolution of civilized manners based on an amalgamation of aristocratic and gradually (after the late eighteenth century) bourgeois behavior. This rise of Western civility,

argues Elias, was a necessary part of the evolution of polities and economies in which the division of labor, monetization, and the accompanying
differentiation of tasks and the integration of different classes and groups
in society, required the personal internalization of various forms of self-
restraint on instinctual drives and passions.[2] The upper classes transmitted
the resulting norms of civilized behavior or manners to their social in-
feriors through works like Erasmus's *De Civilitate Morum Puerilium* (On
Civility in Children).

As Elias notes, the promotion of manners as a socializing process is
based on shame.[3] The civilizing process associated with the absolutist
courts of Europe was based on a social hierarchy and the chain of deference it entailed. The "manners" cultivated by the post-Renaissance courts
embodied this form of social control as it could also encompass the guilt
the Christian morality had embedded in Western minds. Shame and guilt
were thus conjoined in the civilizing process of the West.

The death of God wrought by the scientific revolution and the rise of
Demos—with its attack on social hierarchies and deference—have struck
a double blow to these forms of socialization. Mill, in *On Liberty* had presented an optimistic version of human nature where even without religion
individuals would be able to exercise self control: "The same strong sus-
ceptibilities which make the personal impulses vivid and powerful, are
also the source from whence are generated the most passionate love of
virtue, and the sternest self control."[4] Nietzsche (as we saw in Chapter 6),
who had first pronounced the death of God, would have none of this:

Nietzsche, who took nothing for granted, least of all the virtues of self-control,
self-restraint, and self-discipline, had contempt for those English moralists—that
"flathead" Mill, as he called him, and that "little moralistic female" George Eliot—
who thought they could secularize morality by divorcing it from Christianity.
Beneath their "insipid and cowardly concept "man" lingers the old "cult of Christian morality." What these "moral fanatics" do not realize is how conditional their
morality is on the religion they profess to discard. And it is only because of the
persistence of that religion that, for the English "morality is not yet a problem."[5]

Time, unfortunately, shows Nietzsche to have been right. The guilt
underwritten by Christian morality has been gradually eroded. Worse,
the gradual acceptance of Mill's individualistic principle has led to relativ-
ism, argues Himmelfarb[6], both in morality and epistemology. The postmodernism that this death of certainty has bred, conjoined with the
questioning of all social hierarchies and forms of deference, has increasingly dissolved that other component of the West's social cement, the
shame based on "manners." This latter process has gone farthest in that

unique Western society that emerged newborn as a child of the Enlightenment—the United States.[7] It may be instructive to see why.

As de Tocqueville[8] noted, the Americans had taken over the new Enlightenment ideal of the equality of men *as entailing their similarity*, resulting in an individualist society different in character from the hierarchical aristocratic societies that had arisen in the absolutist states of Europe. Nearly a century later Myrdal also discerned the uniqueness of what he called the American Creed, in which the two basic Enlightenment norms of liberty and equality are represented, but which accepts *inequality of economic outcomes* based on competition.[9]

This rugged individualism and social egalitarianism was helped by America's factor endowments.[10] With abundant land there were no land rents for a substantial landowning class to develop.[11] Unlike the tropical parts of the Americas, grains were the most suitable crops for cultivation. These have constant returns to scale in their production, unlike plantation crops such as sugar that have increasing returns to scale. The same is true to a lesser extent of tobacco and coffee.[12] Where climatic conditions in the Americas were suitable for these latter crops, the use of coerced labor had enormous cost advantages over free labor, and a more highly socially and economically differentiated society with great inequalities of wealth resulted.[13] By contrast, given its factor endowments (including the climate) in most of the United States (except for the South) the family farm became the backbone of the colonial economy[14] and a society with fairly egalitarian mores could develop.[15] This was a society committed to a view of the world in which men are "conceived no longer as hierarchically ranked in various social or cultural species, but as essentially equal and identical."[16]

What was the basis of socialization in the United States? Because it was secular, no state religion could enforce a social ethic. Here, as usual, de Tocqueville is prescient. He finds that the basis lies both in religion and citizenship. He notes the

innumerable multitude of sects in the United States.... Each sect worships God in its own fashion, but all preach the same morality in the name of God. Though it is very important for man as an individual that his religion should be true, that is not the case for society. Society has nothing to fear or hope from another life; what is most important for it is not that all citizens should profess the true religion but that they should profess religion.[17]

He also noted that "while the law allows the American people to do everything [which allows them to be bold and enterprising], there are things, which religion prevents them from imagining and forbids them to dare."[18] Finally, and this is still by and large the case,[19] "all the sects in the United States belong to the great unity of Christendom, and Christian morality is everywhere the same"[20]—a morality dependent upon the inculcation of guilt. That it was an essential element in promoting the social cement of American society is also emphasized by Tocqueville:

Religion, which never intervenes directly in the government of American society, should therefore be considered the first of their political institutions, for although it did not give them the taste for liberty, it singularly facilitates their use thereof.... I do not know if all Americans have faith in their religion—for who can read the secrets of the heart?—but I am sure that they think it necessary for the maintenance of republican institutions.... For the Americans the ideas of Christianity and liberty are so completely mingled that it is almost impossible to get them to conceive of the one without the other.

It is not surprising, therefore, that in a West that is increasingly secular-ized, the proportion of Americans professing "to zealously perform all the external duties of religion,"[21] is still the highest of any other advanced country.[22] But this is probably becoming more of an obeisance. For if other aspects of current American behavior concerning Christian moral injunctions are taken into account—against adultery and divorce, for instance—to an outsider these figures for professed religious belief appear to be merely a sign of hypocrisy, or a manifestation of the fractured American self outlined by MacIntyre (and discussed in the last chapter).[23]

The second form of social glue was provided by the law and the Con-stitution. Alone among the states of the contemporary world, the Ameri-cans have based their mode of association, as did the ancient Greeks, on *citizenship*. Most other states are based on ethnicity or the vagaries of conquest and colonialism. America alone provides a basis of association on the granting of citizenship. This allows numerous different ethnic groups and nationalities to become Americans despite their past loyalties, while the all-powerful American Creed, through a socialization process of loyalty to civics rather than ethics, has created the American melting pot.[24] The importance of public education in this process of socialization cannot be disputed.[25] Thus we have that unique civilization: "the product of two perfectly distinct elements which elsewhere have often been at war with one another but which in America it was somehow possible to incorporate into each other, forming a marvelous combination. I mean the *spirit of religion* and the *spirit of freedom*.... Religion is considered as the guardian of mores, and mores are regarded as the guarantee of the laws and pledge for the maintenance of freedom itself."[26]

An essential element in this unique American process of socialization were, as de Tocqueville noted, the myriad civil associations he found in the country. According to de Tocqueville, once the traditional aristocracy with its sense of noblesse oblige, which usually stood between the rulers and the ruled in the anciens regimes in Europe, had been extinguished with the rise of democracy, these myriad voluntary associations (or NGOs, as they would be called today), provided the bulwark against the tyranny of the central executive in democracies. By providing an inter-mediating layer between the ruling elites and the masses, they prevent the elites from abusing power and allow ordinary citizens to participate in the political process.

This civic society was held together, as was the ancient Greek one, by shame as much as by the guilt fostered by the Pilgrim fathers. But it was a shame based on civics, and ultimately on a form of patriotism arising from the duties of citizenship.[27] The death of God as well as the decline in certainty, as we have discussed earlier, has been particularly deadly for the social cement of American society.[28] The former has eroded that personal sense of guilt that provided a personal ethic to much of the Western streams of American society, which still remain dominant. The latter has eroded the belief as we saw earlier in the legitimacy of the nation-state, and hence of patriotism. Witness the growing reluctance of many-American to die for the flag![29] But if citizenship is increasingly considered irrelevant[30] and the legitimacy of the Eurocultural melting pot is eroded by multiculturalism,[31] and with personal morals increasingly being based on "anything goes," the only basis of social cooperation becomes the law.[32] Hence the growth of that particularly American phenomenon I call "rights chatter." This is a recent version of Oakeshott's "enterprise association" viewpoint of the state.

Ken Minogue calls this new voice "constitutional mania." It emphasizes substantive social and economic rights in addition to the well-known rights to liberty—freedom of speech, contract, and association—emphasized by classical liberals. It seeks to use the law to enforce these "rights" based partly on "needs" and partly on the "equality of respect" desired by a heterogeneity of self-selected minorities differentiated by ethnicity, gender, and/or sexual orientation. But no less than in the collectivist societies that have failed, this attempt to define and legislate a newly discovered and dense structure of rights (including, for some activists, those of nonhuman plants and animals) requires a vast expansion of the government's power over people's lives. The economic costs of this are self-evident.

But these trends also lead to the common impression of the "disuniting of America,"[33] of the erosion of "trust,"[34] or that unlike the dense civil society celebrated by de Tocqueville, Americans are now increasingly "bowling alone."[35] But as I have tried to suggest, to the extent that these diagnoses are correct, they are specifically American. For unlike America, many other parts of the West can still count on the social cement provided by the "manners" associated with the remnants of older social hierarchies. I suspect that as these social norms are eroded by the process of democratization,[36] they too will face the problem of maintaining "civil society" as so many in the West are now posing its central problem.[37] The fractured American self identified by MacIntyre (and discussed in the last chapter) is likely to spread throughout the West.

The role that the shame generated by manners can play in reversing these trends is being supported by many observers in the West,[38] as well as by its politicians. Nothing provided a more fulfilling validation for me of the thesis of this section than General Colin Powell's speech announcing his decision not to run for the presidency. Powell said that had he been elected, his priorities in office would have been to "try to restore a sense of family, restore a sense of *shame* in our society, help bring more civility into our society"![39]

The Welfare State

Nothing illustrates the resulting contrast in what is likely to be the most important aspect of culturally mediated differences in economic performance between the West and the Rest better than the paradox of the Western welfare state. As we saw in our discussion of the Western family in Chapter 5, one consequence of Pope Gregory I's family revolution, which led to the breakdown of the traditional Eurasian family patterns in the West, was the growth of various public social-safety nets for the destitute whom their families were no longer able or willing to support. The most important of these, of course, were provided by the church itself.[40]

The ensuing rise of individualism and the industrialization and urbanization that was associated with it increased the need to provide for "the poor," who had previously been looked after within the communal frameworks of medieval society. Until fairly recently, the poor were clearly identified as those who were destitute. The mass of able-bodied or "structurally" poor was a perennial feature of organic economies, and their poverty could only be alleviated—as it has been—with the unlimited opportunities that Promethean intensive growth has opened up. But for the destitute, who because of physical infirmities and lack of family members, and those who temporarily fell below the poverty line because of conjunctural events, like climatic crises or political turmoil in the predominantly agrarian economies that existed, there is a need for income transfers to alleviate their poverty. Starting with the Elizabethan Poor Law, Western nation-states have been forced to find public ways of dealing with this problem, if private transfers proved inadequate. Though it is arguable whether the system of private transfers augmented by some targeted public assistance was inadequate to deal with destitution and conjunctural poverty,[41] in most advanced Western states, partly spurred by the specter of socialist- or, worse, Communist-inspired social unrest, public transfers replaced private ones not merely for dealing with nature's victims, and those adversely affected by the trade cycle's downturn, but also those whose household income fell below some socially determined poverty norm. This was part of the "egalitarian" voice of Oakeshott's enterprise association.

But the subsequent creation of vast systems of entitlements into gigantic transfer states in the West has had some surprising unintended consequences. Some of these are economic, as the system of incentives and disincentives created by the welfare state have led in some cases to the perpetuation of the very poverty the public transfers sought to redress,[42] to a corruption of their polities as politicians scrambled to buy votes with other people's money,[43] and to endemic fiscal crises.[44]

The more serious unintended consequences are cultural—in the erosion of the shame-based and guilt-based cement of these societies. To delineate these twin effects, it is useful to contrast Western systems of public transfers with the systems of predominantly private transfers, the traditional and current method of dealing with destitution and conjunctural poverty in the Rest. In assessing the case for Western-style welfare states in dealing with the continuing problems of destitution and conjunctural poverty, it is useful to distinguish between social safety nets and welfare states.

The distinction between the "welfare state" and a "social safety net" essentially turns upon the universality of coverage of transfers under a welfare state as opposed to the restriction of collectively provided benefits under a social safety net to the truly needy. The World Bank's *Poverty Reduction Handbook* noted two essential elements in any design of a social safety net: "Identifying the groups in need of assistance, and the means of targeting assistance to those groups cost-effectively." It went on to ask: "Are these questions for public policy, or are they adequately addressed by the traditional family network?"[45]

By contrast, welfare-state advocates favor universality. In their view, it alone provides a feasible means to achieve the ends sought to be sub-served by a social safety net, because of problems concerned with obtaining the requisite information for targeting. Some[46] have argued that because of the ubiquitousness of imperfect information, markets for risk will be inherently imperfect. Hence, universal welfare states are required as part of an efficient solution to deal with "market failure." To deal with this argument would take me too far afield.[47] Suffice it to say that this is a form of the "nirvana economics"[48] currently fashionable on the left, but it provides no credible justification for a welfare state.

Are public transfers needed, as the welfare-state advocates claim, to deal with destitution and conjunctural poverty, and, as some assert, even to deal with mass structural poverty? We need to examine the relative efficacy of private versus public income transfers. As private transfers have become a quantitatively insignificant portion of total income transfers in the West, much of the evidence on the issue comes from the Rest.

Private Transfers

Kin-based transfers, reciprocity arrangements, and interlinked-factor market contracts have been the major ways that traditional societies have dealt with income risk. They have been fairly effective.[49] With the inevitable erosion of village communities it is feared that these private insurance arrangements will break down and that no private alternative will be available to counter destitution and conjunctural poverty in increasingly atomistic industrial economies.

It is in this context that the role of private inter-household transfers is of great importance. Cox and Jimenez provide evidence to show that in developing countries they are still of considerable quantitative importance.[50] Moreover, since the oil price rise of the early 1970s the poor in South Asia and parts of Southeast Asia have found remunerative employment in the newly rich oil states, and their remittances to their Third World relatives have helped to alleviate their poverty.[51]

The motivation for these transfers is of some interest. If they were purely altruistically determined (as in Becker's famous "rotten kid" theorem),[52] then it would imply that with intergenerational transfers between parents and children there would be dynastic families that would behave as though they were a single infinite lived individual. Barro's famous Ricardian equivalence would then hold, with public policies such as debt

financing and social security being completely neutralized by countervailing private action.[53]

Because these implications seem to be highly unrealistic, attempts have
been made to explain private transfers as part of an exchange process
involving an implicit mutually beneficial contract, say between parents
and children, who in exchange for their educational expenditure are committed to looking after their parents in their old age.[54] Lucas and Stark
have developed an intermediate model in which both altruism and self-
interested exchange are the motives for transfers, and found that it applies
satisfactorily to Botswana.[55] Most of the empirical evidence on the
motives for private transfers finds them to be mixed.[56]

Some studies have instead tried to estimate the crowding out effect of
public on private transfers directly. Most of these have been done for the
United States and find some small crowding-out effect. But as the expansion of the welfare state has made public transfers the dominant component in the total of transfers, studies of private transfers in developed
countries are looking at the effects of changes in only a marginal component of transfers. So it is important to look at the evidence from developing countries on the crowding out of private by public transfers.

There are only two such studies of developing countries. Cox and
Jimenez[57] found that in the absence of social security in urban Peru, private inter-household old age support would have been higher by 20 percent. So there is considerable but not complete crowding out of private
by public transfers. A study of the Philippines by Cox and Jimenez[58] is
probably more relevant.[59] They found that private transfers were large
and widespread. They then simulated the effects on these private transfers
of three public policies: unemployment insurance, social security, and
income grants targeted to the poor. For unemployment insurance they
find that "the reduction in private transfers is nearly as large as the boost
in income that unemployment insurance gives to households. Ninety-one
percent of the increase in household income from unemployment insurance is offset by reductions in private transfers."[60] For retirement income
they find that "private transfers would be 37% higher" if retirement
income did not exist. On a program to completely eliminate poverty by
giving each household the difference between its actual income and poverty line income, they find that after private transfers adjust, 46 percent of
urban and 94 percent of rural households below the poverty line before
the program would still be below the line after the program! Moreover,
they give reasons to believe that their estimates of crowding out are
biased downward. This study should certainly give anyone seeking the

public-transfer route to deal with poverty related to risks in the labor market considerable cause to pause.

These doubts concerning the relative efficacy of private versus public transfers are further strengthened by noting that private transfers, by relying on locally held information and on extra economic motivations like trust and altruism, can overcome many of the problems of adverse selection, moral hazard, and the like, which have so exercised the "nirvana" economics "market-failure" school. For as Cox and Jimenez, summarizing the empirical evidence, conclude: "private transfers equalize income; private transfers are directed toward the poor, the young, the old, women, the disabled and the unemployed."[61]

Public Transfers

Perhaps public transfers can do even better, so that we should not worry if they crowd out private transfers? Public subsidization of the two merit goods—health and education—are the major public transfers in nearly all developing countries and a major part of those in developed ones. In addition, social security is important in many Latin American countries and is one of the rising components of public transfers in developed ones.[62]

One question on which there is some empirical evidence is the incidence of the benefits from subsidies for merit goods in developing countries. Beginning with the pioneering studies of Meerman for Malaysia and Selowsky for Colombia, a number of other studies have addressed this issue. Jimenez,[63] summarizing the studies done till 1987, concludes:

Students from the highest quartile of the income distribution profile in Chile, Colombia, Indonesia, and Malaysia receive between 51 and 83% of all public expenditures on higher education, whereas those from the lowest 40% receive between 6 and 15%. The effect is only partly counterbalanced by the concentration of primary education subsidies among poor families, which have most of a country's younger school children. The net result is a distribution of overall educational subsidies roughly proportional to each income group's population share, with the exception of the Dominican Republic where the poor's share is still less. The income bias is less for health. Health subsidies for Colombia and Malaysia are roughly proportional to each income group's population share. But in Indonesia, the poorest 40% capture only about 19% from public health centers and hospitals.[64]

In developed countries the fall in the quality of public education is now widely recognized. Thus a recent study by Evans and Schwab[65] found that Catholic schools in the United States outperformed public schools in their quality of education as judged by their relative effectiveness in ensuring that their pupils finish high school and enter college.[66]

Other studies of the effectiveness of public transfers in developing countries are summarized in Lal-Myint. The general impression is that their incidence is generally regressive, and that they are very imperfect means of helping the poor. A similar "middle class capture" of the welfare state has been documented for a number of Western democracies.[67]

One revealing piece of evidence suggesting that public transfers not only are more inefficient in poverty redressal than private transfers but also crowd them out is provided by a 1990 World Bank study. This

traced public social sector expenditures for nine Latin American countries in the 1980s ... [and] found that real per capita public social spending on health, education, and social security fell during some part of the 1980s in every country in the study. The share of health and education expenditures in total government expenditures also fell, even as that of social security rose. In spite of lower funding, and no apparent increases in equity and efficiency, social indicators generally improved in the 1980s.[68]

Apart from obvious statistical and other biases which might explain this anomaly, the most plausible explanation provided is that, it might be due to "the growing role of non-governmental organizations, and the response of the market oriented private sector to enhanced expectations and demand." That is there was probably a "crowding in" of more equitable and more efficient private transfers to replace the decline in public ones![69]

Political Economy of Transfer States

Enough has been said to suggest that public transfers are clearly not the panacea being touted by socialists of varied hue.[70] Their efficacy in achieving ends like improved educational and health outcomes are dubious and the incidence of their benefits tends to be regressive—certainly as compared with the evidence on private transfers summarized earlier. My general conclusion therefore echoes that of a World Bank report on Honduras: "Most [public] social programs benefit primarily the middle class and rich, through spending on curative hospital care, pension benefits and higher education. Social spending pays for services that might be financed by the private sector."[71]

This "middle class capture" of the benefits of social expenditure is not confined to developing countries. It has also been documented for the welfare states of the OECD.[72] A systemic process is clearly at work—the political economy of redistribution in majoritarian democracies. In a two-party majoritarian democracy, politicians will bid for votes by offering transfers of income from some sections of the populace at the expense of others. Models of this political process (which do not need to assume a democracy, but rather the interplay of different pressure/interest groups)[73] show that there will be a tendency for income to be transferred from both the rich and the poor to the middle classes—the so-called median voter. Even if social expenditures are initially intended to benefit only the needy, in democracies such programs have inevitably been "universalized" through the political process, leading to what are properly called transfer rather than welfare states, which primarily benefit the middle classes.

The poverty alleviation that may occur as a by-product of the expansion of the transfer state is, moreover, bought at a rising dynamic cost. With the universalization of various welfare schemes, political entitlements are created whose fiscal burden is governed more by demography than the conjunctural state of the economy. With the costs of entitlements rising faster than the revenues needed to finance them, the transfer state finds itself in a fiscal crisis sooner or later. This process is discernible both in developing and developed countries.

For developing countries the Lal-Myint study shows how this process is clearly visible in those countries in our sample (Uruguay, Costa Rica, Sri Lanka, and Jamaica) that under the factional pressures of majoritarian democracies have created and expanded welfare states. All four welfare states were financed by taxing the rents from their major primary products. With the expansion of revenues during upturns in the primary product cycle, political pressures led to their commitment to entitlements, which could not be repudiated when revenues fell during the downturn in the price cycle. The ensuing increase in the tax burden on the productive primary sector (to close the fiscal gap) led to a retardation of its growth and productivity, and in some cases to the "killing of the goose that laid the golden eggs." Thus, although there was undoubtedly some poverty redressal as a result of the expansion of these welfare states, over the long run the entitlements created damaged the economic growth on which they were predicated, and hence eventually became unsustainable. Similar processes leading to the fiscal crisis of the state are to be found in many other developing and developed countries.[74] Not surprisingly, many of these countries with overextended welfare states are now seeking to rein them back.

Cultural Aspects

These unintended economic and political consequences of the welfare state have been accompanied by equally serious effects on the social cement of the West. Thus Magnet has recently argued that the pathologies associated with the welfare state, such as exploding divorce rates, rising numbers of single-parent households headed by teenage mothers, exploding rates of illegitimacy, drug abuse, and crime all seemed to occur at about the same time in the late 1960s (see figure 9.1). The Sexual Revolution was launched by the technological marvels of the Pill as well as a series of decisions by the U.S. Supreme Court from 1965 to 1977 that "created a constitutional right of sexual or reproductive autonomy, which it called privacy."[75] The guilt associated with original sin in the West was now finally at an end.

A purely economic explanation based on the perverse incentives created by the Great Society programs is insufficient[76] to explain why all these trends

took off for the stratosphere in tandem, beginning in the mid 1960s and accelerating in the early 1970s. They don't explain why men and women become degraded into the underclass at exactly the same time, even though the incentives to fail were different for women than for men. Indeed, why did so many of the incentives to fail, such as judicial leniency or welfare generosity, fall into place at the same time? The answer is that all these manifestations were emanations of the same spirit of the age, of that great cultural shift that transvalued values and transformed the way the Haves, and soon the Have-Nots, conceived of authority, equality, justice, law, morality, poverty, race and the social order. What turned poverty pathological, in other words, wasn't just a series of institutional changes, but the cultural revolution that informed those changes and that conveyed to the poor a new and destructive set of norms and values.[77]

Similarly, Phelps-Brown, in trying to explain the simultaneous burst of industrial unrest in Europe in the late 1960s, found the explanation in the loosening of the traditional mores of the European working classes in the 1960s culminating in the events of 1968. Scott also notes, in his examination of the causes of the stagflation that resulted in many OECD countries after the first oil shock, the effects of the "cultural evolution" of the 1960s in changing "people's expectations and attitudes"[78] and finds the major cause for the stagflation in "expectations of better and better collectively provided services and more generous pensions and other transfers from the state" colliding "with a lower ceiling imposed by worsening terms of trade in the early 1970s."[79]

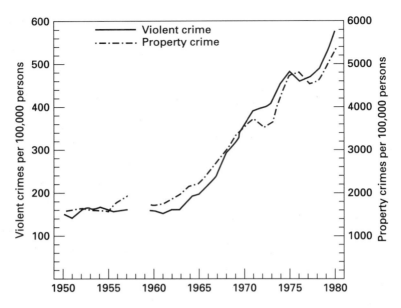

Figure 9.1a

U.S. crimes reported to the police: indexes for 1950–1980

Note: Data for 1950–57 are based on 353 cities of 25,000 population or greater. Data for 1960–80 include all reporting jurisdictions.

Source: Murray 1984, p. 114.

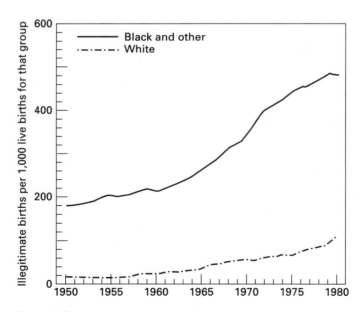

Figure 9.1b

U.S. illegitimate births per 1,000 live births by race, 1950–1980

Source: Murray 1984, p. 126.

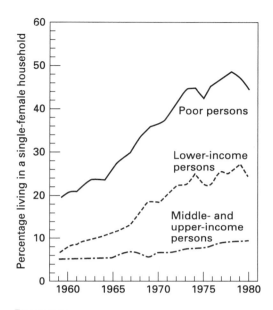

Figure 9.1c
U.S. persons in single-female households by income group, as percentage of persons living in families, 1959–1980

Source: Murray 1984, p. 130.

Magnet maintains that the "cultural revolution" of the "Haves" is to blame. Propelled by the desire for personal liberation—the apotheosis of Mill's simple principle in *On Liberty*[80]—a strange alliance in the United States between the Haves and Have-nots destroyed that sense of personal responsibility (and thus the basis of guilt and shame, in our terms) for the very people who most needed it to ascend the economic ladder. He argues that there was a dual revolution. The first was a social revolution seeking to liberate the poor from political, economic, and racial oppression. The second was a cultural revolution offering the same liberation that the Haves had achieved from the moral restraints of bourgeois values. "The first created the welfare programs of the Great Society, which provided counterincentives to leaving poverty. And the second disparaged the behavior and attitudes that traditionally made for economic improvement."[81] These were "deferral of gratification, sobriety, thrift, dogged industry, and so on through the whole catalogue of antique-sounding bourgeois virtues."[82] Together these twin revolutions

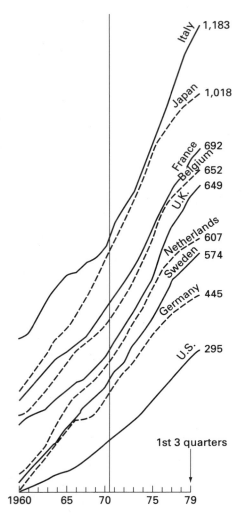

Figure 9.1d
Rise of hourly rates or earnings, mostly in manufacturing, in nine countries of OECD, 1960–1979, showing change in rates of rise about 1969–70. Ratio scale: number at end of each curve gives hourly rates or earnings in 1979 (average of first three quarters) as relative to 1960 = 100.

Source: Phelps-Brown 1983, p. 156.

had the unintended consequence of creating the demoralized and self-perpetuating "underclass," which is a feature not only of urban America, but, if Murray[83] is to be believed, also increasingly of the United Kingdom.[84]

Thus, the cultural consequences of the welfare state may be as momentous as the economic or political ones. As sociologists such as Robert Nisbet (in his *The Quest for Community*) and Nathan Glazer (in his *The Limits of Social Policy*) have noted, the conversion of welfare into transfer states in the West, and their inevitable universalization under the pressure of democratic politics, has led to an attack on civil society from above and below. From above, the intermediate institutions of civil society are forced to surrender their functions and authority to professional elites and the bureaucracies of centralizing states. From below, "rights-chatter"—the clamor for numerous and newly discovered individual rights—undermines the authority of those traditional civil institutions (family, church, school, neighborhood) that in the past promoted both private benevolence and the lower-order "vigorous virtues." The acceptance of claims to various welfare rights substitutes public for private benevolence, sapping the latter, which for classical liberals is the highest (though scarce) virtue. These longer-run, unintended social (and fiscal) consequences of the welfare state are now leading to its questioning and in some cases partial dismantling in the West—the most dramatic example of the latter being the virtual abandonment of the New Zealand welfare state by its chastened socialist party!

The Western welfare state has also sapped the family bonds that provide the safety nets in Asia. This is of relevance because of the oft-repeated claim that "aging populations, growing urbanization and the rising number of nuclear families have weakened the traditional support provided by the family and increased the need for formal provision."[85] But are extended families in the Third World necessarily likely to be extinguished? Is the decline of not only extended but also nuclear families in the West due to some inevitable process associated with economic growth? or, as Murray and many others maintain, is it the unintended consequence of well-intentioned welfare policies that subsidize teenage mothers, promote single parent families, and make the type of reciprocal exchange relationships—outlined in our discussion of private transfers—more and more redundant? If the family has been an institution that has to some extent been created and preserved as a form of mutual insurance against life's risks, is the transfer of these insurance functions to the state not likely to undermine the very institution whose decline politicians in all the Western welfare states are currently bemoaning? One cannot assume that the type of individualistic as opposed to dynastic motivation for marriage, which seems to predominate in the West, is a universal human characteristic, nor that it is a necessary accompaniment of growth.[86] Many Third World cultures—for example, the Indian and Chinese—seem to be relatively immune to these Western cultural norms. As Lee Kwan Yew suggests, the family in many Third World cultures may be *relatively* immune to the specifically Western social developments that have undermined it in the West.[87] But of course, because economic incentives matter, as in the West, Third World families *could* be undermined by similar welfare-state policies.

There are, however, some hopeful auguries for at least two of the major non-Western civilizations, the Sinic and the Hindu. The form of mutual assurance provided within families ultimately depends upon some internalized moral codes. In the West, until the Enlightenment, this morality was underwritten by the guilt promoted by various Christian churches. The fear of God and of burning in Hell was a potent goad to doing the "right thing" even in increasingly individualistic societies. But once God died, this religious bulwark for the morality which provided the cement of these societies has been greatly eroded. "Anything Goes"— their current norm—does not help to engender the requisite social virtues. The attempts to found a secular morality based on reason rather than the revelations contained in the Holy Book, have failed (see Chapter 6). But the crux is that Christianity and its Semitic cousin Islam were (in the religious underpinnings of their social morality) all expressions of people of *the* Book.[88] When that was undermined, so was the traditional social fabric it underwrote. No wonder one of the remaining civilizations still believing in the Book—the Islamic—should take such a dim view of blasphemy,[89] the questioning of the divine revelation contained in their Book. They at least recognize that any such questioning will undermine their social fabric.

But the death of God, which is perhaps inevitable in the modern world, is of less concern for the Sinic and Hindu civilizations. For their religions, unlike the Semitic ones, are not religions of the Book. They have no organized churches, and "these religions" are more a way of life. Their morality is underwritten by cultural processes of socialization that emphasize shame, rather than guilt based on a belief in God. The death of God—following from the secularization that has accompanied modernization—is not as likely to undermine the internalized morality that has underwritten the social fabric of these civilizations. If, as in Japan, that proves to be true, their social institutions, most importantly the family, may prove to be more resilient than those in the West. They may not need the welfare state, with all its deleterious unintended consequences, as Lee Kwan Yew has asserted, and it should not be thrust on them by "do-gooders" from the West!

10 Conclusions

At the end of our long journey, what can we say about the evolution of the civilizations of Eurasia over the millennia?

First, the geography of these civilizations has been important in molding their cosmological beliefs and their polities: the centralized authoritarian bureaucratic state of China; the decentralized polities of Hinduism, Islam and Christendom, politically disunited though culturally united; and the democratic assemblies of ancient Greece and the Aryan republics in the Himalayan foothills.

Second, these civilizations, as well as the Japanese under the Tokugawa, saw periods of Smithian intensive growth, largely as a result of the knitting together of areas of diverse resources into a larger common market under Pax Greco-Roman in the ancient world, Pax Islam under the Abbasids, Pax Buddhist under the Mauryas, Pax Hindu under the Guptas, Pax Tokugawa in Japan, and during the Pax Sung's extension to the Yangtze valley in China. But in none of these civilizations, with the exception of Sung China, was there any likelihood of Promethean growth. That merely technological and scientific developments were insufficient to deliver the Industrial Revolution is borne out by the failure of Sung China to do so, although it had these ingredients. It was a "package" of cosmological beliefs, political decentralization, and the application of the "inquisitive Greek spirit" that uniquely led to Promethean growth and the ascendancy of the West.

The failure of both the Abbasids and the Sung to put together such a package is plausibly ascribed to the respective closing of their peoples' minds by the victory of their respective orthodox clergies. This victory is not surprising inasmuch as all the ancient Eurasian civilizations depended upon maintaining a particular social order that would deliver the "surplus" to feed the cities (the very definition and emblem of "civilization") where the wielders of the sword and the book lived. The merchants (also city-dwellers) were tolerated as a necessary evil but were distrusted, their activities being seen as potential threats to the social order. Likewise, despite variations, there was a common problem faced by these relatively labor-scarce civilizations of tying workers to the land. The solution they found, from the Indian caste system to European serfdom and the "cift-hane" system of the Ottomans, depended as much on their polities, shaped by geography (and thus material factors), as on any particular set of cosmological beliefs. In this sense, as the materialists believe, many aspects of human culture and politics can be explained in terms of eco-logical and material factors.

Third, as I hope I have showed, cosmological beliefs—an essential ele-ment of "culture"—have been crucial in the rise of the West and the sub-sequent evolution of its political economy. The midwife in delivering the package that led to Promethean growth in the West was the Christian church. The individualism it inadvertently promoted is the unique cosmo-logical belief of the West. The Rest have been and continue to be com-munalist. To that extent Max Weber was right, he just got his dates wrong. It has generally been accepted that the instrumental rationality that individualism bred was responsible for the scientific and industrial revolutions that generated Promethean growth. On the origins of this "strange" belief I find Goody's explanation the most persuasive: it arose as the unintended consequence of the Roman Catholic church's acquisi-tive hunger. Thus there would seem to be a "materialist" origin for the "idealism" that led to the rise of the West. But it was historically contin-gent. For we have charted how the growth of individualism was asso-ciated with the twin papal revolutions of the two Popes Gregory, which brought the church into the world and created the cosmological beliefs and legal institutions of a market economy, which in turn eventually led to Promethean growth.

We have seen that this unique trajectory was not predetermined by geography or the polity of post-Roman Europe, nor by differences in the original religious beliefs of Christianity as compared with Hinduism or Islam. It had nothing to do with monotheism; in both pantheistic Hindu India and the monotheistic lands of Islam, the state effectively came to be separated from society. Their conjoining in Western Christendom was the result of contingent factors in which the church's greed for bequests of land played a major role. That this was a mutation of the original Chris-tian doctrine by Augustine is showed by the very different course the Eastern Christian church took in its relationships with the secular power.

Fourth, the papal revolution of Gregory I concerning the family has cast a long shadow over the West. It led to a break with the traditional "family values" previously common among Eurasian civilizations, which were aimed at keeping various self-aggrandizing instincts and basic emotions such as romantic passion in check. To counter these deleterious effects on the internalized mores that had hitherto maintained social order, the church, through, what I have called Augustine's "mutation," put original sin at the fountainhead of its doctrines and created a guilt society wherein the fear of Purgatory was enough to make Christians eschew as best as they were able the seven deadly sins or else seek absolution from the church's functionaries.

The subsequent course of the West's cosmological beliefs has been to reconcile Augustine's medieval philosophical system set out in his *City of God* with the scientific fallout from the individualism it also inadvertently promoted. From the Enlightenment to Marxism to Freudianism to Eco-fundamentalism, we have seen the tenacious hold on the Western mind of Augustine's vision of the Heavenly City. The same narrative, with a Garden of Eden, a fall leading to original sin, and a day of judgment with redemption for the elect and purgatory for the damned, keeps recurring. But these variations on a cosmological theme have had political consequences in the rise of both the demos and the nation, and in the domestic domain in destroying any basis for morality, when, after Darwin, God was seen as the Blind Watchmaker.

The fifth and final conclusion, which gets to the heart of the central concern of these lectures, is the paradoxical nature of what individualism has wrought and its implications for the West and the Rest. Thus, individualism has created the instruments of Promethean growth. But once discovered, these can be, as they have been, diffused worldwide to very different societies that do not have to adopt the cosmological beliefs that led to their creation.[1]

It has created the institutions of the market economy, the most important being the commercial law, including the law of contract and that of incorporation, which (after some kicking and shoving) have been accepted worldwide because of their instrumental efficiency in promoting the material prosperity that is universally desired. This has meant that even in the ancient agrarian civilizations of India and China the workings of the "economic principle" are now gradually undermining their atavistic attitudes toward trade and commerce—the lifeblood of a market economy. The ancient global separation after the last Ice Age of the descendants of

Lucy[2], a common African ancestor, has now been replaced by their effective unification through trade and investment, in what looks more and more like interregional trade and investment in a global economy. The effective competition among these regions for two of the increasingly most mobile factors of production—financial and human capital—has also begun to rein in the traditional predatoriness of the state, which humans have had to suffer at least since the emergence of agriculture and the rise of "civilization."

But individualism has paradoxically undermined the very cement of the prosperous societies it has created. Across time and space, as de Tocqueville rightly notes, this cement has been provided by the emotions of "guilt" or "shame" engendered in the process of socialization. The triumph of science that individualism has wrought has led to the death of God in the West, and thus of the guilt that underwrote its personal morality, whereas the democratization promoted by individualism has undermined the traditional hierarchical bases of these societies and eroded the set of "manners" based on deference, which evinced shame in these societies in their process of socialization. In the exceptional Western country that was born individualistic and democratic—the United States—the sense of shame was inculcated as part of a civic culture glorifying citizenship. This patriotism engendered by the nation-state also played its part in continuing the shame-based component of the process of socialization in other Western societies. But it is increasingly being undermined by the secularization and democratization that individualism has bred. With the rise of postmodernity and the decline of the center at the expense of the border, this patriotism and the shame-based socialization it engenders are also in decline.

In many ways, at the frontiers of the West—for example, U.S. cities— there is a return to the Middle Ages, as "decent" citizens, irrespective of race, increasingly live (or want to live) in gated communities or distant suburbs from which they commute to privately policed workplaces. The only danger lies in the public places they have to traverse in getting from home to work. These are infested with the modern versions of medieval highwaymen—muggers and carjackers. This growing failure of Western states to provide the most basic of public goods—guaranteeing their citizens' safety—is eroding their legitimacy, but it need not dissipate the economic vigor of the West, *pace* the Middle Ages. This failure, however, will make the West a dangerous place in which to live.

The religious void in the West left by what individualism has wrought is increasingly being filled by the bizarre worship of nature of the eco-fundamentalists, while in personal morals "anything goes" is the motto. Having thus greatly undermined the two processes of socialization that humankind has used to turn the evolutionary psychologists' Naked Ape into a moral animal, individualism has thus paradoxically loosened the glue of the very societies it has made unimaginably prosperous.

A Western anthropologist wrote a book against the relativist approach to other cultures called *Sick Societies*.[3] A non-Western anthropologist looking at the West—particularly at its frontiers in America—would have to use the same epithet of what individualism in its full flower has wrought in these societies.

Western social science, until recently, has been infected by a particular form of dualism going under the label of "modernization theory." In this "modernization" and "westernization" were lumped together and contrasted with "backwardness and tradition." It was believed that to achieve Promethean growth and thence the material fruits of modernization, the Western package of ethical beliefs and political forms would also have to be accepted. The current U.S. project of global legislation of its perceived mores—human rights[4] and democracy—goes back at least to the unholy alliance of utilitarian administrators and Christian missionaries in nineteenth-century India, whose White Man's Burden was to save the heathens' souls so that they could achieve prosperity. But, as I have been at pains to show, the contemporary notion of "rights" is a latecomer even within the Western cosmology, and though it was linked to the individualism that led to the West's unique trajectory, there is nothing universal about the notion. Nor is there anything universal about egalitarianism, which is confined to the religions born among the southern nomads of ancient civilizations. Nor is democracy essential for development. After all, hereditary monarchy has been the most common form of government through human history, and it, not democracy, delivered the Industrial Revolution. Nor, as we have seen, is the Western family a cause or consequence of the West's economic progress. These aspects of Westernization, though contingently tied with the West's modernization, are not necessarily so: it is possible to modernize without Westernizing.[5]

If the evolutionary psychologists are to be believed, our basic instincts—the human nature that they are charting—have been fixed through evolutionary processes during the millennia when we were hunter-gatherers. One essential component of these instincts, it now appears from the archaeological record, was to trade—to truck and barter. This is Hicks's Economic Principle: "People would act *economically*; when an opportunity of an advantage was presented to them they would take it".[6] This economic behavior must be part of our makeup just as much as the other instincts and passions. With settled agriculture and the need to regulate opportunistic behavior, social mores developed to rein in all these passions. One way of looking at the twin papal revolutions that led to the rise of the West is to see them as removing these traditional restraints and substituting the powerful but ultimately self-destructive mores based on the concept of original sin. The concomitant unleashing of the instinct based on the economic principle has played an important part in promoting intensive growth. This is a lesson all civilizations have now learned. But the unleashing of the other passions was a contingent and unintended consequence of the development of Western cosmological beliefs that grew from the papal revolutions. They have destroyed both the novel (guilt) and the traditional (shame) cements of Western societies.

By contrast, as Japan has showed, and as India and China are beginning to show, the Rest do not have to make this Faustian compact. It is possible for these non-Western societies to adopt the West's means to attain prosperity without giving up their souls. Their social cement is unlikely to be undermined by secularization, insofar as it does not depend on a belief in God. In these hierarchically ordered societies, the social cement was provided by ancient processes of socialization based on shame. It is not surprising, therefore, that rather than succumb to the current attempt by the West to legislate its unique value—individualism—these ancient civilizations are instead deriding it by invoking that ancient Biblical injunction: "Physician, heal thyself."

Appendix

Four theoretical models underlie the argument of these lectures: the Boserup model, the model of the predatory state from Lal (1988), the model of dual preferences from Kuran (1995), and the model of an economy where land is abundant and labor scarce (due to Domar 1970).

The Boserup Process

Boserup (1965) has argued that population pressure is a necessary but not sufficient condition for technical change in agriculture (in the form of an intensive use of both labor and capital). She identifies the differing labor input per hectare requirements of different agrarian systems by the frequency with which a particular piece of land is cropped. Thus settled agriculture is more labor- and capital-intensive than nomadic pastoralism, which in turn is more intensive in these inputs than hunting and gathering or the slash-and-burn agriculture practiced until recently in parts of Africa. Contrary to Malthusian presumptions, she argues that population growth leads to the adoption of more advanced techniques that raise yields per hectare. Because these new advanced techniques require increased labor effort, they will not be adopted until rising population reduces the per capita food output that can be produced with existing techniques and forces a change.

The model has been formalized by Pryor and Maurer (1982), who also produce a more general model that includes both the Malthusian and Boserupian positions as special cases. The essence of the Boserup process can be depicted by figure A.1., where in (A) we have a production function summarizing agricultural techniques in terms of labor input (labor hours) OY. Each point on this can be thought of as a different agrarian system. There are diminishing returns to labor. In the second quadrant we depict the original population (all assumed to work equally, and share

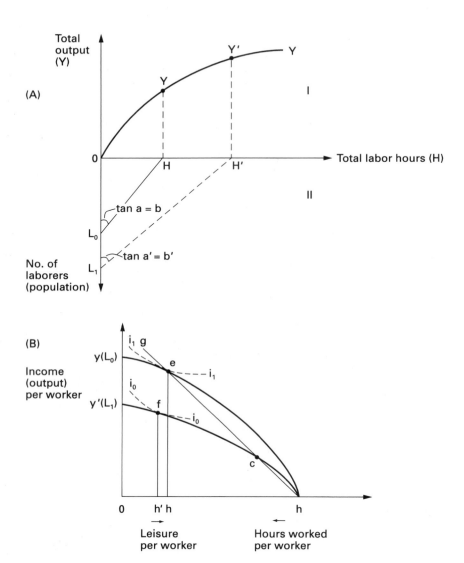

Figure A.1

equally in output) by OL_0. The "intensity" of work effort per worker in the "primitive" system of agriculture system—say, hunting and gathering—is given by tan $a = b$, which yields a total input of labor hours of OH and hence total output of YH. Part (B) of figure A.1 shows the output per worker as related to hours worked per worker, $-hy$. OH being the total hours per worker available, the difference between hours worked and total hours available is leisure per worker. We can also then draw in indifference curves between income and leisure to determine the individual worker's income—leisure equilibrium given hy—which is just OY scaled by the population OL_0.

Suppose population expands to OL_1 in (A). Then the income per worker curve in (B) will shift downward. It can be constructed by noting that the slope of the ray hg measures the average product of labor (apl) when total labor input is OH and output HY in (A). Becuase hy' is just a scaled-down version of OY—the scalar being OL_1—at the point e there will be the same apl and hence marginal product of labor as at c. Clearly, income per worker will fall as a result of population growth, inasmuch as hy' lies below hy. If both income and leisure are normal goods, the new work-leisure equilibrium will be at f, implying a rise in hours worked per worker to hh', and thus an increase in the intensity of work to tan $a' = b'$ (in A). This will raise total labor input to OH', and output will rise to YH' in the new, more labor-intensive agrarian system—say, settled agriculture.

What is more, as Pryor and Maurer show, if population is growing at a constant rate then agricultural output will also be growing at that rate in the steady state of the model. This is the process observed in the form of the Ishikawa curve in both India and China.[1]

The Model of the Predatory State

The following model is based on Lal (1988). Consider a simple model of a predatory state whose only source of revenue is a proportional tax on agricultural output (Y) at the rate t.[2]

Suppose that the area controlled by the state is divided into M identical villages, each with a fixed labor supply of L working on a fixed supply of land in each village of N. For simplicity assume (as in much of the development literature) that there is equal work and income-sharing in each village, so that each worker receives the (net of tax) average product of labor ($y(1 - t)$) in agriculture (where $y = Y/L_A$, and L_A is the labor force in each village engaged in agriculture). The state uses part of the revenue it obtains to hire public servants from each village (L_g) to administer the village and provide any other public goods, such as irrigation or police, either at the national or local level. The cost of hiring a marginal public employee will be equal to the supply price of rural labor, which in turn will be equal to the net of tax-average product of labor. Moreover, following Findlay and Wilson (1987), we assume that the provision of these public goods raises the productivity of the economy above what would exist in the absence of the state—namely, under anarchy.

Thus in each of the M villages we have

$$L_g + L_A = L \tag{A.1}$$

and

$$Y = A(L_g)F(L_A, N) \tag{A.2}$$
$$A'(L_g) > 0 : A''(L_g) < 0; \quad A(0) = 1$$

with L and N fixed, we can, using (A.1), write (A.2) as

$$Y = Y(L_g; L, N) \tag{A.3}$$

with $Y = Y^0 > 0 = A(0)F(L_A, N)$ when $L_A = L$ and $L_g = 0$; and $Y = 0$, when $L_A = 0$ and $L_g = L$.

The total revenue (TR) the predator controlling the state earns is given by

$$TR = M \cdot t \cdot Y. \tag{A.4}$$

The total variable costs (TVC) of the predatory state are

$$TVC = M \cdot L_g(1 - t)y(L_g) \tag{A.5}$$

where

$$y(L_g) \equiv \frac{Y(L_g)}{L_A}.$$

In addition to these variable costs, the incumbent predator controlling the state will have had to expend fixed capital costs of K to capture and maintain the state, of which we assume αK are sunk costs. So the "effective" fixed costs of the incumbent (FC_I) will be $(1 - \alpha)k$.

$$FC_I = (1 - \alpha)K \tag{A.6}$$

The total cost curve (TC_I) of the incumbent will therefore be from (A.5) and (A.6)

$$TC_I = M \cdot L_g(1 - t)y(L_g) + (1 - \alpha)K \qquad\qquad\qquad (A.7)$$

By contrast, a new entrant seeking to control this natural monopoly, whom we assume to have access to the same military technology, would incur the same variable costs as the incumbent, but will have to expend the full fixed costs (that is, inclusive of the sunk cost αK) in capturing and replacing the incumbent. The new entrant's total cost curve TC_E will therefore be

$$TC_E = TVC + K \qquad\qquad\qquad (A.8)$$

and this will lie above the incumbent's total cost curve by the fixed amount αK, as in figure A.2a.

If the size of the territory to be controlled (M) lies within the decreasing average cost portion of the total cost curve, the incumbent will be able to find a tax rate t and earn a "monopoly" profit equal to the sunk cost αK, which makes his monopoly sustainable in the sense that the new entrant cannot charge a lower tax rate and break even. Thus, as in figure A.2(A), for territory size M, the incumbent will charge a tax rate t, such that the total revenue line intersects the entrant's cost curve at C_E. Because the incumbent's costs are C_I, he will make a profit of αK. The net revenue-maximizing predator state's profit π function will be:

$$\pi = TR - TC_I = \alpha K \qquad\qquad\qquad (A.9)$$

Substituting for TR and TC_I from (A.4), (A.3), and (A.7), we can determine the optimum tax rate t and level of public employment L_g, by maximizing

$$\pi = M[tY(L_g) - (1 - t)y(L_g) \cdot L_g] - (1 - \alpha)K \qquad\qquad\qquad (A.10)$$

with respect to L_g, that is setting $\dfrac{\delta \pi}{\delta L_g} = 0$, which yields

$$tY'(L_g) = (1 - t)[y(L_g) + L_g, y'(L_g)] \qquad\qquad\qquad (A.11)$$

namely, as is to be expected, the marginal revenue equals marginal cost of public employment, at which the profit from equation (A.9) equals αK. From (A.9), (A.6), and (A.5), the total surplus (S) between the total revenue (TR) and total variable costs (TVC) earned by the incumbent is

$$S = TR - TVC = K \qquad\qquad\qquad (A.12)$$

with the surplus per identical village being K/M.

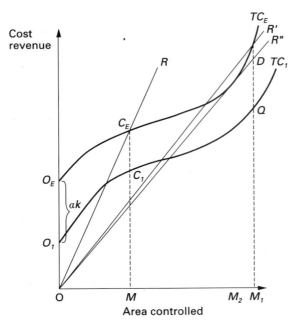

Figure A.2a
Determination of area controlled

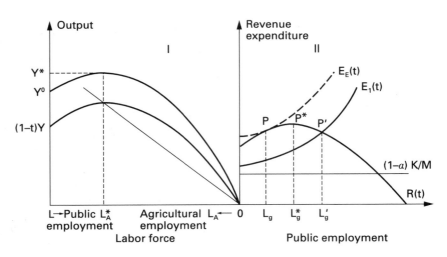

Figure A.2b
The equilibrium of the predatory state

The resulting general equilibrium of this agrarian predatory state can be depicted in figure A.2b. The first quadrant depicts the total agricultural output curve of each identical village with respect to the given labor force OL working on the fixed acreage N. If there are no government employees—hence no state—then the whole of the village's labor force works in agriculture and produces output LY^0. This is the "anarchy" level of output. With some government employees being hired to provide public goods, the agricultural labor force shrinks but total output increases, until the allocation of the labor force is such that there are $LL_A^* = L_g^*$ workers in public employment, and OL_A^* working in agriculture producing the maximal attainable output Y^* (higher than Y_0, because of the public goods provided by the L_g^* public employees).

For a given tax rate t on rural output, the vertical distance between the $Y(1-t)Y$ curves in quadrant I gives the total revenue available for a particular level of public (L_g) employment. This per-village revenue function $(R(t))$ is plotted in quadrant II of figure A.2b. For any given tax rate (t) it reaches a maximum where $L_g^* = L - L_A^*$ workers are employed in the public sector. The competitive wage for public employees is equal to the supply price of rural labor, which *ex hypothesi* is the net of tax average product in agriculture, given by the slope of the ray Oy, when the level of rural agricultural employment is L_A^* and public employment is L_g^*.

Thus, by a similar construction for each level of L_g, and for the given tax rate (t), the village-level variable-cost function $VC(t)$ can be derived in quadrant II. Adding the "effective" fixed costs per village that the incumbent of the predatory state has to incur to maintain its natural monopoly of $(1-\alpha)K/M$ yields the per-village expenditure function $E_I(t)$ of the incumbent, which is a vertical displacement by $(1-\alpha)K/M$ of the variable cost $(VC(t))$ function. The per-village expenditure function of a potential entrant to this natural monopoly $E_E(t)$ will lie at a vertical distance equal to $\alpha K/M$ above the incumbent's expenditure function. The optimal tax rate for the net revenue-maximizing predatory state will be determined by the tangency of the entrant's expenditure function with the revenue function for this optimal rate, as at P in quadrant II of figure A.2b. For suppose the tax rate were higher ($t' > t$), then the incumbent's and entrant's expenditure function ($E(t')$) would shift downward and the revenue function ($R(t')$) upward (not drawn). The incumbent's monopoly would no longer be sustainable in the range where the new entrant's expenditure function ($E_E(t')$) now lies below the revenue function $R(t')$. Similarly, if the tax rate were lower ($t'' < t$), the revenue and expenditure functions would shift downward and upward respectively and the incumbent would not be maximizing net revenue. Thus we have shown that there will be a unique tax rate and fiscal-cum-public employment equilibrium, determined by the underlying production function and the net barrier to entry costs facing a new entrant. The net revenue-maximizing predatory state will chose a tax rate (t), and public employment level (L_g) (for each village) such that the vertical distance between the $E(t)$ and $R(t)$ function at its maximum equal the per-village sustainable rent it can charge of $\alpha K/M$. It is also obvious from the shapes of the production, revenue, and expenditure functions that the net revenue-maximizing public-employment level will be less than the socially optimal level L_g^*.

Hitherto we have assumed that the size of the territory to be controlled lay within the decreasing average cost portion of the total cost curve of the state monopoly in figure A.2a, which yielded a sustainable equilibrium. Suppose, however, that either the size of the territory to be controlled was larger (say $M1$ in figure A.2a), or else the fixed costs were low enough so that the increasing average costs (for the given tax rate t) occurred within the range OM in figure A.2a. The incumbent may no longer be able to extract a sustainable rent equal to the maximum "natural rent" given by his sunk costs αK. Thus, if for the cost curves depicted in figure A.2(A) the area to be controlled is $M1$, setting a tax rate that yields total revenue given by points on the ray OR' would, while yielding the incumbent the "natural rent" αK, make his monopoly unsustainable. For a new entrant can now set a slightly lower tax rate and still cover total costs by controlling between M_2 and M_1 villages (in figure A.2a), where his total revenue curve (just slightly lower than OR') lies above his total cost curve. The incumbent can guard against this possibility by setting his tax rate at a level that yields a total revenue line OR'', tangent to the incumbent's total cost curve (TC_E). The incumbent's sustainable rent will then only be DQ; which is less than αK.

However, depending upon the shape of the fixed-cost curve in controlling the given territory, it is possible (see Baumol and Willig 1981) that there may be no tax rate which will be sustainable against entry, and political instability in the territory will be the norm. Moreover, if the territory is large enough (a large alluvial plain such as the Indo-Gangetic region in northern India) and the fixed costs required to establish a state are prohibitive for one sovereign to control the whole territory, there may be a number of states in an otherwise homogeneous region. Even if all their cost curves are identical, there may also not be a stable equilibrium in the *number* of states in the territory (see Baumol and Fischer 1978).

This model emphasizes the importance of fixed costs (K) and the extent of sunk costs (αK) as barriers to entry in the "optimal" fiscal and public employment equilibrium of the predatory State.

Barriers to Entry

We need to distinguish between internal and external competitors to the rulers of a state, though of course there are many historical examples of claimants of both sorts combining to overthrow the incumbent natural monopolist.

For potential external predators, the geography of the particular region and "amalgamation costs" are relevant in determining the barriers to entry. The early European city-states that first established a market system could exist independently because of their geography. Later, with changes in military technology, the feasible territorial size of a state grew. The "core areas" of the new European states were alluvial plains on which plow husbandry could be practiced to yield the tax base for military control. Though the intervening areas could be and were brought into polities linked to the core areas as communications and military technology improved, there were a number of natural barriers—the sea that protected England, the Pyrenees, and the Alps, and the northern marshes that defined the "natural" defenses of Spain, France, the Netherlands, and Italy. These raised the entry cost for external predators.

Also, paradoxically, modern-day countries such as Switzerland and the Netherlands (the old United Provinces) found that economic disadvantages such as difficult terrain also proved to be their political strength, inasmuch as external predators found it too costly (in terms of net returns) to control them.

In addition there were the amalgamation costs faced by external predators. Given ethnic, linguistic, and religious differences between the external predator and the peoples in an incumbent's territory—differences in Europe "dating from early folk movements and settlement history"—the incumbent could count on a form of "loyalty" that the external predator could not.

What of entry barriers to challenges from internal competitors? This depended upon military technology and the physical size of the "naturally" defensible territory. Ceteris paribus, a physically smaller territory would be easier to take over than a larger one, whereas the changing technology of warfare, which made large scale an advantage in the violence industry, would tend to favor the incumbent. For instance, the development of the cannon in the mid-fifteenth century removed the security of baronial fortifications in Europe and shifted the balance of advantages to an incumbent centralizing predator who could build larger and more expensive castles.

Thus the resource base for extracting revenue and the geographical area "naturally" defensible with available military technology would determine the "optimal" territorial size of the state in a particular region as well as the stable sustainable "natural" rent that could be extracted by the predator. But what shapes the system of property rights that these factors will tend to enforce?

North and Thomas argue that this will depend upon the relative "bargaining strengths" of the rulers and constituents. But this "bargaining strength" has in effect been subsumed in the "entry barriers" that determine the sustainable "natural" rent the incumbent predator can extract.

The lower the entry barriers to internal rivals, the more likely it is that the reduction in natural "rents" represented by the property rights required for an open market will be instituted. However, the effects of entry barriers facing external rivals may be more ambiguous. The higher these barriers, the smaller the incentive for the incumbent predator to come to terms with his prey, something he might have to do to increase their "loyalty" and hence the "amalgamation costs" faced by external competitors if external barriers were lower. But equally, to the extent that the constituents fear amalgamation by an external predator, they are less likely to press their case against an incumbent predator the lower the entry barrier, and vice versa.

The system of efficient property rights based on the relative bargaining strength of the prey is most likely to emerge in regions where geography and military technology allow the "natural" territorial size of the state to be such that barriers to internal and external entry are high enough to prevent the endemic political instability associated with internal baronial warfare or external invasions, but not so high as to make the incumbent secure enough to extract the maximum feasible revenue from his prey. It is the uniqueness of Europe, as Jones emphasizes, that it provided the ecological environment for the development of a "states system" after the Renaissance, which bucked the historical trend toward organizing large regional populations into empires. In Europe no empire was built after the fall of Rome; overseas empires came later. Though Europe thereby lost some economies of scale, the predatory power of the individual states was lowered compared with an imperial monopoly over the region. The environmental characteristic was "the scatter of regions of high arable potential set in a continent of wastes and forests."

A second factor, perhaps of equal importance, is the structure of the economy, which determines the feasible set of taxes—their relative structure, if the monopoly is to be sustainable, being determined by the Ramsey Rules à la BBW (Baumol, Bailey, and Willig (1977)). Here the important distinction (as Hicks notes) is the relative importance of internal versus external trade. As in premodern economies this is likely to depend upon natural-resource endowments, particularly the availability of rich arable land relative to the population, we would expect external trade to be more important for the *relatively* resource poor countries. The Greek city-states, the Netherlands, and England would fall in this category.

The self-interest of the predator in expanding the tax base of an economy dependent on external trade should induce him to set up the property rights for a mercantile economy. The economic history of Britain and the Netherlands vis-à-vis France and Spain can (as North and Thomas show) be written in terms of different systems of property rights that were established after the Renaissance, and there were good ecological and economic reasons why this should have been so.

If the incumbent predator is far-sighted he will charge Ramsey prices for the multiproduct natural monopoly he owns, extracting the "natural" rent equal to the present discounted value of the internal and external entry costs. However, even if these costs do not change over time (which is unlikely) they cannot be ascertained with any exactitude. Their estimates will be probabilistic. Depending upon differences in subjective probabilities and/or different degrees of risk aversion on the part of the incumbent and his rivals, what may "objectively" seem to be a sustainable equilibrium may or may not turn out to be one. There may thus be sustainable equilibria in practice that involve extracting more or less than the "natural" rent that is entailed by "objective" entry barriers. There may then be long-run "predatory" cycles in which the *long-run* sustainable equilibrium is undermined over time by predators beginning to charge more than the Ramsey prices. The higher prices make entry profitable. This leads in the medium run (which of course could be more than a century!) to the eventual overthrow of the incumbent and the establishment of a fresh sustainable equilibrium by a new group of predators.

Cycles in Fiscal Predation

Military technology has obviously been important in determining the degree to which the natural monopoly that has been periodically established in the Indo-Gangetic plain is contestable by internal rivals. Once a new entrant established his dominance, the sustainability on a dynamic basis of the newly established monopoly depended upon his heirs being far-sighted enough not to extract more than the natural rent. If they did, then there would be an incentive for internal competitors to arise and attempt to provide a competitive supply. The rebellions at the edge of the empire (where, because of costs of transport and communication, rival entry, would be easier) which have plagued (as they still plague) India's imperial rulers would then become endemic. The ensuing breakdown of the empire would be followed by another period of chaos until one or the other of the feuding chiefs succeeded in establishing his hegemony but refrained from overcharging for the natural monopoly he had acquired. If the underlying ecological, demographic, and economic conditions did not alter markedly—as they did not until very recently—there would be cycles of growth and decay of empires linked to cycles in "rents" that the predatory state sought to exact, with the "stable" equilibrium corresponding to the sustainable "natural" rents extractable under the rules of BBW!

Dual Preferences and Changes in Public Opinion

The model that explains shifts in "public opinion" and hence the cosmological beliefs that are an important part of culture is due to Kuran (1995). The persistence of "core beliefs" in the ancient civilizations noted in the text, as well as the rise of Christianity, can be explained in these terms.

Kuran defines *public* opinion as the distribution of public preferences, and *private* opinion as the corresponding distribution of private preferences. Individuals are expected to care about their reputational utility, which will depend in part upon public opinion. Individuals may therefore find that total utility, which consists of both reputational utility and the intrinsic utility from his private preferences, may be maximized by falsifying private preferences and thereby gaining reputational utility.

Suppose reputational utility is a function of the mean of all public preferences (opinion).

Then consider an individual's public preference declaration on some sensitive issue. In figure A.3a, suppose his preferred position is $x = 20$.

Given a choice between 0 and 100, he will support 0. If pressures from both groups are the same he will choose 0 as his public preference. But now suppose the mean of public opinion shifts toward 100, then the advantage to supporting 0 steadily weakens and at some point, say $x = 70$, the individual becomes indifferent between supporting 0 or 100. This is his political threshold.

The distribution of these thresholds is shown in the next figure, figure A.3b. The propagation curve plots for each Y between 0 and 100 the percentage of society with thresholds at or below that level. In the diagram, 30 percent of all thresholds are at 0, 80 percent below 100, and, naturally, 100 percent at or below 100. This curve will determine the propagation of preference falsification.

There will be some expectation that every individual will have about public opinion in the next period. Assume that this expected public opinion is the same for everyone. Given this, the propagation curve will yield a realization of public opinion. In figure A.3c on the X axis is expected public opinion, on the Y axis actual public opinion. The 45° line shows where the two are the same—as they must be for equilibrium. Suppose expected public opinion starts at 20. The propagation curve indicates that 35 percent of the population has a threshold at or below 20. So this part of the population will give its public support to 100, and the remaining 65 percent will support 0. An expectation of 20 has thus generated a public opinion of 35. The expectation will be revised upwards. To be self-fulfilling, the expected public opinion must rise to 40. In this case there is a single unique equilibrium. But there could be corner equilibria and multiple equilibria as in the next two figures (figure A.3d and A.3e). Considering the latter, public opinion will go to one or the other equilibria depending upon whether the *initial* expectation is below or above 60. This can lead to bandwagon effects, which can be triggered by small events which change the initial expectations.

Thus sudden changes in public opinion are possible, as happened for instance in Eastern Europe in 1989. A similar process would account for the 1960s "cultural" revolution in the West.

Factor Proportions and Agrarian Structure

Domar (1970) has shown that free land, free peasants, and a nonworking group of landlords cannot exist simultaneously. Any two can, but not all three.

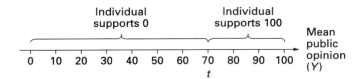

Figure A.3a
The individual's political threshold. If public opinion is sufficiently favorable to 100, he will
publicly support 100.

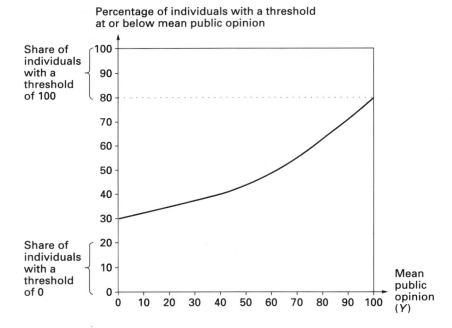

Figure A.3b
The propagation curve. Half of all thresholds are at 0 or 100, with the remaining half distributed between the extremes.

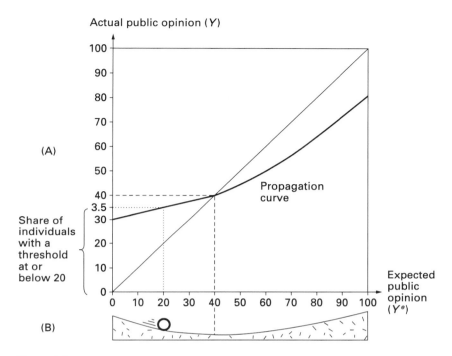

Figure A.3c
Expected public opinion and its motion. Only an expectation of 40 is self-fulfilling and self-reproducing. Any other expectation will result in adjustments toward 40.

Thus consider the case where land and labor are the only two factors of production. Land is so abundant that there are no diminishing returns to labor, whose marginal and average product are the same ($mpl = apl$). If employers seek to hire labor, they will have to pay a wage equal to this common marginal *and* average product of labor, leaving no surplus rents from land for the employer. Hence the agrarian form that will emerge is family labor-based farms, inasmuch as any form of hired labor or tenancy will be unprofitable and landlords who have to depend on one or the other cannot exist. By dunning this independent peasantry through direct or indirect taxes, a government could support a nonworking class of retainers; but the latter or an independent nobility of landlords could not support themselves from land rents because none would be available.[3]

This is very much the form of North American agrarian structure and development in the colonial period. With an important variation it is also the "cift-hane" system under the Ottomans. Here a predatory state has

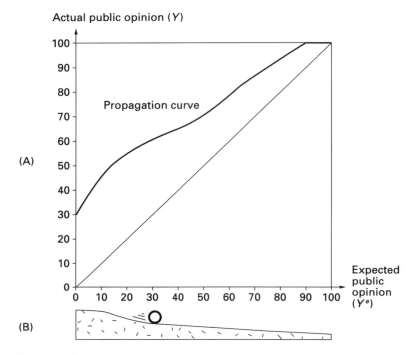

Figure A.3d
A unique corner equilibrium. Any expectation below 100 will induce upward self-corrections.

title to all the land in its domain. It then allocates a part of the available land to the existing peasants on the basis of the family labor each household can provide. It then taxes these family farms to support its revenue maximizing objectives. Because the state policed its estates and the only way peasants could obtain land was through the allocations by the state (which were altered with changing demography), there was no way in which they could become an independent yeomanry, as in the United States.

Next, suppose the government wants to create an independent class of landowners and grants the chosen few sole rights of ownership to land. If the peasants are free to move, competition among landlords will drive the rural wage up to the marginal product of labor, which is close or equal to its average product because of the abundance of land. There will be little or no surplus left for the landlords. In order to provide this surplus some means will have to be found to restrict or abolish the peasants' freedom to move. Serfdom, slavery, and the caste system, as we have seen, were

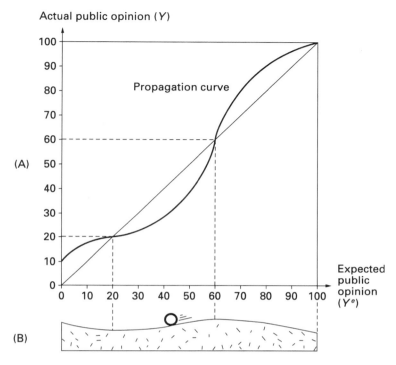

Figure A.3e
A case with three equilibria. Expectations below 60 will result in corrections in the direction of 20; and ones above 60 will generate adjustments toward 100.

forms of tying labor down to land. These emerged in the great civilizations to create a landowning class that derived a rent not from land but from the peasants by expropriating a large part of their income above a subsistence level.

Finally, as the labor force expands from natural increase and/or migration and land becomes scarce relative to labor, diminishing returns to labor appear (*mpl < apl*). This allows landlords to obtain the rents from land and an assured labor supply to work it by being paid by its marginal product (mpl), or else through various forms of tenancy.

Notes

Introduction

1. Huntington (1993).

2. Hicks and Redding (1983).

3. This is ironic because a variant of this "religion" is also present in Kim Il Sung's North Korea.

4. Reynolds (1985). He ascribes it in turn to Ashoh Guha (1981).

5. Skinner (1985), p. 19. But this does not mean that I subscribe to any crude geographical or historical determinism. Nor do I believe in producing a theory of history, for the reasons cogently set out by Peter Bauer (1981). But what I will be doing is looking at parts of world history through a very, very wide lens!

Chapter 1

1. But see Becker (1996), where he argues for a richer "extended utility function," which besides goods also includes "personal" and "social" capital as its arguments. The notion of social capital has also been developed and used by the sociologist James Coleman (1990). Becker's extended utility function can lead to very different subutility functions over goods, which determine consumption choices. These could, therefore, be very different in countries with "different traditions" with different stocks of social and personal capital (Becker, ibid., pp. 5–6). "Culture" is part of social capital and is only likely to change slowly (p. 16). He also notes that his and Stigler's (1977) view only applied to *meta*preferences, and that in his latest work he tries to show "that the past casts a long shadow on the present through its influence on the formation of present preferences and choices" (ibid, p. 132). I have little quarrel with this "new" Chicago viewpoint. My purpose in these lectures can be seen as delineating these links between the past and the present and to make the nature of the hysteresis in some beliefs arising from culture more transparent.

2. Elster (1979), p. 113, n. 4.

3. Gellner (1988) has pilloried this view as follows:

This Hayek/Popper vision might well be called the "Viennese Theory." One might well wonder whether it was not inspired by the fact that, in the nineteenth century, the individualistic, atomized, cultivated bourgeoisie of the Habsburg capital had to contend with the

influx of swarms of kin-bound, collectivistic, rule-ignoring migrants from the eastern marches
of the Empire, from the Balkans and Galicia. Cosmopolitan liberals had to contend, in the
political sphere, with the emerging breed of *national* socialists. This "Viennese" vision is an
inversion, a denial all at once of romanticism—it elevates ... (society) ... over ... (community)—and of Marxism. Marx anticipated the restoration, rather than the overcoming, of the
alleged social proclivities of early man. (pp. 28–29)

But this passage could equally represent a Czech getting back at an Austrian!

4. For a history of these disputes within the field which is defined by the study of culture—
anthropology—see Marvin Harris's (1969) entertaining account. Harris of course remains
the economist's favorite anthropologist given his commitment to "cultural materialism." See
Harris (1989) for *his* account of humankind.

5. It appears from recent archaeological evidence that trade and specialization go back to the
earliest hunter-gatherer phase of human history. See Ridley (1996), chap. 10, for a succinct
discussion and references.

6. Cited in Brems (1987), p. 698.

7. Ruttan (1988) has a whole appendix listing various definitions of culture.

8. Gellner (1988), p. 14.

9. North (1990), Ch. 5.

10. Gellner (1988), p. 14.

11. See Colinvaux (1983).

12. Hahn (1973).

13. Hahn (1973), p. 28.

14. It is now largely accepted as a result of the psycholinguistics pioneered by Chomsky
(1957) that the capacity for language is an innate capacity of our species. See also Pinker
(1994).

15. See Searle (1992).

16. See Dawkins (1976).

17. The naturalistic fallacy states that one cannot derive an "ought" from an "is." The evolutionary biologist Alexander (1987, p. xvi) "explicitly reject[s] the attitude that whatever biology tells us is so is also what ought to be (David Hume's so-called naturalistic fallacy), as
offered by such biologist-philosophers as Julian Huxley (1947) and Wolfgang Wickler
(1972)."

18. Darwin (1871), vol. 1, pp. 88–89, cited in Wright (1994), p. 344.

19. See Trivers (1985), Tooby and Cosmides (1989). Popular accounts can be found in
Wright (1994) and Ridley (1996).

20. Rousseau's *Emile* provides the text for the education of children who are not repressed
by unhealthy and superstitious social norms. This text has of course been the main inspira-
tion behind various forms of progressive education ever since.

21. Hume (1750), p. 271.

22. See Alexander (1987), who notes that modern biology is resolving the

problem of duality (selfishness and altruism) in human nature, paradoxical to the earliest philosophers ... with Hume's "elements of the serpent and the wolf" referring to the serving of
our own interests at others' expense, and his "particle of the dove" representing the serving
of our own interests through: (1) relatives who carry our genetic materials and (2) friends and
associates who may be expected to reciprocate our kindness with interest. (p. 4)

See also Nesse (1990).

23. But this does not mean that human beings are "general purpose inclusive fitness maximizers." As Tooby and Cosmides (1990) note,

humans are adaptation-executers, not fitness-strivers. For this reason, human behavior is not
well explained by attempts to show how it corresponds to contextually appropriate fitness
pursuit. Instead it should be explained as the output of adaptations (using present circumstances as input), which are themselves the constructed product of selection under ancestral
conditions. Far from being governed by "rational fitness-maximization" ... the operation of
human psychological mechanisms are orchestrated by emotions that frame present circumstances in terms of the evolutionary past. (p. 420)

It is the central role of these evolved human emotions, in particular the moral ones—shame
and guilt—in the process of civilization that we examine below.

24. Bonner (1980), p. 55. Bonner also notes that there are "rarer but well known cases, such
as those involving hybridization where new species are formed, or rather begun, in one generation" (ibid).

25. Thus Cosmides, Tooby, and Barkow (1992) note, "The few thousand years since the
scattered appearance of agriculture is only a small stretch in evolutionary terms, less than 1
percent of the two million years our ancestors spent as Pleistocene hunter-gatherers" (p. 5).
This leads them to conclude that "the evolved structure of the human mind is adapted to the
way of life of Pleistocene hunter-gatherers, and not necessarily to our modern circumstances." Hence while there is "a universal human nature ... this universality exists primarily
at the level of evolved psychological mechanisms, not of expressed cultural behaviors" (ibid).
    Crawford, Salter, and Lang (1989) provide a particularly interesting experiment that sup-
ports the view that many of our emotions evolved in the Pleistocene. They examined grief.
Darwinian logic would suggest that the value of a child's life to its parents should vary
during its life cycle, growing till it reaches its peak when its reproductive potential is at its
highest. For then the parent will have made all the earlier investment in nurturing the organ-
ism which is of parental value in passing on their genes. This leads to the prediction that
parents should experience more grief at the death of an adolescent than of an infant. Crawford et al. (1989) asked a sample of Canadian parents to imagine the death of their children at
various ages and estimate which would cause different degrees of grief. As predicted, grief
grew until adolescence and then declined. From Canadian demographic data on reproductive
potential, the expected pattern of grief with the age of the child at death can be determined.
When the experimental estimates were compared with specific Canadian demographic estimates, the correlation coefficient was 0.64. But when these experimental estimates were
compared with the demographic estimates of reproductive potential of the hunter-gatherer
tribe—the Kung—the correlation was 0.92.

26. The theory of "reciprocal altruism" based on the strategy of "tit-for-tat" in an infinitely
repeated game of the "prisoners dilemma" predicts some cooperation. See Axelrod (1984),
Trivers (1985). But see Hirshleifer and Martinez Coll (1988) for the many restrictive assumptions on which Axelrod's results depend, and hence why in general, "tit-for-tat" need not
necessarily generate the social equilibrium posited.

27. For Smith (1759/1966) "sympathy" was the supreme moral virtue. The emotions he described as the moral sentiments were anger, contempt, disgust, envy, greed, shame, and guilt.

28. The most detailed account by an economist is Frank (1988), who sees various emotional responses as a form of credible precommitment that, though going against narrow self-interest, could have been an advantage in the prehistoric repeated prisoner's dilemma game in which our instincts were born. He builds on earlier work by Schelling (1978), Akerloff (1983), Hirshleifer (1984), Sen (1977, 1985).

29. See Arrow (1974), North (1990).

30. See Campbell (1975), who commends psychologists to see the "possible sources of validity in recipes for living that have been evolved, tested, and winnowed through hundreds of generations of human social history.... The religions of all ancient urban civilizations (as independently developed in China, India, Mesopotamia, Egypt, Mexico and Peru) taught that many aspects of human nature need to be curbed if optimal social coordination is to be achieved, for example, selfishness, pride, greed, dishonesty, covetousness, cowardice, lust, wrath (pp. 1103–4)."

31. Freud (1930/1969). As Campbell (1975) notes in contrast with the moral traditions of the ancient civilizations,

psychology and psychiatry, on the other hand, not only describe man as selfishly motivated, but implicitly or explicitly teach that he ought to be so. They tend to see repression and inhibition of individual impulse as undesirable, and see all guilt as a dysfunctional neurotic blight created by cruel child rearing and a needlessly repressive society. They further recommend that we accept our biology and psychological impulses as good and seek pleasure rather than enchain ourselves with duty. (p. 1104)

As we saw in Chapter 9, this has had important social consequences for the West.

It should also be noted that, in contrast with Darwin, Freud's own scientific credentials have not stood the test of time. Thus the anthropologist Kroeber (1948), writing about Freud's psychoanalytic explanation of culture, claims it "is intuitive, dogmatic, and wholly unhistorical. It disregards the findings of prehistory and archaeology as irrelevant, or at most as dealing only with details of little significance as compared with its own interpretation of the essence of how culture came to be. In condensation, Freud's own theory is that 'the beginnings of religion, ethics, society and art meet in the Oedipus complex'.... The theory is obviously as arbitrary as it is fantastically one-sided" (p. 617).

For a critique of Freud's project by a philosopher of science see Patricia Kitcher (1995), and for a devastating appraisal of Freud's whole career see Webster (1995).

32. Mill (1874), p. 393.

33. Campbell (1975), summarizes these as "social mechanisms of child socialization, reward and punishment, socially restricted learning opportunities, identification, imitation, emulation, indoctrination into tribal ideologies, language and linguistic meaning systems, conformity pressures, social authority systems, and the like" (p. 1107).

34. But many sociobiologists have succumbed to this temptation. See, for example, the contributions to Betzig, Mulder, Turke (1988). Hard-hitting attacks on this misuse of Darwinism are by Tooby and Cosmides (1990) and Symons (1992). See also Philip Kitcher (1985)—a philosopher of science—who distinguishes between pop sociobiology of the above sort and of sociobiology that has advanced our theoretical understanding of evolution by natural selection. But for a critique of Kitcher in turn see Alexander (1987).

35. Campbell (1975), p. 1111.

36. One finding of sociobiology may help to explain the ubiquity of preference falsification; this concerns self-deception. Trivers (1985) explains how the strategic animal who was our forebear would have found it useful to indulge in self-deception to allow subtle cheating in its social interactions to get a larger share of the available cooperative gains. One of the dangers with deception is that it might be betrayed by various physical signs (sweaty palms, shifty eyes, and the like). If the individual can convince himself of the truth of his lie "he or she can lie without the nervousness that accompanies deception" (p. 416). So sociobiologists argue that self-deception would have evolved as a trait in our prehistoric environment to enable "hiding the truth from the conscious mind the better to hide it from others" (p. 415). Trivers also reports on an experiment by Gur and Sackeim (1979) that demonstrated that "(1) true and false information is simultaneously stored in a single person. (2) The false information is stored in the conscious mind, the true information is unconscious. In this sense we may speak of self-deception, keeping information from the conscious mind. (3) Self-deception is motivated with reference to others" (p. 417).

This notion of self-deception together with the other basic instincts, combined with the role of learned cultural traits, could also provide a rationale for Freud's model of the mind in terms of the id, ego, and superego (see Badcock (1991)), but clearly not for the fantastical "history" that Freud claims for its development, and not the "scientific" claim he makes for it (see Webster (1995)).

37. A study by Demos (1996) shows how in New England shame rather than guilt was the major form of social control in the century preceding the American revolution. This gave way in the first half of the nineteenth century to guilt.

38. The English journalist Paul Johnson is one example among many. See his continuing debate with the biologist Richard Dawkins in the pages of the British weekly *The Spectator*.

39. It is worth noting that the Marxist notion of primitive communism was based on the anthropologist Morgan's (1877) delineation of primitive society. Morgan claimed that primitive societies were promiscuous and stateless, with communal ownership of reproductive and property rights. The growth of private-property rights led to inequality and the rise of the state and despotism. This romantic but false view of primitive society was lifted wholesale by Engels (1884) into his history of the family; see Bloch (1983), Betzig (1986). By contrast, the Darwinian view, which emphasizes the competition for reproductive rights in which inequalities in property ownership could matter, views primitive societies as being much more individualistic and would deny that communal reproductive rights were common; see Betzig (1986). This view is substantiated by recent anthropological work on the family (see Kuper, chap. 7), which finds "the nuclear family, complete with a father figure, hedged around with incest taboos ... [as] very ancient" (ibid, p, 171). The powerful, however, monopolized a larger share of women; see Betzig (1986).

40. Triandis (1995). He, however, calls what I have labeled communalism "collectivism." But given the association of the latter term with a particular type of economy—viz. Communist—it is better to use the former term.

41. Triandis (1995): "The majority of the world, roughly 70 percent of the population is collectivist" (p. 13).

42. Triandis (1995), p. 26, reporting the results of his statistical work on societies reported in Mead (1967).

43. See Ekman and Davidson (1994).

44. See Ekman and Davidson (1994), Harre and Parrott (1996), and in particular Le Doux (1996), written by a neural scientist, which provides evidence for his thesis that emotional responses are hardwired into the brain's circuitry but that what evinces these emotions is learned through experience.

45. Ekman and Davidson (1994), p. 176.

46. Scherer and Wallbott (1994), Wallbott and Scherer (1995).

47. Ekman and Davidson (1994), p. 176.

48. Freud (1930/1969) in a footnote (p. 54) does talk about sexual shame, which he claims was the "consequence of man's raising himself from the ground, of his assumption of an upright gait; this made his genitals, which were previously concealed, visible and in need of protection, and so provoked feelings of shame in him." The rest of his book is about guilt, particularly that instilled by the Judeo-Christian tradition.

Darwin (1872), however, in his discussion of blushing clearly notes the distinction between shame and guilt. He writes, "With respect to blushing from strictly moral causes, we meet with the same fundamental principle as before, namely regard for the opinion of others. It is not the conscience which raises a blush.... It is not the sense of guilt which crimsons the face" (p. 332) but rather shame, modesty, or a breach of etiquette, which depend "in all cases on the same principle; this principle being a sensitive regard for the opinion, more particularly for the depreciation of others, primarily in relation to our personal appearance, especially of our faces; and secondarily, through the force of association and habit, in relation to the opinion of others on our conduct" (pp. 335–36). Later he writes, "with respect to real shame from moral delinquencies, we can perceive why it is not guilt, but the thought that others think us guilty which raises blush" (p. 345).

By contrast, Wright's (1994) discussion of various psychological experiments, which he claims show that guilt is a primary emotion, in fact offers examples of shame. For instance, as an example of guilt he cites the twinge of conscience when we make eye contact with a beggar: "We may feel uncomfortable about failing to help.... We don't seem to mind not giving nearly so much as we mind being *seen not giving*" (p. 206, emphasis added). But from the emphasized passage it is clear this is an example of shame. Darwin, considering a very similar case, wrote: "A lady by herself may give money to a beggar without a trace of a blush, but if there are others present, and she doubts whether they approve, or suspects they think her influenced by display, she will blush" (p. 333). Darwin, as the above passages make clear, rightly associates blushing with shame, not guilt.

49. Talk of emotions will upset many economists of the hard rational-choice persuasion. Except for some honorable exceptions cited in note 28, economists have by and large ignored emotions. They have looked upon them as being irrational. But in the past social thinkers have always emphasized the importance of emotions for practical reasoning. See Nussbaum (1990) for a spirited defense of the Aristotelian view that "practical reasoning unaccompanied by emotion is not sufficient for practical wisdom; that emotions are not only not more unreliable than intellectual calculations, but frequently are more reliable, and less deceptively seductive" (p. 40). Against this is the rationalist view that either "emotions are unreliable and distracting because they have nothing to do with cognition at all"—a view of emotions as blind animal reactions which has been "decisively rejected by cognitive psychology ... anthropology ... psychoanalysis ... and even by philosophy"—or that emotions "have a great deal to do with cognition, but they embody a view of the world that is in fact false" (ibid). Much of Nussbaum's book seeks to counter the second claim. But as regards the counterarguments to the first claim, it is important for my purpose to note that, as she claims, there is interdisciplinary agreement that "emotions are very closely linked to beliefs in such a way that a modification of beliefs brings about a modification of emotion" (p. 41). The cos-

mological beliefs I have identified as an important part of the "culture" that could effect economic performance are thus closely tied with emotions as we shall see. Nussbaum also notes that the father of political economy Adam Smith also placed great import on the role of emotions in practical reasoning in his *Theory of Moral Sentiments*, excluding only love and lust! See Nussbaum, pp. 338–46.

50. Scheff (1990), p. 80. Shame is also different from embarrassment, even though the physical signs of the two (e.g., blushing) may be the same, as Darwin (1872, pp. 333–35) explicitly noted. Thus, as the psychologist M. Lewis (1992) notes,

we often experience embarrassment when being complimented.... In the case of shame, the experience is produced by the negative evaluation of the self in regard to standards, rules and goals.... Since praise cannot readily lead to an evaluation of failure, it is likely that embarrassment due to compliments has more to do with the exposure of the self than with evaluation. In other word, this type of embarrassment is related to self-consciousness. It is often associated with public exposure. (p. 82)

It should be noted that although Lewis's book is the only one by a psychologist I have been able to find that deals exclusively with shame, it is marred by the unstated assumption of his discipline that "shame" is dysfunctional, which, as we saw in note 31, some psychologists themselves are coming to question. Second, it has some bizarre characterizations of shame and guilt; for instance, Lewis claims that "Judaism focuses on guilt, whereas Christianity focuses on shame" (p. 249). The latter will come as surprising news to the French cultural historian Jean Delumeau (1990), who has written a seven-hundred-page book, *Sin and Fear*, charting the emergence of a Western guilt culture based on Christianity between the thirteenth and eighteenth centuries.

51. Williams (1993), p. 78.

52. Ibid., p. 219.

53. Ibid., p. 219.

54. Ibid., p. 221.

55. Williams, in his brilliant account of "shame and necessity" in ancient Greece, argues that one of the tenets of post-Enlightenment Western philosophy, starting with Kant, has been the primacy of guilt over shame. Similarly, "in modern societies" the sociologist Scheff tells us,

It is taken for granted that shame is a rare emotion among adults, prevalent only among small children.... This belief is reflected in the division made in anthropology between shame cultures and guilt cultures, with traditional societies relying on shame for social control; and modern societies, guilt. A similar premise is found in orthodox psychoanalytic theory, which places almost total emphasis on guilt as the adult emotion of self-control, with shame thought of as "regressive," that is, as childish. (p. 79)

Not surprisingly, therefore, Western moral philosophers have viewed the Greeks with their reliance on shame in the process of socialization as premoral or amoral—like children. But, as Williams notes,

One thing that a marked contrast between shame and guilt may express is the idea that it is important to distinguish between "moral" and "non-moral" qualities. Shame itself is neutral on that distinction: we, like the Greeks, can be as mortified or disgraced by a failure in prowess or cunning as by a failure of generosity or loyalty. Guilt, on the other hand, is closely related to the conceptions of morality, and to insist on its particular importance is to insist on those conceptions.

But if with the death of God the basis for this guilt-based morality dies, and despite the ink spilled by philosophers there is no rationalist substitute that will command universal assent, what process of social control is left? The clue lies in recognizing that, as Williams notes, "we can feel both guilt and shame towards the same action. In a moment of cowardice, we let someone down; we feel guilty because we have let them down, ashamed because we have contemptibly fallen short of what we might have hoped of ourselves" (p. 92). Shame can encompass guilt, "for the structures of shame contain the possibility of controlling and learning from guilt, because they give a conception of one's ethical identity, in relation to which guilt can make sense. Shame can understand guilt, but guilt cannot understand itself" (p. 93). Thus, concludes Williams, shame works

by giving through the emotions a sense of who one is and of what one hopes to be, it mediates between act, character, and consequence, and also between ethical demands [those of a particular morality evincing guilt] and the rest of life. Whatever it is working on, it requires an internalized other, who ... embodies intimations of a genuine social reality—in particular, of how it will be for one's life with others if one acts in one way rather than another. (p. 102)

56. It should, however, be noted that the distinction between "shame" and "guilt" cultures introduced by anthropologists like Mead and Benedict no longer finds favor with anthropologists. See, for instance, Strathern (1977). But I think their reasons for repudiating this distinction are unpersuasive. All Strathern shows is that the New Guinean tribe he studied had terms for both shame and guilt, with shame "showing" on the skin, unlike guilt. But this is exactly the distinction between the two emotions we have known since Darwin. It does not tell us, nor does Strathern, which emotion is dominant in the socialization process.

Similarly, Peristiany and Pitt-Rivers (1992) in their introduction to a book called *Honor and Grace*, repudiate their own earlier use of "shame" in defining Mediterranean cultures (Peristiany 1965). They write,

It appeared to us that the distinction has been lifted from the popular moral philosophy of the Anglophone countries and applied in fields where its relevance was dubious, for the sentiment of shame appears to be universal and guilt is simply internalized shame, so that though the degree of internalization of the sanctions varies, no culture can be unequivocally called one or the other. In addition the subject which tends to be internalized varies: Western Europe from one period to another internalized its sexual shame in different degrees; the Protestant ethic, in addition, internalized financial shame. The Trobrianders feel it on neither of these counts, but many primitive peoples feel guilt with regard to the violation of taboos which Europeans might regard as morally neutral ... susceptibility to shame does not entail either the presence or absence of guilt. The opposition then is a false one as far as cultures are concerned, however useful it may be in the discussion of individual personalities within our own society" (pp. 6–7)

In terms of the different psychological dispositions of the two emotions noted in the text, this account is clearly incoherent. The authors, moreover, cite the authority of Kroeber for their position. But here is what Kroeber (1948) wrote: "Shame is partly externalized: it is a feeling with reference to others. Sense of sin, however, is internal. One can feel sinful in solitude, over an act involving no hurt to others. Sin implies a disapproving conscience at work within oneself; shame the knowledge that others disapprove; though shame can also be superadded to sense of sin—perhaps normally is so added. The distinction is not hard and fast; but it is polar" (p. 612).

Quite! This account of the distinction between shame and guilt conforms to that given in the text. The reason why Kroeber thought it was not useful in classifying other cultures was because past studies

leave little explicit sin sense to any culture but our own Occidental one.... Shame as a deterrent factor and a social force is probably operative in nearly all cultures. It is perhaps generally expectable except in the special cases—like our own or Manus civilization—where it has been overlaid by some special development such as masochistic preoccupation with evil—preoccupation with other people's sins or our own" (ibid).

But if guilt is part of the exceptionalism of Western culture, this is a fact of great importance for my subject matter, and the reasons for this exceptionalism as well as its consequences are, as we will see, relevant in judging the role of the cosmological beliefs associated with the rise of the West.

57. But see Kuper (1994). He begins his book by stating that "we are all Darwinians now. Darwin's is the one great Victorian theory that still commands assent from almost all who understand it.... Specialists debate technical side-issues, express sophisticated reservations, propose refinements, but virtually all natural and social scientists are Darwinians now, and with good reason. I take that as read."

58. Pryor (1977).

59. This has also been used by Betzig (1986) to test statistically her thesis that political power is translated into reproductive success with powerful men acquiring and monopolizing a disproportionate share of the available young women. She finds this holds for most of the preindustrial societies but has broken down in modern ones.

60. See Birdsall (1989).

61. Sociologists (e.g., Garnovetter) have seen a contradiction in the stance of the "new" institutional economics in that it has an "oversocialized" and "undersocialized" conception of human behavior. But, as Garnovetter notes, disapprovingly, both conceptions

have in common a conception of action and decision carried out by atomized actors. In the undersocialized account, atomization results from narrow utilitarian pursuit of self-interest; in the oversocialized one, from the fact that behavioral patterns have been internalized and ongoing social relations thus have only peripheral effects on behavior. That the internalized rules of behavior are social in origin does not differentiate this argument decisively from the utilitarian one, in which the source of utility functions is left open, leaving room for behavior guided entirely by consensually determined norms and values—as in the oversocialized view. (p. 484)

Social influences are all contained inside an individual's head, so, in actual decision situations, he or she can be atomized as any *Homo economicus*, though perhaps with different rules for decision. (p. 486)

Quite! Thus there is nothing contradictory for example in the Victorian entrepreneur's relentless pursuit of profit (undersocialization) and his using the wealth thereby obtained to buy a landed estate to gentrify himself and his progeny (oversocialization)! On the usual complaint by sociologists, including Granovetter, that the new institutional economics falls afoul of some methodological prescription concerning "functionalism," see Lal (1988) pp. 4–7.

62. Hallpike (1986), p. 150.

63. Ibid., p. 166.

64. Ibid., pp. 181–82.

65. Ibid., p. 290.

66. Ibid, p. 293.

67. But see Engerman and Sokoloff (1995) for counterevidence that differences in relative factor endowments determined the divergent paths of North and South America. They argue convincingly that the type of crops that the natural resource endowment (including climate) in the United States allowed peasant farming, whereas in most of Latin America, crops required plantations that in turn needed hired (or slave) labor. See also Lal-Myint (1996), which emphasizes the effects of these differing ecological circumstances in affecting the polity.

68. Boyd and Richerson (1985), pp. 56–60.

69. Ibid., p. 60.

70. An example being two violinists playing in an orchestra, as compared with "discovering, while I am practicing my part, that someone in the next room is practicing her part, and thus discovering that by chance, we are playing the same piece in a synchronized fashion" (Searle [1995], p. 24). The former represents collective, the latter two person's individual intentionality.

71. "Such rules not merely regulate [but] also create the very possibility of certain activities. Thus the rules of chess do not regulate an antecedently existing activity.... Rather [they] create the very possibility of playing chess. The rules are constitutive of chess in the sense that playing chess is constituted in part by acting in accord with the rules." Searle, ibid, pp. 27–28.

72. Ibid., p. 33.

73. Ibid., p. 92.

74. See, for instance, Bernheim (1994) and Becker and Murphy (1988).

75. Whenever I write "him" I of course mean "her"!

Chapter 2

1. Wrigley (1988).

2. Wrigley (1988), pp. 5–6.

3. Wrigley, p. 6.

4. Parker (1982) terms it Schumpeterian growth. But I think this term applies more often to those on the technological frontier, whereas my term encompasses the late industrializers who can adopt the fruits of Schumpeterian growth.

5. Jones (1988).

6. Archaeologists seem to be divided as to whether the Boserupian process can explain the rise of settled agriculture. Thus Fagan denies that there is "any evidence for rapid population increase in the centuries immediately preceding civilization" (p. 170) in Egypt and Mesopotamia. By contrast, Renfrew (1973) argues in favor of the Boserup thesis. Locay, in terms of an explicit model, shows that

many of the widespread changes preceding the transition to agriculture could be accounted for either by increasing population density [the Boserup thesis] or by deterioration in hunting-gathering productivity [Vernon Smith's hypothesis]. The two hypotheses yield almost identical implications, but they differ in that the environmental deterioration hypothesis does not require positive population growth. (p. 754)

She notes that although the archaeological evidence is inconclusive, there is some evidence that tends to support the Boserup thesis. "This model implies that prior to agriculture [there would have been] declining standard of living both in terms of parental consumption and in terms of utility.... Analysis of skeletons from the Eastern Mediterranean from about 32,000 B.P., a period during which large game was important and people were fairly nomadic, indicates that the life expectancy of adult males was 33.3 and of adult females 28.7. By 11,000 B.P. when fish and wild grasses were the important sources of food and people were fairly sedentary, adult male and female life expectancy had fallen sharply to 32 and 24.9 years, respectively. The drop in stature was even more dramatic. Average heights for the earlier periods were 177.2 cms for males and 165 cms for females. This compares with 164.6 cms for males and 152.5 cms for females for the more recent period." (p. 748)

It should be noted that, as she emphasizes, in the earlier period, "as all labor and land were devoted to hunter-gathering ... hunting-gathering becomes more labor intensive as land becomes scarce. This is precisely what the archaeological record shows. As the importance of large game in subsistence declined, people exploited more intensely aquatic resources, plants, and small game, all of which are less land intensive" (p. 749).

   Pryor and Maurer (1982) surveying the evidence summarized in Wright (1971) and Cohen (1977), claim that "it appears that both per capita income levels and population growth rate declined and that, intensification of production occurred from the upper paleothetic to the early bronze age. Thus a model incorporating both Boserup-type and Malthus-type responses to standard of living changes induced by population changes seems superior to either model separately" (p. 490). This would also take account of the worries expressed, for instance, by Mokyr about the relevance of the Boserup process to the adoption of deep plowing in Europe.

7. Broadly, these ecological differences correspond to those between areas of hoe and plow agriculture. These material differences have subsequently had important social consequences, for instance in the differing status of women in the relevant societies; see Boserup (1970) and Goody (1976).

8. Cameron (1993), p. 24.

9. Gellner (1988), p. 277.

10. The steppe nomads provided the impetus for most of the technological development associated with warfare.

11. McNeill (1979), pp. 23–25. The role of warfare in the evolution of technology has been well documented by Keegan. But as his chapter headings show, these are few and far between: stone, flesh (horses), iron and fire (from cannon to the nuclear bomb). Little (1981) and Scott (1989), have argued that "science and technology" are not an important dividing line between the West and the Rest. As Little notes, until the eighteenth century technological

improvements and dissemination seem to have been almost incredibly slow. The breastplate harness of horses, which tended to throttle them, reduced their efficiency, as compared with a padded collar, from 15 manpower to 4 manpower. It took 3000 years or more for a rudimentary padded collar to evolve, and another 1000 years for it to develop and become general. It similarly took thousands of years for fore and aft rigging and a swinging boom to appear. Yet such improvements did not have to—wait upon new materials, or concentrated power; nor did they require, by way of "science", more than observation, wit, and ingenuity.

   Glancing through the 3000-odd pages of the *Oxford History of Technology*, one finds dozens of statements like—"the general form of war galley had not changed very greatly 1500 years later" (i.e., in A.D. 1500), or "Thus by c. 1500 B.C. three basic glass-making techniques were in use. It was not for another 1500 years or so that a new process was developed (glass blowing). (p. 66)

I agree with him and Scott (pp. 307–10), therefore, that "science and technology" cannot explain the rise of the West. This, of course, is also the view of Joseph Needham (1963), the leading scholar of Chinese science, who writes:

Not to put too fine a point on the matter, whoever would explain the failure of Chinese society to develop modern science had better begin by explaining the failure of Chinese society to develop mercantile and then industrial capitalism. Whatever the individual pre-possessions of Western historians of science, all are necessitated to admit that from the 15th century A.D. onwards a complex of changes occurred: the Renaissance cannot be thought of without the Reformation, the Reformation cannot be thought of without the rise of modern science, and none of them can be thought of without the rise of capitalism.... We seem to be in the presence of a kind of organic whole, a packet of change. (p. 139)

It is an investigation of this "packet," which is a major purpose of these lectures, in which "technology and science" are a mere by-product and not the independent prime movers in the rise of the West.

For a contrary view see Mokyr (1990), who considers differences in technical creativity as explaining the different wealth of nations. But his evolutionary theory about technical creativity is not very persuasive. Furthermore, what he identifies as the West's exceptional technical creativity remains a "black box," unless—as I will do—it is identified with a unique trait, which led to it, which I claim is individualism. Many of the historical puzzles he alludes to can then be more readily explained. Instead of trying to explain why something as nebulous as "technological creativity" was sustained in the West, the question then becomes the one I pose: Why did individualism uniquely arise in the West? The role of the Western Christian church is crucial in this, as we shall see, but in surprising ways not noted by economic historians! In this context, mention should also be made of White (1978), who is again a "technologist," but whose linkage between the West's technological exceptionalism and the medieval Christian church has resonances with the story I tell.

12. Frankfort (1948), pp. vi–viii.

13. Ibid., pp. 4–5.

14. Ibid., pp. 4–5.

15. Ibid., p. 5.

16. Ibid., p. 337.

17. I Sam 8:19–20 (Ibid., p. 339).

18. Ibid., p. 339.

19. Ibid., p. 341.

20. McNeill (1979), pp. 71–72.

21. Ibid., pp. 72–73.

Chapter 3

1. This part is based on Lal (1988), which also provides extensive references.

2. Domar (1970).

3. This can be shown more rigorously in terms of a model developed by Akerloff; see Lal (1988), pp. 42–44.

4. Basham (1971), p. 156.

5. Ibid., p. 157.

6. Also see Srinivas (1965) pp. 554 and following.

7. Singh (1986), p. 96.

8. Ibid., p. 96.

9. Ibid., p. 100.

10. For a good discussion of the anglicization of brahminical and other Indian law under the British, see Pt. 3 of Rudolph and Rudolph (1967).

11. Srinivas (1966), p. 144.

12. Singh (1986), p. 97 (emphasis added).

13. Cohn (1987), p. 105.

14. Singh (1986), p. 101.

15. See, for instance, Goode (1963).

16. Goody (1990), p. 457.

17. Singh (1986), p. 177.

18. Desai (1964), Kapadia (1956), Kolenda (1968), Shah (1974), Srinivas (1966). See also the references cited in Roland (1988).

19. Srinivas (1966), p. 138. Goody (1990) provides a magisterial cross-cultural study of "systems of marriage and the family in the pre-industrial societies of Eurasia"—as the subtitle of the book has it. His main purpose is to show the similarities between the systems in preindustrial Eurasia as contrasted with their differences with Africa. With land intensive shifting agriculture based on the hoe, there was little social differentiation in Africa. Hence there was little need for the kinship strategies commonly found in the agrarian civilizations of Eurasia. Based on the plow, often requiring irrigation, and with land relatively scarce in contrast with Africa, their agrarian systems led to economic and social differentiation, and thence the common need for what he terms "strategies of heirship." These would differ regionally within Eurasia because of differences in ecology—for instance, those between the irrigated, wet rice-producing areas of southern India and China, as compared with the rainfed wheat-producing areas of northern India and China. Within regions there would be differences in these customs depending upon differences in wealth—with the poor, having less "land" wealth to pass on to their heirs, adopting different domestic customs from those of the rich. For the latter, their status depends

principally (though never entirely) upon the estate ... [whose] continuity is a matter of securing the personnel to exploit and maintain the property as well as the offspring to inherit rights in it. What we are talking about is a type of domestic group, a family, referred to as a "house" or JUF [joint undivided family], which is not necessarily a household nor yet a houseful since individual members maybe working abroad, but a group of variable size having claims on a particular estate by virtue of ties of filiation, of marriage and of their variants such as adoption and concubinage. (p. 469)

He then shows how in China, India, Tibet, Sri Lanka, ancient Egypt, Mesopotamia, and Israel, Greece and Rome, material considerations determined the differences concerning inheritance within a broadly similar pattern of marriage and family structures. This explains customs such as adoption, polygyny, marrying-in sons-in-law (filiacentric unions), close-kin marriages, remarriage of widows, and divorce.

His second purpose is to establish that these differences

neither prevented the development of a mercantile capitalism in Asia long before it made its mark in Western Europe nor did they prevent the development of exhaustive proto-industrial activity in China and India. Nor again have family variables done anything to inhibit the very rapid industrialization in East Asia—indeed there is much evidence that its progress has been assisted by joint undivided families, the "house." (p. 482)

He thus seeks to counter the thesis of a number of recent historians and demographers—see Hajnal (1982), Laslett (1977), Stone (1977), MacFarlane (1979), Shorter (1975), and Kertzer and Saller, eds., (1991) for a detailed examination of the applicability of their thesis to Italy from antiquity to modern times—who see differences in the family between East and West as explaining the rise of the West. Except for the specific changes wrought by Western Christianity (on which more later), Goody shows as flawed these claims that the uniqueness of the West

resided in the development of the elementary nuclear family (or household), the presence of bilateral institutions (kindreds) rather than unilineal ones (clans), in the late age of marriage of males and females (which supposedly encouraged mobility) and the closer relations between parents and children ("parental love") and between the couple themselves ("conjugal love").

For, as Goody documents, these features were not unique to the West. "They can be found among some of the societies we have studied. While it can be argued that only in Western Europe were they found as a particular cluster of weighted variables or relations ... there was no question of any being unique to, or probably 'invented' in that region" (p. 486).

But as Whyte (1996) has argued, in trying to distinguish Eurasian from African domestic customs, Goody fails to emphasize the important differences between the Western family as it emerged in Western Christendom and in the other continuing Eurasian civilizations—the Sinic, Hindu, and Islamic.

20. Maddison (1971), p. 18.

21. Lal (1988).

22. See Ishikawa (1967). It should, however, be noted that a Malthusian process of increasing pressure on land would also yield the Ishikawa curve.

23. B. Wilson (1982), pp. 27–28.

24. Dumont (1986).

25. Gellner (1988), p. 121. Gellner goes on to identify the essential features of a society that individualism has wrought in the West: "A society ... in which single individuals could apparently carry the entire culture within themselves, unaided, and if need be reproduce it single-handedly on their island. This is intimately linked to the emergence of a society in which knowledge was autonomous, a judge but not the judged."

26. Boyd and Richerson (1985), p. 47, summarizing the evidence in Werner (1979).

27. See Roland (1988). He notes from his detailed psychological studies of urbanized Indians today that in child-rearing practices "shaming is used as one of the paramount means of instituting controls in child rearing and seems very effective" (p. 265). "Thus how he will be

regarded by others becomes a central inner dynamic, rather than a feeling of inner guilt over aggressive impulses per se, which is more characteristic of the Western superego" (p. 264).

28. *Times Concise Atlas of World History*, p. 8.

29. Perkins (1969), p. 6.

30. Ibid., p. 6.

31. Ibid., p. 23.

32. Ibid., p. 24.

33. Ibid., pp. 23–24.

34. Elvin (1973), p. 113.

35. Ibid., p. 83.

36. Ibid., p. 234.

37. Ibid., p. 255.

38. Ibid., p. 248.

39. Ibid., p. 250. He also notes:

Chinese rural society in the 19th century and early 20th century was thus one of the most fluid in the world, lacking any of the status or caste restraints which typified late pre modern Japan or India. (p. 258)

It was a society that was both egalitarian and riven with mutual jealousies. The economic closeness of exploiter and exploited, and the lack of any ideologically sanctioned inevitability in the social differences between them, made for hostility rather than harmony. (p. 259)

Power in the countryside no longer resided solely or even primarily in the ownership of land, though obviously it might sometimes be *reflected* in such ownership. In what then did it primarily reside? The short answer is: trade, finance, education, and institutional position, in ascending order of importance. (p. 267)

40. Elvin (1973) notes that "medieval China was distinguished not only by the productivity of its farming but also by the cheapness and, on the whole, the good organization of its water transport system" (p. 144).

41. Ibid., p. 149.

42. Ibid., p. 170.

43. Ibid., p. 167.

44. Elvin (1973) states: "they were not centers of political or personal freedom, nor did they possess distinctive legal institutions. Their inhabitants developed no civic consciousness ... nor served in any autonomous citizen armies" (p. 177).

45. Jones (1988), p. 76.

46. McNeill (1983), Jones (1988), and Lin (1992).

47. McNeill (1983), p. 31.

48. Ibid., p. 40.

49. Ibid., pp. 50–51.

50. Elvin (1973), pp. 226–27.

51. Ibid., pp. 233–34.

52. Hallpike (1986) defines the core principles

which produced by Han times a society with a non-theistic religion and with no organized priesthood distinct from the secular authorities; a highly moralistic, paternal conception of the ideal relationship between government and people; a civilian bureaucracy chosen by merit through examination (more than one and a half millennia before this appeared in Europe); a marked lack of esteem for warfare and military glory; a legal system in which administrative and penal law were greatly elaborated by comparison with civil law; and a merchant class which, despite its great wealth, enjoyed neither prestige nor any legal autonomy that might have led to the emergence of capitalism. (p. 295)

53. Jenner (1992), p. 22.

54. Ibid., p. 23:

The Shuihudi documents show that the bureaucracy reached into every village, conscripting men for forced labor and military service, running a Gulag economy of permanent and temporary state slave laborers, enforcing ideological and administrative unity on the conscripted territories, imposing draconian discipline on the officials themselves as well as the general population and doing things with the sort of methodical efficiency that we do not associate with late Imperial China. This was all different in kind from anything in western Eurasia before the 18th, if not the 19th century.

55. Ibid., p. 5.

56. Ibid., p. 6.

57. Ibid., p. 7.

58. Ibid., p. 10.

59. Ibid., pp. 10–11.

60. Keightley (1990), p. 48.

61. Jenner (1992), p. 3.

62. Keightley (1990), p. 48.

63. There is no support for Wittfogel's (1957) view that Chinese oriental despotism was created to manage large irrigation schemes. As both Keightley (1990, p. 49) and Jenner (1992) note, Chinese civilization and its bureaucratic absolutism arose very early when the cradle of the civilization was in areas of dry-farming of wheat and millet. This did not require any elaborate water-control projects. When a need for them arose during the later medieval economic revolution under the Sung, the traditional Chinese state was already in place and obviously facilitated their execution and maintenance.

64. Elvin (1973), p. 220.

65. Needham (1956) 544; cited in Hallpike (1986, p. 309).

66. See also Goody (1990). He notes one important difference found in marriage and domestic arrangements within China (and also in India), between the north and the south. These concern lineages, marriage transactions, divorce, widow remarriage, adoption and fila-

centric unions, type of marriage, and the importance of women's labor. It seems in both India and China the north is less "permissive" than the south in all these respects, and this is also the case with differences between higher- and lower-status groups in the two regions of both countries, with the "upper" groups behaving generally more like the north and "lower" groups like the south. "The practices prevalent in the North and among upper groups are closer to Confucian norms, that is, closer to those of the original core of culture, Confucian and neo-Confucianism" (p. 109). He attempts to relate these to ecological differences (p. 284). This conjecture is broadly right, if instead of concentrating purely on "inheritance strategies," we go a step backward and look upon these customs as different ways of dealing with the different sources of uncertainty of income in agrarian economies subject to climatic risk.

67. Keightley (1990), pp. 44–45. Jenner (1992) tells us,

Members of the family are bound together not only by common descent; they are also held in closed circles of debts and obligations that have to be honored if one is to hold one's head high in the world. Few cultures place as much emphasis on the absolute nature of debts and the absolute need to repay them as do China's. When as a child you become more aware of the world you are taught that your parents have run up a huge credit balance with you by investing much time, effort and wealth in creating you and bringing you up. This is a debt that has to be repaid to them as your creditors in this life if you are to be a real human being. If you are a good son, you will do this by keeping your parents in dignity and comfort in their old age and by burying and mourning them properly after their death. (pp. 108–9)

68. Jenner (1992), p. 124.

69. See e.g., deBary (1991), Weiming Tu (1990), Redding (1990).

70. See Hicks and Redding (1983) and Vogel (1991).

71. Baum (1994).

72. Jenner also notes that the essential feature of the "high culture" that has dominated China is one which has promoted the values of a premodern imperial bureaucracy. "There is plenty of evidence that China's business cultures have long been able to flourish if only they were allowed to, but for over two thousand years states have preferred to keep business divided, confined and controlled" (Jenner [1992], p. 178).

73. See Redding (1990).

Chapter 4

1. Crone (1996), p. 2.

2. Ibid., p. 5.

3. Ibid., p. 7.

4. McNeill (1963), p. 424.

5. Ibid.

6. Crone and Cook (1977).

7. Ibid., p. 73.

8. Ibid., p. 74.

9. Ibid., p. 74.

10. Ibid.

11. Ibid, p. 75.

12. Ibid., p. 77.

13. Ibid.

14. Ibid.

15. Ibid.

16. McNeill (1963), p. 431.

17. Ibid., p. 434.

18. As Crone and Hinds (1986) note,

the widespread insistence that the caliphate be elective (al-amr shura), the endless demands for observance of "kitab" and "sunna," good practice and past models, the constant objections to Ummayad fiscal policy, and the general readiness to take up arms against what was perceived to be oppressive rule, all these are features indicative of so stubborn a determination to keep government under control that one might have credited it with a good chance of success. (p. 106)

19. "The caliph Umar created a system of stipends for those who had fought in the cause of Islam, regulated according to priority of conversion and service, and this reinforced the cohesion of the ruling elite, or at least their separation from those they ruled." Hourani (1991), p. 24.

20. Ibid. p. 107.

21. Crone (1980) provides a succinct analysis of the evolution of this conquest society.

22. McNeill (1963), p. 429.

23. McNeill (1979), p. 390.

24. B. Lewis (1994), p. 5.

25. Ibid.

26. Thus Ashtor (1976), the leading economic historian of medieval Islam, notes:

The Abbasdis succeeded in ... realizing their great scheme of knitting together the lands conquered by their predecessors into a uniform empire.... Islamization and Arabization made great progress, and at the same time the countries of the Near and Middle East became an economic unit, which distinguished itself by intense industrial and commercial activities. It is not an exaggeration to speak of a true economic miracle, performed under the guidance of the Abbasid government. (p. 77)

27. Ibid., p. 71.

28. Ibid., p. 78.

29. Ibid., pp. 98–99.

30. Ibid., p. 77.

31. Ibid., pp. 80–86.

32. Ibid., p. 101.

33. Issawi (1981) p. 85. By contrast, Marshall Hodgson (1974) in his monumental study *The Venture of Islam* maintains that there was no such decline. All that happened, he argues, was that the West began to overtake Islamic civilization from the seventeenth century onward. The continuing expansion of Islam as well as its superior military power based on keeping abreast of advances in military technology in the West are adduced as evidence. For a robust response see Issawi (1981).

34. Issawi (1982).

35. Owen (1981).

36. Issawi (1981), p. 86.

37. Ibid., p. 89.

38. Ashtor (1976), p. 111, citing the findings of Cohen (1970).

39. Ibid., p. 114.

40. Also see Jones (1988) who also argues a variant of the "economic irrelevancy of Islam" case. Kuran (1997) provides a succinct survey of the various ideas, and also to my mind a convincing case based on his theory of preference falsification (see the appendix) for the view that Islam as it was codified after the Abbasid settlement did inhibit economic development in the countries of its sway.

41. Cook (1983) notes that Mohammed cleverly used the Biblical divide between the children of Abraham—Isaac, the son by his wife Sarah, and Ishmael, the son by his Egyptian concubine Hagar—by "opening up the Ishmaelite dead end, thereby creating a second line of sacred history that was specifically Arabian" (p. 36). The Arabs became the descendants of Ishmael, just as the Jews and Christians were those of Isaac. "The effect of these ideas is simple but crucial: they endow Arabia and the Arabs with an honored place in monotheist history, and one genealogically independent of the Jews and Christians" (p. 38). Also see Crone and Cook (1977).

42. McNeill (1963), p. 421.

43. Hourani (1991), p. 147.

44. McNeill (1963), p. 421.

45. Ibid., pp. 421–22.

46. Ibid., p. 431.

47. Cook (1983).

48. Cook (1983), p. 30.

49. See Rahman (1979), who gives a good account of the Mutazila movement of the eighth and ninth centuries. That movement

had generally developed under the influence of Hellenic rationalism, thereby creating the first major tension in the religious history of Islam. The leaders of Muslim orthodoxy, representing the old tradition, at first suffered at the hands of this rationalist movement ... but subsequently, by mustering political strength and by borrowing the very weapons of Greek dialectic, effectively gained the upper hand. Gradually, the orthodox "ulama" brought almost all education under their control, and worked out and implemented curricula to realize their own intellectual and spiritual ideals. (p. 5)

50. Ibid.

51. Crone and Cook (1977), p. 126.

52. "Still in the last resort a despot, the Christian god was nevertheless by Hellenic standards a passably enlightened one. He himself was no longer given to very strenuous activity; but as a symbol over and above the impersonal laws, he evinced a compensatory stability" (Crone and Cook [1977], p. 127).

53. Hourani (1991) notes:

The assumption of philosophy was that human reason rightly used could give man certain knowledge of the universe, but to be Muslim was to believe that some knowledge essential for human life had come to man only through the revelation of God's Word to the prophets. If Islam was true, what were the limitations of philosophy? If the claims of the philosophers were valid, what need was there for prophecy? ... Al-Farabi (d. 950) [argued that] philosophy and the religion of Islam do not ... contradict each other. They express the same truth in different forms, which correspond to the different levels at which human beings can apprehend it.... Implicit in the ideas of al-Farabi was the suggestion that philosophy in its pure form was not for everyone. The distinction between the intellectual elite and the masses was to become a commonplace of Islamic thought. Philosophy continued to exist, but was carried on as a private activity, largely by medical men, pursued with discretion and often met with suspicion. (pp. 77–8)

54. Crone and Cook (1977), p. 128.

55. Ibid., pp. 128–29.

56. Cook (1983), pp. 84–85. Though scholars usually date the rise of nationalism to the nineteenth century, Cook's insight is surely valid that the fusion of politics and religion in Islam is like most modern nationalisms where "men confront the problem of remaining themselves while adopting the belief of others" (ibid.). This newfound cultural and religious identity was indispensable for the southern nomads who had adopted Islam to maintain their distinctive identity, when various northern barbarians, from the Goths in the West to the Mongols in the East were acculturated in the civilizations (Latin Christendom and Confucian China) they had conquered.

57. This is not to deny that after the rise of Sufism there are great similarities between the conversion of pagans on the edges of the initial Islamic empire by Sufi missionaries, and that of the German tribes in medieval Europe by Christian monks. In both cases one of the major inducements was that both set of missionaries could remove the terrors of the natural world from the minds of simple people which allowed an extension of cultivation into what were considered to be areas which were terrifying. For a detailed study of this process of the disenchantment of nature in the Islamic conversion of the peasantry of Bengal see Eaton (1993).

It should also be noted that, as Rahman (1979) states, although the view that "Islam was propagated 'by the sword'" is a travesty,

it is also a distortion of facts to say that Islam spread in the same way as, say, Buddhism or even Christianity.... Whereas the Muslims did not spread their faith through the sword, it is, nevertheless, true that Islam insisted on the assumption of political power since it regarded itself as the repository of the Will of God which had to be worked on earth through a political order. From this point of view, Islam resembles the Communist structure which, even if it does not oblige people to accept its creed, nevertheless insists on the assumption of the political order. To deny this fact would be both to violate history and to deny justice to Islam itself. (p. 2)

58. Crone and Cook (1977), p. 145.

59. See Delumeau (1990) and Chapter 9 of this book.

60. Ruthven (1984), p. 125.

61. Ibid., p. 138.

62. Ibid., p. 139.

63. See Ibn Khaldun (1379/1958).

64. See e.g., Gellner (1981), and Hall (1985).

65. My model of the contestable predatory state (see Appendix) fits this view very well.

66. P. Anderson (1979).

67. Crone (1980), p. 79.

68. Ibid.

69. Ibid., p. 80.

70. Ibid., p. 84.

71. These were Christian children obtained as a "tax" on Christian subjects in the Balkans, who were then enslaved, converted, and manumitted and who rose to high office under the Ottomans.

72. With the end of parricide, unelevated princes from among a sultan's palace were confined in gilded "cages" in the harem. "Here pillow talk was of politics, and women and eunuchs conspired to secure the succession for a potential patron from among the sultan's brood.... For much of the 17th century the effective chief executives of the state were queen-mothers who knew nothing first hand of the world beyond the harem walls" (Fernando-Armesto [1995], p. 239).

73. Crone (1980), p. 90.

74. See Crone and Hinds (1986), and Rahman (1979).

75. Crone (1980), p. 81.

76. See Crone (1980), Pipes (1981), M. Rodinson (1974), Garcin (1978).

77. Garcin (1978).

78. Cook (1988).

79. Ibid., p. 134.

80. Ibid., p. 133.

81. Cook (1983), p. 44.

82. Hourani (1991), p. 161.

83. Ibid.

84. Anderson (1979), p. 497.

85. Ibid., p. 498.

86. Crone and Hinds (1986), p. 109.

87. Ibid. It is not surprising that the Muslim conquest of India did little to change the political parameters of what I have termed "the Hindu equilibrium" (Lal [1988]).

88. Ruthven (1991), p. 178.

89. Ibid., p. 176.

90. See B. Lewis (1982) pp. 229–30.

91. See Rahman (1979), chaps. 11 and 14.

92. Rahman notes that during this medieval flowering "difficult and delicate matters like unbiased descriptions of non-Islamic religions had developed so much that the famous al-Baruni complains in the introduction of his work on India that while the Muslims had been able to produce fairly objective works on such religions as Judaism and Christianity, they had been unable to do so with regard to Hinduism, and that, therefore, he was going to attempt the task" (Ibid., p. 4).

93. Ibid., p. 296.

94. Kuran (1997), p. 5.

95. Crone and Cook, pp. 142–44.

96. Ibid, p. 143.

97. See Elvin (1973).

98. Fernandez-Armesto (1995), p. 35.

99. Inalcik (1994), pp. 44–54.

100. This was the system of family labor based farms common under Roman, Byzantine, and Ottoman rule in the area. A. V. Chyanov (1966) argued that it was the most economically efficient form of rural organization, and as such remained the basic form of land settlement for millennia. See Inalcik (1994), chap. 6, for a detailed analysis of this system during Ottoman rule.

101. Kuran (1993), p. 294.

102. This is also the main plea of Rahman (1979), a Pakistani Islamic scholar.

103. Ruthven (1991), p. 302.

104. See Roy (1994), and Ruthven (1991).

105. Ruthven, op. cit., p. 352.

106. An excellent account of the reasons for the Shah's downfall and Khomeini's success is provided in Abrahamian (1981).

107. But Huntington's (1993) fears of a threat to the West by some unified Islamic civilization is grossly exaggerated. See Said (1994), p. 347, for an intemperate riposte.

108. There is a further cultural aspect of Muslim societies noted by Gellner (1992) that makes them unstable. Harking back to Ibn Khaldun, he makes a distinction between high and low Islam, the former was the Islam of the scholars, the latter of the people. The scholars were concerned with "the three central, pervasive and actually invoked principles of religious

and political legitimacy [within Islam]: the divine message and its legal elaboration, the consensus of the community, and finally, sacred leadership (by members of the House of the Prophet, or by specially selected members of it" (Gellner [1992], p. 8) The coexistence of the tribal polity with this high Islam meant that there was a perpetual danger facing Muslim rulers of a fusion of the two forces: a revivalist movement insisting on the maintenance or restoration of uncompromising religious truth and sustained by the support of low Islam with its cohesive, armed and militarily experienced rural self-governing communities. These communities *normally* practiced a culturally "low" variant of Islam, with its belief in magic rather than learning, and its saint cults, but were eager to embrace the purer, unitarian "high" form under the influence of a wave of enthusiasm, and in the hope of urban booty and political privilege (ibid. p. 11).

In the past, these movements of reformist Islam rose and fell in cycles. "The reformers prevailed ... and having re-established a purified order, things slowly returned to normality. The spirit is willing but the social flesh is weak" (p. 14). But the coming of the modern world has changed this. "The old *status quo* was based on a military and political balance of power, in which the central authority simply lacked the means to assert itself effectively in the desert and in the mountains, and, in a large part of the countryside, left the maintenance of order to self-administering local groups, normally known as 'tribes'" (p. 14). With the political centralization made possible by modern technology, these "erstwhile local mutual aid groups" have been eroded. There has thus been

an enormous shift in the balance *from* Folk Islam *to* High Islam.... Urbanization, political centralization, incorporation in a wider market, labor migration, have all impelled populations in the direction of the formally (theologically) more "correct" Islam.... Identification with Reformed Islam has played a role very similar to that played by nationalism elsewhere. (p. 15)

Gellner sees Islam as uniquely placed to escape the perennial question faced by Third World elites: should they emulate the West and attain material prosperity at the expense of tradition (as many see it), or should they maintain traditions and forego material advantage? For the fundamentalists of High Islam do not recommend an emulation of the West "nor idealization of some folk virtue or wisdom ... but a return to, a more rigorous observance of High Islam" (p. 19). Moreover, they could blame their past weakness in facing the West to the prevalence of low Islam.

But unless high Islam can reform itself through interpretation, then, as Kuran (1997) has argued, Islam is likely to remain a brake on economic progress. As parts of high Islam can be used to preach all the virtues that Weber identified as essential to the spirit of capitalism, it can (if suitably reformed) also promote the economic development through free markets that leads to material prosperity. But whether that will happen remains an open question. Meanwhile, with secular regimes from Algeria to Turkey under threat from Islamicists, there is as yet no likelihood of fundamentalism dying out with the secularization that accompanies industrialization.

109. Crone and Cook (1977), p. 129.

110. Ibid., pp. 147–48.

111. Kuran (1997) quoting Ulgener.

Chapter 5

1. Finley (1974), p. 91.

2. See McEvedy and Jones (1978), p. 26.

3. See Reynolds (1985).

4. Gellner (1988), pp. 130–31.

5. Gellner (1988), p. 276.

6. Hicks (1969).

7. Anderson (1979), p. 429, emphasis added.

8. McNeill (1979), p. 99.

9. Ibid.

10. Ibid., emphasis added.

11. Ibid.

12. Finley (1974), pp. 39–40.

13. Macfarlane (1979).

14. Ibid., p. 196.

15. Ibid, pp. 197–98.

16. Ibid., pp. 170, 206.

17. Thus see the essays by Elvin (1978) on China, Sanderson (1978) on India, and Jean La Fontaine and Godfrey Lienhardt on Africa in Carrithers et al. (1978), which delineate the concept of the "person" in these other cultures and show that they differ substantially from that based on Western individualism.

18. The classical historian Robin Lane Fox (1988), in his vivid reconstruction of the Roman world—in particular the Eastern half where these various cults were competing for the loyalty of the citizens of many cities in Asia Minor—notes that "one of the fundamental contrasts between pagan cult and Christianity was this passage from an oral culture of myth and conjecture to one based on written texts" (p. 304).

19. Lane Fox (1988), p. 609.

20. Ibid., p. 314.

21. Dumont (1986), p. 26.

22. Ibid., p. 27.

23. Ibid., p. 31.

24. Ibid., p. 47.

25. Troeltsch (1931), p. 64, cited in Dumont (1986), p. 33.

26. Dumont, p. 34.

27. Dumont (1986), p. 39.

28. Dumont (1986) writes,

When justice is Christianized in this manner, reason is made not only to bow to faith but to recognize in faith something akin to itself, as it were reason itself raised to a superior power.... [This is] Augustine's apparently extravagant claim: to philosophize from faith, to set faith, i.e., experience of God, at the foundation of rational thought … here, under the aegis of the Christian God, the modern era begins, when men will increasingly struggle to embody their personal experience in reason, that is to reduce the gulf that initially separated reason from experience…. Augustine inaugurates a millenary, protean, existential struggle between reason and experience, a struggle unceasingly renewed and propagating from one level to another, which will in the last analysis modify the relation between the ideal and the actual, and of which we are in some manner the products. (pp. 40–41)

29. Ibid., p. 50.

30. Dumont notes that "the antagonistic worldly element that individualism had hitherto to accommodate disappears entirely in Calvins's theocracy. The field is absolutely unified. *The individual is now in the world, and the individualist value rules without restriction or limitation.* The in-worldly individual is before us" (p. 52).

31. Gurevich (1995) also dates the rise of European individualism to Augustine.

32. Hicks (1969), pp. 78–79. The most thorough and devastating critique of the Weber-Tawney thesis of a direct correlation between Puritanism and economic progress is by the Swedish economic historian Kurt Samuelsson (1961).

33. McNeill (1979), p. 268.

34. Dumont 1986), p. 71.

35. Jones (1981), p. 106.

36. See Jones (1988).

37. Mann (1986), p. 407.

38. Southern (1970).

39. Southern (1970), p. 16.

40. Mann (1986), p. 407.

41. Lal (1988).

42. Berman (1983), p. 87.

43. See Duby (1974), Postan (1975), and Mann (1986).

44. Southern (1970), pp. 34–35.

45. Thus Berman (1983) notes, "It is wrongly supposed that Roman Catholic thought was fundamentally otherworldly and ascetic; in fact, in the late eleventh and twelfth centuries Roman Catholic theology broke away from the predominantly otherworldly, ascetic ideal which had prevailed earlier and which still prevails in much of Eastern Orthodoxy" (p. 337). He goes on to say:

The Western Church of the late eleventh and twelfth centuries—in contrast to the Eastern church, and also in contrast to the entire Church both in the East and in the West, prior to the Papal Revolution—believed in the possibility of reconciling commercial activity with a Christian life…. The secular activities of those engaged in commercial enterprise were to be organized in ways that would redeem them from the sin of avarice. The merchants were to form guilds that would have religious functions and would maintain standards of morality in commercial transactions…. Thus the church-state set an example for the city-state, and church law set an example for city law and for commercial law…. From the point of view of the Christian social theory which prevailed in the formative period of Western commercial institutions, the economic activities of merchants, like other secular activities, were no longer to be considered as necessarily "a danger to salvation"; on the contrary, they were considered to be a path to salvation, if carried on according to the principles laid down by the Church. These principles were spelled out in the canon law. From the Church's point of view, the law developed by the merchants, the *lex mercatoria*, was supposed to reflect, not contradict, the canon law.... Law was a bridge between mercantile activity and the salvation of the soul. (pp. 338–39)

46. Berman (1983), pp. 348–49.

47. Berman (1983), pp. 349–50.

48. Canon law also developed a law of usury that "developed as a system of exceptions to the [old and new testament] prohibition against usury." It became "a flexible rule against unconscionability and against unfair competition.... Indeed the canonists first used the Roman word 'interest'... to mean a lawful charge for the loan of money, as distinguished from the sin of usury" (Berman [1983], p. 249).

49. Southern (1970).

50. Berman (1983), p. 521.

51. Berman writes:

Christianity taught a ... practical doctrine—that hills, valleys, forests, rivers, rocks, wind, storm, sun, moon, stars, wild beasts, snakes, and all the other phenomena of nature were created by God to serve man and were not haunted (as the Germanic peoples believed) by hostile supernatural deities, and that therefore it was possible for the wandering, warring tribes to settle on the land without fear. This was both preached and lived out in the fifth, sixth, seventh, and eighth centuries by tens of thousands of monks, who themselves settled in the wilderness, first as hermits and then in monastic communities, and who attracted many others to join them in tilling the soil. (Berman [1983], p. 62)

52. See Southern (1970). Berman (1983) writes: "Spreading across Europe from Ireland and Wales, the monastic movement fought the superstitions of nature that dominated Germanic religions, and it opposed to the pagan calendar, based on nature and the four seasons, a Christian calendar based on biblical events and the lives of the saints" (p. 63).

53. Berman (1983), p. 66.

54. For sixth to eighth century Europe see Southern (1970, chap. 6). For India for the same period see Lal (1988, chap. 3.9).

55. The Papal Revolution gave birth to a new formulation of the doctrine of the two swords that

had been introduced five centuries earlier by Pope Gelasius I. The earlier formulation had been concerned with the relation between earthly and heavenly spheres of Christian living. For the theorists of the Papal Revolution, however, the main problem was the relation between the ecclesiastical and lay authorities in the earthly sphere itself. It was the church as a visible, corporate, political and legal entity that was to wield the spiritual sword; and that sword was to control not only life in the next world but also a large number of matters in this world as well, including administration of church property, activities of clerics, family relations, business morality, indeed, anything that could be brought under the heading of morals or belief. (Berman [1983], p. 521)

56. Berman (1983), p. 520.

57. Goody (1983), pp. 34–35.

58. Ibid., p. 39.

59. Ibid., p. 43.

60. See Goody and Harrison (1976); Wrigley (1978).

61. Goody (1983), p. 45.

62. Ibid., p. 45.

63. Lane Fox (1988), p. 311.

64. That this was recognized by contemporaries is noted by Lane Fox (1988):

In July 370, the Emperor Valentinian addressed a ruling to the Pope of Rome that male clerics and unmarried ascetics must not hang around the houses of women and widows and try to worm themselves or their churches into their bequests, to the detriment, even, of the women's families and blood relations. It is even more revealing that, twenty years later, in August 390, his successor deplored these "despoilers of the weaker sex," yet admitted reluctantly that the law was unworkable and would have to be abolished. Ingratiating monks and clergymen had proved too strong for secular justice. (p. 310)

It is also worth noting the rise of the Benedictine order, which from A.D. 700 to 1100 "was held to be the highest form of religious life" (Southern (1970, p. 217). They served an important social function:

At no time in the Middle Ages, and least of all in the early centuries, were the resources of society expanding fast enough to provide honorable positions in secular life for all the children of noble families. There were severe, and well-justified, restrictions on the practice of splitting up the family property, and it was a very serious problem to provide secure and acceptable positions for those members of the family for whom no sufficient endowment could be provided. The problem was especially serious for the girls of a family. They were not exposed to the hazards of an active military life, which created gaps and unexpected opportunities for the boys. There were not enough suitable marriages for all of them; and those who married were often widowed at an early age. A great family had to make provision for all these eventualities, and the monasteries performed an essential service in helping to solve this problem. They provided the children of noble families with a reasonably aristocratic life and with opportunities of great splendor. The use of monasteries for this purpose naturally imposed on families an obligation to make suitable provision for their upkeep. Parents commonly gave large gifts to the monasteries to which they offered a child: the gift of an estate was not unusual. (Ibid., p. 228)

Finally, Gibbon (1880) notes: "The Christians of Rome were possessed of a very considerable wealth.... Many among their proselytes had sold their lands and houses to increase the public riches of the sect, at the expense, indeed, of their unfortunate children, who found themselves beggars because their parents had been saints" (II, 132).

65. I have thought for some time that a great book is waiting to be written of the Roman Catholic church as a business enterprise. Viewed as such, it is probably the longest-lasting and most global and financially successful business corporation the world has ever known. Its product, "salvation," has had an enduring appeal that must be the envy of any modern corporation. An attempt has been made by Ekelund et al. (1996).

66. Goody (1983), p. 105.

67. Herlihy (1961), p. 87.

68. "In England the great build-up of Church lands occurred during the period A.D. 600–1100, that is, beginning with the arrival of Augustine down to the Norman Conquest. Devotion and the new monastic orders of the sixth and tenth centuries played their part; so did royal patronage. Much was alienated in the ordinary course of seeking salvation, by gift and by bequest" (Goody [1983], p. 105).

69. Goody (1983), p. 115.

70. Herlihy (1961), p. 97.

71. Goody (1983), p. 118.

72. Southern (1970), p. 130.

73. Ibid., p. 125.

74. Ibid., p. 21.

75. There has been a century-long debate among anthropologists about the nature of the primitive family. Kuper (1996), chap. 7, provides an excellent summary of this debate. Early anthropologists believed that promiscuity and polygyny was rife among savages. Darwin and in particular Westermarck demurred. "The licentiousness of many savages is no doubt astonishing" Darwin wrote, "but it seems to me that more evidence is requisite, before we fully admit that their intercourse is in any case promiscuous" (*The Descent of Man*, p. 896). He also noted that no other primates were known to be sexually permissive. The anthropologists believed that some cultural rule had been invented to regulate the free play of humans' promiscuous basic instincts; this was the incest taboo. Westermarck supported Darwin's position and argued that the incest taboo was part of human nature and that marriage and the family were universal among primates. Freud, in his *Totem and Taboo*, argues that incest was a cultural construct: "the incest taboo checks natural drives and ... diverts a growing boy's sexual energy away from his mother, liberating energies that can be turned to cultural creativity. Civilization, according to Freud, was built upon the repression of instinct" (Kuper, p. 162). Lévi-Strauss, in his *Elementary Structures of Kinship*, argues that the incest taboo allowed marriage alliances that promoted a broader sociality. When a man gave up his sexual rights to his sister and daughter, he had to marry them outside the family, which gave him a claim on the sisters and daughters of other men. All the anthropological theories apart from Westermarck's were based on the assumption that zoologists observing primates in zoos had found them to be incestuous, so that the incest taboo was supposed to distinguish man from the apes. "As it turns out this conclusion was false. Incestuous sexual contact is uncommon among most animals in nature" (Kuper, p. 166). Moreover, recent research on children brought up on Israeli kibbutzim, and the practice of child marriages called "sim pua" in China, has shown that children brought up as siblings have a natural aversion to mate with each other; see Shepher (1983), Wolf and Huang (1980). It seems that Westermarck was right. Other evidence summarized in Kuper shows that monogamous marriage is the rule in most human societies. Oddities like the polygyny among the Nairs of Kerala (see Fuller (1976)) is exceptional, as is that among high-status groups surveyed in Betzig (1986). The Nair case can be explained in terms of material factors: the unusual economic specialization of its men as mercenary soldiers, who were absent for long periods. "The female-based family arrangements they had developed made this way of life possible" (Kuper, p. 169). When, on annexing Malabar in 1792, the British suppressed the military system that had underwritten this domestic system, by the "early 19th century the polyandrous system died out, and increasingly the Nayar [Nairs] began to favor permanent relationships between a single man and woman" (Ibid).

76. See Goody (1983).

77. See Laslett and Wall (1972); Laslett (1977); Hajnal (1965); Hajnal (1982); Wrigley and Schofield (1981).

78. Macfarlane (1979, 1986), Goody (1983, 1990).

79. Hajnal (1982).

80. "Late marriage for both sexes (mean ages at first marriage are, say, over 26 for men and over 23 for women); after marriage [the couple] are in charge of their household (the husband is head of the household); before marriage young people often circulate between households as servants." By contrast with these "simple households," in the rest of Eurasia there were "joint household" systems characterized by

earlier marriage for men and rather early marriage for women (mean ages at first marriage are under 26 for men and under 21 for women; a young married couple often start life together either in a household of which an older couple is and remains in charge or in a household of which an unmarried older person (such as a widower or widow) continues to be head. Usually the young wife joins her husband in the household of which he is a member; households with several married couples may split to form two or more households, each containing one or more couples. (Ibid., p. 452)

For the pitfalls in categorizing the complexity of family systems into some simple dichotomies or other schemata, see Wrigley (1977).

81. The unmarried could survive as servants and postpone marriage for as long as they liked. These "servants," however, were not necessarily distinguished by class. They are better looked upon as the medieval equivalent of modern au pairs!

82. That this homeostatic fertility behavior characterized England and was linked to changes in the marriage age and the extent of "living-in" is conclusively established in the detailed study by Wrigley and Schofield (1981).

83. Goody (1996), p. 14.

84. See Wolf (1995).

85. Goody (1996), p. 15.

86. Ibid., p. 17.

87. Macfarlane (1979, 1986).

88. Hajnal (1982), p. 477. Also see Smith (1979).

89. Macfarlane (1986), p. 335.

90. Ibid., p. 334.

91. See references in Macfarlane (1986), p. 108.

92. Ibid., p. 116.

93. See Lal-Myint (1996), chap. 9.

94. Duby (1978), p. 17.

95. Goody (1983), p. 155.

96. Crone and Cook (1977), p. 147. As they note: "Ibn Hanbal would not have climbed a palm tree for a pretty girl in the manner of Rabbi Atim; but neither did he need to climb a pillar in pursuit of God in the manner of St. Simeon Stylites" (Ibid.).

97. See Bloch (1965), Southern (1953).

98. Jankowiak and Fischer (1992).

99. Jankowiak, ed., (1995), p. 5.

100. Liebowitz (1983). Fisher (1995) provides a succinct outline of the sociobiological evidence about theories of love.

101. Liebowitz (1983), p. 200.

102. Tennov (1979); Money (1980).

103. Fisher (1992).

104. Fisher (1995), p. 33.

105. See Buss (1994), Daly and Wilson (1983), Fisher (1992).

106. Lancaster and Lancaster (1983); Fisher (1992).

107. The emotion of love is not exclusive to our species. It is worth noting that it has been found that the neurochemicals associated with the sensations of attraction and attachment are also found in birds and nonhuman mammals. See Shepherd (1988) and Fisher (1995).

108. Brain (1996), p. 6.

109. See Singer (1984) for a comprehensive account of the philosophical and literary origins of the concept of love. He distinguishes between two conceptualizations in Western thought. The first looks at love as being a matter of calculated self-interest. The sociobiological view would fit in here. The second is what Lindholm (1995) labels "the experience of transcendence": "the beloved is adulated as an earthly and imperfect expression of divine harmony and beauty ... love for a person ... is a means to a higher end, much like the contemplation of a work of art" (p. 58).

110. Lindholm (1995), p. 58.

111. Lindholm (1995) pp. 66–67.

112. Singer (1984), vol. 1, p. 340.

113. Delumeau (1990).

114. Arapura (1972).

115. Ibid.

116. Delumeau (1990), p. 246.

117. Ibid., p. 9.

118. St. Augustine, *City of God*, chap. 14.

119. Delumeau (1990), p. 259.

120. Ibid., p.1.

121. St. Augustine, XIV, 24, cited in Delameau (1990), p. 16.

122. Ibid., p. 16.

123. Everyone could be subject to one of the seven deadly sins: pride, envy, anger, sloth, avarice, gluttony, lust.

124. Delumeau notes that like most other peoples early Europeans "found it difficult to accept the abrupt disappearance of those with whom they shared their lives. Hence they believed in ghosts.... This belief was so strong in our civilization that Christianity integrated it quite spontaneously and used parts of it as part of the pedagogy of salvation .... Ghosts are but souls in Purgatory" (p. 37). However, in most other civilizations "the death of an individual is secondary to the survival of the community, and where both living and dead maintain social ties and solidarity. This concept which is shared by many civilizations, has found its expression in ancestor cults and in the casual use of death images in everyday lie" (Ibid.). By contrast the Christian attitude was summarized by Luther's complaining against the practice of using cemeteries as places for social gatherings; a graveyard should instead be a "venerable and almost sacred place, where one would walk with respectful awe" and be led to "reflect upon death, the Last Judgment and the Resurrection, and pray" (Ibid., p. 39).

In the past, another person's death was regarded with indifference; it shocked no one. Everyone was used to death, and nobody was surprised when it was their turn to go. Seen in these terms, it is quite legitimate to compare the attitudes toward death decried by Luther with those of "primitive" peoples who, contrary to European civilization today, attribute little importance to the individual. The participatory mentality of such peoples prevents them from "experiencing death as a separation or as a kind of dereliction." (Ibid., p. 39)

125. Ibid., p. 54.

126. "It was in the 16th century, and specifically in Protestant theology, that the accusation of man and the world reached its climax in Western civilization." Delumeau (1990), p. 27.

127. Ibid., p. 31.

128. Arapura (1972), pp. 95–99.

129. Arapura (1972), pp. 101–102.

130. Delumeau (1990), p. 556.

131. Cited in Eisenstadt (1996), p. 6.

132. It should be noted that many economic historians have also emphasized that the individualism of the medieval Italian city-states fostered by both the Christian church's growing in-worldliness and rising humanism was an essential element in the rise of the institutions such as codified commercial law, banking, joint stock companies and an incipient stock market, which led to the rise of capitalism and the West. Greif (1994) has recently produced evidence and a game theoretic model to show how it was this individualism which impelled the Genoese in the twelfth century to establish these institutions, in contrast with their major competitors the Maghribis. The latter, he argues relied on traditional familial contacts and informal collective economic punishments to overcome the inevitable problems of moral hazard and adverse selection involved in choosing agents to conduct long distance trade. By contrast in the individualist Genoese society, such familial (collective) forms of dealing with the principal-agent problem were not available. They were then impelled "to develop formal legal and political enforcement organizations ... to support collective actions, and to facilitate exchange, [including] a formal legal code ... to facilitate exchange by coordinating expectations and enhancing the deterrence effect of formal organizations" (p. 936). He then

goes on to show how these different cultural aspects of the two groups led the Genoese but not the Maghribi to develop the family firm, "which was a permanent partnership with unlimited and joint liability" (p. 940). This led in time to

family firms beginning to sell shares to non-family members.... [These] tradable shares required a suitable market, and "stock markets" were developed. Furthermore, the separation between ownership and control introduced by the family firm motivated the introduction of organizations able to surmount the related contractual problems, such as improvement in information transmission techniques, accounting procedures, and the incentive scheme provided to agents. (p. 941)

But, as I hope the text has shown, it was the papal revolution of Gregory VII that established these legal reforms and that the individualism of the "West" predates the rise of the city-states of medieval Italy, spanning the doings of the two popes Gregory between the sixth and eleventh centuries.

133. Ware (1993), p. 134.

134. Ibid.

135. Ibid., p. 135.

136. Riasanovsky (1993), p. 35.

137. Ibid., p. 36.

138. Fernandez-Armesto (1995), p. 93.

139. Ibid., p. 94.

140. As Domar (1970) notes, the scarcity of labor and serfdom as the answer to provide a surplus for the nobility is attested to by two facts:

The first ... [is] the replacement of the basic land tax by a household tax in the seventeenth century and a poll tax under Peter the Great. The second is ... [a] cultural trait ... as late as in the first half of the nineteenth century, the social position of a Russian landowner ... depended less on his landholdings ... than on the number of *souls* (registered male peasants) he owned." (Domar [1970], p. 232).

141. This is the traditional family-labor based agrarian system that was the basis of Chyanov's famous study.

142. Domar and Machina (1984) try to ascertain whether serfdom became unprofitable because of the rise of grain prices following the repeal of the British Corn laws, which acted like an expansion of population. They do not find much empirical support for the "unprofitability" thesis for the abolition of serfdom.

143. Pintner (1995), p. 9.

144. Ibid, p. 5.

Chapter 6

1. McClelland (1996), p. 171.

2. The following is based on Minogue (1995), chap. 6.

3. Minogue (1995), p. 49.

4. Ibid, p. 175.

5. Ibid.

6. Collectivism was defined by Dicey (1914) as "government for the good of the people by experts or officials who know or think they know what is good for the people better than any non-official person or than the mass of people themselves" (p. lxxiii). Hayek (1944) defined it as "the deliberate organization of the labors of society for a definite social goal" (p. 56).

7. Skidelsky (1995), p. 45.

8. Ibid.

9. In his collection of aphorisms called *The Dawn*, 571.

10. Laslett (1989), who writes, "It was then that consensual unions began to be widespread, abortions to be exceedingly common, contraception to be universal and the numbers of births to fall so far that it is now doubtful if many Western populations can maintain their numbers in the long run" (p. 843).

11. C. L. Becker (1932), p. 31.

12. Ibid.

13. Ibid., p. 73.

14. Ibid., p. 65.

15. Locke (1690/1947), Bk. I, Ch. II, Sec. I.

16. Hume (1779/1948), p. 134.

17. Hume (1777/1987), II, 94.

18. C. L. Becker (1932), p. 108.

19. Ibid., p. 118.

20. Ibid., p. 130.

21. Ibid., p. 161.

22. Ibid., p. 74.

23. Dawkins (1986).

24. C. L. Becker (1932), pp. 161–62.

25. Matthew 7:12.

26. See Singer (1982) on Hegel, p. 32.

27. Ibid., p. 33.

28. Nietzsche, *Daybreak*, p. 230.

29. Nietzsche, *Skirmishes of an Untimely Man*, 5, in Kaufman (1954), pp. 515–16. Tanner (1994), who provides a succinct and sympathetic account of Nietzsche's thought, also notes after quoting this passage that the Wittgensteinian contemporary philosopher Elizabeth Anscombe has made much the same point in ignorance of this precursor. See Tanner (1994), p. 34, and Anscombe (1968).

30. Hume (1740/1985), Bk. III, Pt. III, Sec. I, p. 640.

31. Ibid., Bk. III, Pt. II, Sec. I, p. 535.

32. Ibid., Bk. III, Pt. II, Sec. I, p. 551. Hume earlier has clearly set out the origins of morality as essential to control man's self-aggrandizing instincts to garner the gains from cooperation, as I have set out in Chapter 1. Thus Hume writes:

After men have found by experience, that their selfishness and confin'd generosity, acting at their liberty, totally incapacitate them for society; and at the same time have observed, that society is necessary to the satisfaction of those very passions, they are naturally induc'd to lay themselves under the restraint of such rules, as may render their commerce more safe and commodious.

He goes on to note that what would today be called reciprocal altruism in a repeated "prisoners dilemma game" will not work "when society has become numerous and has encreas'd to a tribe or a nation" and hence general moral rules emerge to prevent self-serving cheating so that even

when the injustice is so distant from us, as no way to affect our interest, it still displeases us; because we consider it as prejudicial to human society, and pernicious to every one that approaches the person guilty of it. We partake of their uneasiness by *sympathy*; and as everything which gives uneasiness in human actions, upon the general survey, is call'd Vice, and whatever produces satisfaction, in the same manner, is denominated Virtue; this is the reason why the sense of moral good and evil follows upon justice and injustice. (Ibid.)

33. Ibid.

34. One other aspect of the difference between the views of the sages of the Scottish and Continental Enlightenment needs to be noted: in the language of the eighteenth century the "enthusiasm" of the latter as contrasted by the "skepticism" of the former. The "enthusiasm" concerned the possibility of creating a new and better world based on reason. This view leads directly to the social engineering that has been a part of this particular liberal tradition, which in turn leads through other mutations to collectivism. But this particular divide in the legacy of the Enlightenment is better viewed through Oakeshott's spectacles, and will be taken up later. There was, however, one other divide in the liberal heritage, as has been noted by Skidelsky (1995), that fits in here. He notes that the nineteenth-century liberalism that emerged from the Enlightenment and the French Revolution had two partly conflicting aims, only one of which was compatible with individualism. The first sought to release the individual from social fetters, the second to disperse power. For liberal-conservatives like de Tocqueville the major aim was decentralizing power. It was not unfettered individualism they sought to promote but a moral order that could withstand the State's encroachment on liberty. He and the Scottish sages were at one in their aim to disperse power by attacking all forms of despotism, but not necessarily to release them from the tyranny of social custom. Though in the economic arena both groups would support the market, in ethics there was and continues to be a division between liberal social conservatism and libertarianism, depending upon the degree of unfettered individualism they see desirable in an unfettered private sphere.

35. C. L. Becker (1932), p. 164.

36. See Gellner (1993). Webster (1995), a more popular and prolix book, makes the same point and also provides a detailed indictment of Freud as a scientist. Kitcher (1995) provides a scholarly philosophical critique of Freud's science of the mind. Gay (1988) provides the "official" view of Freud's life and works. Also see Hale, Jr. (1995) for a limp defense of psychoanalysis not as a science but as the art of healing.

37. Gellner (1993), p. 36.

38. Gellner (1993), p. 34.

39. Sartre, *Huis Clos*.

40. Gellner (1993), p. 147.

41. Hayek (1979), vol. 3, p. 174, citing Chisholm (1946).

42. Ibid.

43. Douglas and Wildavsky (1983), p. 30.

44. Bramwell (1989), p. 23.

45. Ibid., p. 16.

46. Pepper (1984).

47. Bramwell (1989), p. 4.

48. See Birdsall (1989) for a review.

49. Douglas and Widavsky (1983), p. 125.

50. This section is based on Lal (1995a).

51. A recent history of Western political thought by McClelland (1996) is worth noting. McClelland finds a division in Western political thought with the Reformation. Before that, from Aristotle to Aquinas, it was assumed that there was community of men united in the "objects of their love." The purpose of politics was to create this good society. With the Reformation there was radical disagreement within communities about the ends of life. Locke's theory provided the answer. The ruler is ceded power to protect the life, liberty, and prosperity of his subjects. He does not legislate any particular view of the ends of life, an issue on which subjects can follow their own beliefs. The idea of limited government replaces the classical notion of a state that exists to promote the good life. The subsequent history of Western political thought has been a tussle between these "classical" and "modern" visions, with Rousseau, Hegel, Fichte, and Marx reviving classical arguments and attempting to find new "objects of love" around which communities could unite. This story is not very different from Oakeshott's.

52. Oakeshott (1993).

53. Ibid., p. 24.

54. Ibid., p. 25.

55. Ibid., p. 25.

56. Ibid., p. 25.

57. Oakeshott (1993), p. 27.

58. Hicks (1969), p. 99.

59. Sugden (1993), in his review of Sen (1992), makes much the same distinction between the two divergent views of public policy embodied in the technocratic "market failure" school and those of the neo-Austrians and the Virginia public choice school.

60. For instance by Sen (1992). That they cannot be reconciled in the way Sen proposes—by arguing that classical liberals, too, are egalitarians inasmuch as they are concerned with the equality of liberty—is cogently outlined by Sugden (1993).

61. See Lal-Myint (1996), on which much of this section is based.

62. See Aftalion (1990).

63. B. Anderson (1991).

64. B. Anderson (1991), p. 58.

65. Lynch, p. 276, emphasis added. Cited in B. Anderson (1991), p. 50.

66. Ibid., p. 42.

67. Seton Watson (1977), pp. 28–29, 48; Bloch (1961) vol. 1, pp. 75, 98.

68. B. Anderson (1991), p. 77.

69. Ibid.

70. Ibid., p. 81.

71. Seton Watson (1977), p. 148.

72. B. Anderson (1991), p. 85.

73. See Lal (1988), p. 112.

74. Toulmin, p. 161.

75. Ibid., p. 196.

76. Douglas and Wildavsky, p. 102.

77. Ibid., p. 123.

78. Schumpeter (1918).

79. See Hayek (1978a) and Lal (1994), chaps. 9 and 10.

80. The model of the predatory state is outlined in chap. 13.2 of Lal (1988), vol. 1, and in the Appendix to this book, whereas Lal (1994), chap. 13, shows how democratic states are likely to behave like predatory ones.

81. As he put it: "In a world governed by pressures of organized interests, we cannot count on benevolence, intelligence or understanding but only on sheer self-interest to give us the institutions we want. The insight and wisdom of Adam Smith stand today" (Hayek, 1990, p. 131).

82. See Lal (1994), chap. 9.

83. I may be influenced by the fact that I live part of the year in Los Angeles, where the daily business of domestic life seems increasingly to mirror the Middle Ages. Thus we live in a condominium that has armed guards and requires verified access to all apartments. The university where I work, a five-minute drive away, is similarly protected by the campus police. The only danger I suffer is in the public spaces I have to traverse going from my protected home to my protected workplace—in the form of carjackers, muggers, and other "highwaymen." But this is exactly how medieval life was conducted. The "palazzo" usually had a blank wall facing the street, with a narrow gate leading into the splendid private

dwelling. The public thoroughfares were unsafe owing to highway robbers, and you would have to take private guards to traverse dangerous public places. This is just like contemporary Los Angeles. With even the "respectable poor" demanding "gated" communities in the areas where they live, the reversion to the Middle Ages would seem to be around the corner! This, of course, is the result of the growing failure of overextended centralized states to provide the most basic public good—public order and safety—which was the primary justification for their creation. Their failure in this respect further undermines the "center" at the expense of the "border." The reasons for this strange denouement are addressed elliptically in Chapter 9.

Chapter 7

1. The following is based on Lal (1995b).

2. For India see Lal (1988).

3. Even though this is the result of administrative fiat, as Jenner (1992) documents.

4. See Hicks.

5. Lal (1988), chap. 13.2.

6. Lal (1988).

7. McNeill (1983), p. 49.

8. Rowe (1990), p. 243.

9. Weiner (1991).

10. See Lin (1990).

11. The problems with the Chinese data—which have sadly been used even by reputable international organizations like the World Bank—can be readily highlighted by looking at the implications of the World Bank estimates of per capita GNP and its growth rate between 1965 and 1990 in India and China. According to the World Bank (1992, World Development Indicators, Table 1), the average rate of growth of per capita income was 5.8 percent for China and 1.9 percent for India over this period. The level of per capita income in 1990 was $370 for China and $350 for India. These figures imply that per capita incomes in China in 1965 could only have been 41 percent of India's. As Srinivasan rightly comments, "No knowledgeable analyst of the two countries would subscribe to this relative value of China's GNP per capita in 1965! A plausible explanation for these paradoxical figures is that the figure of $370 in 1990 as China's per capita GNP reflects the consideration that a more realistic figure might soon make China ineligible for loans from IDA, the soft loan affiliate of the World Bank" (p. 5). See also Lardy, appendix B, and Malenbaum (1990).

Nor has the scholarly discussion reached any measure of agreement; see Rawski (1989), Ma and Garnaut (1992), Kumar (1992), Dernberger and Eckaus (1987), and Malenbaum (1990). For the base period, 1950, the most plausible inference is Kumar's: "The per capita income of both India and China was very low in 1949 and given the margin of error, it is not worth arguing about which country was the poorer" (Kumar [1992], p. 30). Furthermore, the distortions in the Chinese relative price structure where there were few links between prices and the respective marginal rates of substitution in consumption or of transformation in production, make any inferences of Chinese productive capacity or welfare from its GNP at domestic prices highly dubious. Purchasing power parity estimates of Chinese GDP have however been made by Heston et al., and by Maddison, and are summarized in Lal (1995b),

Table 1. Given all the problems surrounding the basic data and the price comparisons made, these can at best provide broad orders of magnitude, and of the two, in my judgment, the Maddison estimates ring truer!

These problems of estimating Chinese GDP are compounded by problems in estimating its population. The only proper censuses in China were in 1982 and 1990. All earlier estimates are based on partial surveys. Moreover the numbers emerging from the recent 1990 census are marred by the underreporting of female births due to the "one child" population policy; see Yi et al. (1993).

12. Srinivasan (1993), p. 20.

13. World Bank (1983), Table 3.19.

14. Srinivasan (1993), p. 18.

15. See Lal (1995b) for details of the reform process in both countries till early 1995, and also for an extensive bibliography.

16. This crisis, which threatened international bankruptcy for India, and the response to it was a replay of dramas enacted in many parts of Latin America in the 1980s. I have charted the anatomy of this cycle of economic repression—macroeconomic crisis—reform elsewhere, in greater detail (Lal [1987], [1993], Lal and Myint [1996]). Two points, however, that are relevant for my present purposes may be noted. First, these are fiscal crises caused by the unsustainability of the vast system of politically determined entitlements to income streams created by past dirigisme in the microeconomy. Second they arise when all possible means of financing them seem to be at an end. One means is through taxation. But tax revenues are less than buoyant both because growth has been damaged by the productivity damaging effects of dirigisme and because of the inescapable rise of the "black" economy as more and more seek to escape the taxed economy. With entitlements growing, at some stage a fiscal deficit will emerge. This can only be financed by three means: internal borrowing, external borrowing, or levying the inflation tax. Given underdeveloped domestic capital markets, internal borrowing is limited. So the usual option is to increase foreign borrowing. India did this, and in an echo of China (but with important differences in the form) tried to tap the riches of its worldwide diaspora (nonresident Indians, or NRIs). But as in Latin America this capital inflow was short term and hence volatile. With the continuing political instability and little sign of improvement in the productivity and hence capacity to repay of the economy, these investors are at some stage likely to take fright—as the NRIs did, leading to the balance-of-payments crisis that triggered the latest Indian reforms. This leaves only the inflationary tax. But this too is unsustainable, as economic agents take countervailing action—in a democracy as inflation-shy as the Indian, also through the ballot box! The ensuing crisis appears as a balance of payments and fiscal crisis, and it provides a small window of opportunity for radical reform. This, at the most basic level, involves rescinding all the politically determined entitlements created by dirigisme—and therein lies the rub. For the losers already know who they are, whereas the gainers from the increased productivity that results from liberalization are potential, that is, unknown. For this reason I have been an advocate of a "big bang" when a crisis presents an opportunity for reform.

17. It is worth noting that China's growth rate has been about twice India's. This is because of differences in the rate of investment, which in 1990 was nearly 40 percent of GDP in China as compared with 23 percent in India. There is little evidence that the productivity of investment (and changes in it due to the reforms that have so far taken place) are all that different in the two countries. Thus for China, according to the World Bank, total factor productivity in agriculture and industry combined declined at an annual rate of −1.41 percent between 1957 and 65, rose at only 0.62 percent during 1965−76, and in the reform era

(1980–88) grew at 2.4 percent in the state sector, 4.63 percent in the collective sector, and 6.44 percent in the agricultural sector (World Bank [1992], Table 2.3). Given the statistical difficulties outlined earlier these can not be taken as hard figures but merely as indicating trends. For India, Ahluwalia's estimates for industry indicate that total factor productivity in manufacturing grew at 3.4 percent in the first half of the 1980s as compared with a decline of 0.3 percent per annum in the previous fifteen years.

18. *The Economist*, Nov. 13, 1992 L.A. survey, p. 14.

19. See, e.g., Lal (1988), Bhagwati (1993).

20. See Pocock (1975), Lal (1993, chap. 2).

21. One straw in the wind is the very different reaction that prime minister V. P. Singh's desire to implement the Mandal Report on caste reservations in government jobs evoked from the universities, compared with the virtual silence that greeted the Rao government's actual implementation of the report on instructions from the Supreme Court. Some commentators in India have suggested that with the liberalization undertaken in 1991, job prospects in the private sector look much brighter to the upper-caste young than do those in the public sector, so the policy of reservations is of lesser relevance to their future!

22. E.g., the Ambani group.

23. See Fiszbein, Diwan.

24. Thus *The Economist* (August 6, 1994) reported: "State governments are now bust, largely because they are getting less cash from Delhi, and bankruptcy is now driving radical change.... Uttar Pradesh, India's largest state, has raised power tariffs sharply, put 28 sugar mills up for sale and outlined plans to privatize power generation and distribution. The chief minister of Madhya Pradesh proposes to sack 28,000 workers. Several other states are privatizing loss-making companies and cutting payrolls" (p. 50).

25. But see Baum's reconstruction of the palace struggles during Deng's ascendancy.

26. Evans (1993).

27. Ibid., p. 146.

28. Ibid., p. 236.

29. Ibid., p. 219.

30. See Baum (1994).

31. As Baum notes, by the early 1990s, "with the center controlling a steadily diminishing share of the nation's material and fiscal resources, Beijing's relations with the provinces had come to resemble a semi-anarchic game of mutual bargaining, backscratching, and bickering, rather than a hierarchical game of centralized command and control" (p. 328).

32. Lin et al. (1994) note:

After the reforms a market price existed, legally or illegally, along with a planned price for almost every kind of input or commodity that the State controlled. The difference between the market price and the planned price was economic rent. It is estimated that the economic rent from the controlled commodity price, the interest rate, and the exchange rate was at least 200 billion yuan, about 21.5 percent of the national income in 1988. In 1992 the economic rent from bank loans alone reached 220 billion yuan. (p. 20)

Baum notes that by October 1992, through the anticorruption drive launched in 1990, "the cumulative total had risen to 733,543 party cadres disciplined for economic corruption, of whom 154,289 were expelled from the party" (p. 317).

33. Thus, Baum notes, "According to foreign intelligence estimates, extra budgetary resources generated approximately Y 30 billion in military income in 1992—accounting for almost half the PLA's total outlays" (p. 379).

34. One straw in the wind is the report (*Daily Telegraph*, September 20, 1994, p. 12) that "worried that the relaxation of communist ideology has left Chinese youth drifting, the nation has embarked on a moral education campaign that combines patriotism with old fashioned Confucian values." The important unanswered question is whether Dengism represents the last throw of a dynasty about to lose the mandate of heaven, or a revitalization of the existing dynasty by embracing a mercantile culture.

Chapter 8

1. And given the role of the Chinese business families in their economies, this should also include Indonesia, Malaysia, and Thailand.

2. See Young (1992), Little (1994).

3. See Lal (1994), chap. 7.

4. See World Bank (1993).

5. See Demsetz (1995), chap. 3. He defines the problem as "the inability of owners of a corporation that is very diffusely owned to be motivated or empowered to discipline the professional management that runs the firm" (p. 42).

6. See Young.

7. Jenner (1992), p. 172.

8. Ibid., p. 170.

9. Ibid., pp. 172–73.

10. Pye (1985).

11. Morishima (1982).

12. Vogel (1991).

13. Whyte (1996).

14. Berger (1988) claims that Weber was just wrong.

15. See, for instance, Greif.

16. Hicks (1969).

17. I was impressed by this emerging world division of labor on meeting a number of managers of these virtual factories in California. The growing importance of shifting and volatile "designer" consumer goods was impressed upon me when I went to buy some socks at my local department store in Los Angeles. I was offered a virtual feast of designer label socks, and nothing else. What is more, although each sock had its "Western" designer's logo, inside

a label announced the sock was made "in China" or "in Malaysia" or some other Third World country.

This emerging pattern of the international division of labor also explains the emerging problems that the West is facing in the globalized economy. For the West, which is increasingly the "design" center in this world market for "bespoke" consumer goods, human capital is the source of its comparative advantage. This has raised the premium on education at each level of education as shown by rates of return calculations in the United States. It also explains the stagnation of real wages of the low skilled in the United States and the high unemployment rates in the European Union. As the Fordist industries, as much as the production of "designer" consumer goods shifts to the relatively low labor-cost producers in the labor-abundant economies of the Third World, the West will have to live by its wits, in the highly variegated, human capital-intensive service activities of the "design centers."

18. It is worth noting that as Whyte (1996) summarizing the evidence shows, many aspects of the traditional Chinese family have altered. These are mainly connected with the greatly improved status of women, with fewer joint families, decline in parentally arranged marriages, increased female participation in the labor force outside the home, and the sharp decline in fertility. Nevertheless, some features have not changed: universal marriage still is the norm, extended families are overwhelmingly patrilocal, and "even though there is some increase in older Chinese living by themselves, still the great majority of Chinese spend their final years living with a grown child and his or her (usually his) family." The most important aspect of families that has not changed is "the overwhelming loyalty that Chinese in all settings continue to feel toward their families. Obligations to the larger family are heavily stressed in child socialization in all of these Chinese locales, and young people seem to accept the message and fulfil its obligation" (pp. 16–17).

19. Jones (1988), p. 154.

20. Ibid., p. 153.

21. "The index of total area of paddy-fields rises from 91 in about 930 A.D. to 100 in c. 1450, and steeply to 173 in c. 1600. Under the Tokugawa the gains were greater still, the index reaching 314 in c. 1720. Thereafter the areal expansion was much slower, and reached only 322 by 1874" (Jones 153).

22. Morishima (1982), p. 9.

23. Ibid., p. 35.

24. Jones (1988), p. 153.

25. Ibid., p. 155.

26. Ibid., p. 162.

27. Ibid., p. 165.

28. Morishima (1982), p. 16.

29. Ibid., p. 7.

30. See Lal (1993), chap. 2.

31. Ibid., p. 196.

32. Ibid., p. 18.

33. See K. van Wolferen (1989), S. N. Eisenstadt (1996).

34. C. Gluck (1985) provides the best account of this creation of Japan's modern myths. Also see Waswo (1996).

35. van Wolferen (1989), p. 302.

36. Masao (1964), p. 33.

37. van Wolferen (1989), p. 307.

38. van Wolferen gives an interesting reason for this affiliation. It was connected with the unequal treaties that Japan had to sign on its opening to the West. These included deeply resented provisions of extraterritoriality, which

the foreigners were ready to scrap ... if and when legal trials could be conducted by a competent judiciary. It was the desperate need this created that launched Todai. Its graduates did not, initially, need to pass the civil service exams in order to fill the highest posts, and by 1890 their supply was large enough to fill nearly all administrative vacancies and more than half the judicial vacancies. (1989, p. 308)

39. As van Wolferen notes (Ibid., pp. 155–57).

40. See van Wolferen (1989), Eisenstadt (1996), and Waswo (1996).

41. Patrick and Rosovsky (1976).

42. Emmott (1989).

43. See Tsuru (1993) for a lucid account of the genesis and denouement of Japanese corporatism, or, as I prefer to call it, "crony capitalism."

44. Emmott (1989), p. 264.

45. Scott (1989), Table 16.1.

46. See Ponnuru (1995), Dick (1995).

47. In a very perceptive analysis of "social and cultural factors in Japanese economic growth," Nathan Glazer notes that even if one accepts the difference between Japan and the West as painted by Benedict and Nakane, "a difference exhibited in a net of obligations that binds individuals together and makes strong institutions of the family, principally, but by extension of the school and workplace" (p. 816); this does not explain why these "traditional values of Japan were suited to economic growth, while not so dissimilar values of other societies were not" (p. 817). In particular he cites India and Japan and argues that in fact the differences in the "verticality" in Indian and Japanese "traditional" values would prima facie have favored India. As he notes: "Can the specific differences in social structure and values explain the difference in economic outcome? The suspicion cannot be ignored that if it were India that had turned out an economic success and Japan an economic failure, the ingenious social scientist, also could have explained these outcomes by the two different kinds of verticality in these two societies" (p. 817).

48. Benedict (1946).

49. See Nakane (1972) for an account of how the traditional hierarchical basis of the "shame society" has merely been adapted to the modern world of meritocracy and bureaucracy in both business and government. Even Reischauer (1977), who has been at points to paint Japan as a "normal" country, notes that there is considerable validity in the concept that Japan has a shame rather than guilt culture, "that is shame before the judgment of society is a

stronger conditioning force than guilt over sin in the eyes of God" (p. 142). Conversely, van Wolferen notes that "to understand [the Japanese] moral world one must imagine a situation in which good behavior is constantly determined by individuals' views of how others expect them to behave; in which they can never think 'To hell with them'; and in which conformity to social expectations is not an unfortunate compromise but the only possible way to live" (p. 327).

Both authors also emphasize the absence of any faith in individualism. Thus Reischauer states, "The word "individualism" itself has always been in ill repute in Japan. It suggests to the Japanese selfishness rather than personal responsibility" (p. 160). van Wolferen also notes the ambivalence of the Japanese on individualism (p. 291) and remarks that it goes back to Tokugawa ideology. "In their world-view the moral autonomy of the individual person did not exist; this was the core of the ideology" (p. 256).

50. Ekman (1972). Friesen (1972), cited in Matsumoto (1996), also provides further evidence garnered by social psychologists that points to the "communalist" and shame-based nature of Japanese society.

51. Matsumoto (1996), p. 45.

52. See Matsumoto (1996), for references, along with the studies cited in Chapter 1.

53. See Rosenberger (1992), particularly the introduction and the essay by J. Tobin. See also Tobin, Wu, and Davidson (1989) for an empirical study of preschooling in Japan, China, and the United States.

54. I have found the social psychologists evidence much more persuasive than the shifting position adopted by sociologists and anthropologists on the defining characteristics of Japanese society. The major writings of the latter are Nakane (1972), Doi (1973), (1985), and the collections in Lebra and Lebra (1974) and Rosenberger (1992). As we saw in Chapter 1, the anthropologists' flip-flop on the shame-guilt distinction has also spread to their interpretation of Japanese society, for which it was initially invented by their forebears, Benedict and Mead. It is now being claimed by Lebra (in Rosenberger 1992) that Japan is also a guilt society, in which shame is internalized as guilt. But for the reasons set out in Chapter 1 this will not do, inasmuch as it fails to recognize the very different triggers to these distinct emotions.

55. Related by S. N. Eisenstadt at a colloquium on "Culture, Democracy and Development" at UCLA on Nov. 22–23, 1996.

56. MacIntyre (1990), p. 491.

57. Ibid., p. 492.

58. Ibid.

59. Ibid.

60. Ibid., pp. 493–94.

61. Ibid., p. 495.

62. Ibid., p. 496.

63. Waswo (1996) makes this point lucidly and forcefully.

64. Glazer (1976), pp. 860–61.

65. Ibid., p. 861.

Chapter 9

1. Elias, (1978).

2. See also Hirschman (1977).

3. Thus, he states, "The feeling of shame is a specific excitation, a kind of anxiety which is automatically reproduced in the individual on certain occasions by force of habit," and that "no less characteristic of a civilizing process than 'rationalization' is the peculiar molding of the drive economy that we call 'shame' and 'repugnance' or embarrassment'" (vol. II, pt. I, Ch. VI, p. 492).

4. Mill (1910), p. 118.

5. Himmelfarb (1995), p. 86; Nietzsche (1967), p. 21 (no. 30), p. 186 (no. 340); Nietzsche (1954), pp. 515–16 (no. 5).

6. Himmelfarb (1995).

7. Lipset (1996) is a restatement of this element of American exceptionalism, which his triumphalist book acclaims even though recognizing that it is as the subtitle of his book states a double-edged sword.

8. De Tocqueville (1835/1956).

9. Myrdal (1964). It should be noted that the question of race, the American dilemma discussed by Myrdal still continues to haunt America. It would take me too far afield to discuss this in any depth. But see Lipset (1996) for an empirical survey of what has happened to blacks in general since Myrdal wrote; Tucker and Mitchell-Kernan (1995) on the black family; W. J. Wilson (1987) on the underclass; and Smith and Welch (1986) on black economic progress. Many of the issues touched upon on the cultural aspects of the welfare state of course apply with particular force to the black "underclass."

10. See Engerman and Sokoloff (1994), Solow (1991).

11. See Appendix 4.

12. See Engerman and Sokoloff (1994) and Solow (1991) For evidence on the substantial economies in producing certain crops on large slave plantations see Fogel (1989), Engerman (1983), and Deer (1949).

13. That factor endowments rather than culture influenced the development of these different types of societies in the Americas is fascinatingly illustrated by the case of the Puritan colony of Providence Island, which followed the Caribbean and Latin American pattern of land ownership and settlement than the North American one of its other brethren. See Kupperman (1993).

14. But as Barbara Solow, who explicitly uses the Domar model of an economy with abundant land outlined in Appendix 4, notes, with few land rents there cannot be economic growth as Wakefield (1829/1969) claimed. As labor garners all the returns to land, there would merely be a replication of family farms as the labor supply grows through natural increase or immigration. The returns to capital are potentially very high, "but they cannot be realized without the supply of labor to capitalist landlords that is not forthcoming" (Solow, p. 34). Slavery as in the American South provides the necessary surplus to generate growth, as did the tariff advocated by Hamilton in industrializing the North. The democracy of independent yeoman lauded by Jefferson could maintain its cosmological beliefs even as its

material basis was undermined by Promethean growth. "As Wakefield put it succinctly: In the North the tariff, and in the South slavery, prevent America from becoming Jefferson's republic of independent yeomen, a republic that would be incapable of rapid economic development" (Solow [1991], p. 38).

15. Engerman and Sokoloff (1994) have argued that "substantial differences in the degree of inequality in wealth, human capital, and political power" account for the "variation in the records of growth" of the United States and Canada vis-à-vis other New World economies. I would contest this view. As the Lal-Myint study, which examined the role of different factor endowments and relative degrees of inequality in explaining economic performance across a large number of developing countries found, whereas the former made a difference the latter did not. Moreover, the relatively worse performance of some (but not all) natural-resource abundant countries was found to depend upon the politicization of the natural-resource rents that accrue. There was no association one way or the other between changes in inequality and growth rates.

16. L. Dumont (1970), p. 16.

17. Vol. 1, p. 359.

18. Ibid., p. 361.

19. See Bellah et al. (1986), pp. 237–48.

20. Ibid., p. 359.

21. De Tocqueville (1956), vol. 2, p. 552.

22. Thus Bellah et al. (1986) note, "some 40% of Americans attend religious services at least once a week (a much greater number than would be found in Western Europe or even Canada) and religious membership is around 60% of the total population" (p. 219).

23. Lipset (1996) also uses these figures of church attendance and religious beliefs to show how the processes of cementing society in the nineteenth century noted by de Tocqueville are still active.

24. Fuchs (1991) notes, "When Tocqueville asked what made the Americans a nation, he answered that American patriotism was not based on ancient customs and traditions as in other countries. Patriotism in the U.S., he wrote "grows by the exercise of 'civil rights'. What he called the 'patriotism' of a republic was based on the premise that it is possible to interest men (and women) in the welfare of their country by making them participants in its government, and by so doing to enlist their enthusiastic loyalty to the national community" (p. 3). Almond and Verba (1963) labeled the American political culture as a "civic culture" in which "there is a substantial consensus on the legitimacy of political institutions and the direction and content of public policy, a widespread tolerance of a plurality of interests and belief in their reconcilability, and a widely distributed sense of political competence and mutual trust in the citizenry" (Almond and Verba [1980], p. 179). Fuchs states:

this new invention of America—voluntary pluralism—in which individuals ... who comport themselves as good citizens of the civic culture are free to differ from each other in religion and in other aspects of their private lives ... was sanctioned and protected by a unifying civic culture based on the American founding myth, its institutions, heroes, rules and rhetoric.... [Even after the new immigrants were no longer English and Scots] political principle remained the core of national community. The new immigrants entered a process of ethnic-Americanization through participation in the political system, and, in so doing, established even more clearly the American civic culture as a basis of American unity. (pp. 5–6)

25. As de Tocqueville notes:

In America ... the local community was organized before the county, the county before the state, and the state before the Union.... The towns appointed their own magistrates of all sorts, assessed themselves, and imposed their own taxes. The New England towns adopted no representative institutions. As at Athens, matters of common concern were dealt with in the market place and in the general assembly of the citizens.... They had a higher and more comprehensive conception of the duties of society towards its members than had the law-givers of Europe at that time, and they imposed obligations upon it which were shirked else-where.... [Among these] it is the provisions for public education which, from the very first, throw into clearest relief the originality of American civilization. (vol. 1, pp. 51–52)

26. De Tocqueville (1956), vol. 1, pp. 54–55.

27. See the previous note. The epigraph from de Tocqueville at the beginning of this book is from his chapter "Honor," in which he contrasted "that honor or shame [which] attach[ed] to a man's action's according to his condition—that was the result of the very existence of an aristocratic ordering of society" ([1956] vol. 2, p. 800) with that of a nation like America "in which it is hard to discover a trace of class distinctions, honor will then be limited to a few precepts, and these precepts will draw continually closer to the moral laws accepted by humanity in general" (Ibid., p. 807). Among these he identified three, which were particularly associated with "what one might call the contemporary American conception of honor" (p. 804). The first of these is chastity (see p. 850); the second is courage "which makes a man almost insensible to the loss of a fortune laboriously acquired and prompts him instantly to fresh exertions to gain another" (p. 806); and the third is not to be idle—for "in a democratic society ... where fortunes are small and insecure, everybody works, and work opens all doors. That circumstance has made the point of honor do an about turn and set it facing against idleness" (Ibid.). As argued later in the text, the sexual and cultural revolution of the 1960s has greatly undermined all these three sources of "honor and shame" in the United States.

28. Daniel Bell notes that there was a dramatic shift in the 1960s in attitudes on the influence of religion. Whereas in April 1957 only 14 percent thought it was losing its influence, in April 1962 31 percent and by April 1968 68 percent thought it was. Bell comments: "what is striking ... is that this shift of mood parallels the years of the Kennedy and Johnson admin-istrations, the years of the New Frontier and the Great Society" (pp. 186–87).

29. Lipset (1996), however, notes that a study by Sol Tax found that "as of 1968, the Viet-nam War rated as our *fourth* 'least popular' conflict with a foreign enemy. Large numbers of Americans refused to support the War of 1812, the Mexican War, the Civil War, World War I, and the Korean War" (Lipset, p. 65).

30. Daniel Bell, like so many other U.S. commentators, finds the Vietnam War the turning point. "In most countries," he writes, "there is a distinction between the nation and the administration in office. One can be opposed to a *government* yet not call into question one's allegiance to the *nation*. In the United States the distinction has never been necessary because the government reflected a broad consensus. Yet during the Vietnam War, the rejection of the government led many to reject the nation" (p. 190).

31. Arthur Schlesinger documents this trend and provides a trenchant critique.

32. Edmund Burke realized this when he wrote: "Men are qualified for civil liberty in exact proportion to their disposition to put moral chains upon their own appetites.... Society can-not exist unless a controlling power upon will and appetite be placed somewhere, and the less of it there is within, the more there must be without." Cited in Himmelfarb (1994), p. 51.

33. See Schlesinger (1992).

34. See Fukuyama (1995).

35. See Putnam (1995).

36. Siedentop (1996) claims that one of the unintended consequences of Thatcher's revolution in Britain was that it attacked the old social hierarchies, including meritocratic ones like
the law and the academy. "Just as post-revolutionary French social thinkers had to contemplate a new world without deference, so Britain today is having, at last, to contemplate
such a world. For Thatcherism, whatever it intended, and whatever else it achieved,
destroyed the British *ancien regime*" (p. 3). The social cement provided by shame in a hierarchical society is dissolving in the United Kingdom, as it has already, for different reasons,
in the United States.

37. See Himmelfarb (1994), D. Green (1993), Etzioni (1993).

38. The most eloquent is Himmelfarb (1994). But also see J. Q. Wilson (1993), Bennett
(1993), Dennis and Erdos (1993).

39. From the *Los Angeles Times*, Nov. 9, 1995, p. A17.

40. Goody (1996) questions any cross-cultural variations in the provision of these public
safety nets, which have existed in the West from about the thirteenth century; see Smith
(1979). He rightly claims that there was "public provision for the poor under earlier Christianity outside Northwest Europe, as well as under Jewish, Parsi, Jain, Muslim and Buddhist
dispensations. The idea that only Northwest Europe was charitable to the aged poor outside
the family is a myth that derives from ethnocentric preoccupations with the nature of the
'uniqueness of the West' and of Christian *caritas*" (p. 10). This is no doubt correct, and all
societies have made public provisions for destitutes who cannot be supported by relatives.
The relevant question is a quantitative one: were there more of these public social safety nets
in the West because of the family revolution than in the Rest? Until some quantitative evidence is produced of the relative incidence of public charity in the two "areas" I find the
inductive argument flowing from Goody's (1983) own delineation of the papal family revolution, would support the case made for differences between the West and the rest, e.g., by
Hajnal (1982).

41. See Green (1993).

42. Murray (1984) remains the most powerful indictment on this score.

43. Ralph Harris (1988) provides the most concise and eloquent statement of this charge.

44. See Lal and Wolf (1986).

45. PH, pp. 2–13.

46. See, e.g., Barr (1992).

47. But see Lal (1993b).

48. The term is due to Demsetz (1969). For an explication in terms of the recent controversy
surrounding the minimum wage see Lal (1995a).

49. As Platteau (1991) concludes:

Even though empirical evidence is scanty (but not altogether absent), the case can reasonably
be made that, barring exceptionally unfavorable circumstances (such as repeated crop failures

or crop diseases affecting entire communities), traditional methods for controlling the risk of falling into distress have usually enabled the people to counter natural and other hazards in a rather effective way. (p. 156)

50. Cox and Jimenez (1990) remark

For example, among a sample of urban poor in El Salvador, 33% reported having received private transfers, and income from private transfers accounted for 39% of total income among recipients. Ninety-three percent of a rural south Indian sample received transfers from other households. In Malaysia, private transfers accounted for almost half the income of the poorest households. Nearly three quarters of rural households in Java, Indonesia, gave private transfers to other households. About half of a sample of Filipino households received private cash transfers. (p. 206)

Also see Rempel and Lobdell (1978), Knowles and Anker (1981), Collier and Lal (1986), Oberai et. al. (1980), and Lucas and Stark (1985) on the significant size and effects of remittances within the rural and between the rural and urban sectors in Ghana, Liberia, Nigeria, Pakistan, Tanzania, Kenya, India, and Botswana.

51. See G. Swamy (1981).

52. The rotten kid theorem states that

when one member [of a family] cares sufficiently about other members to be the head, all members have the same motivation as the head to maximize family opportunities and to internalize fully all within-family "externalities," regardless of how selfish (or, indeed, how envious) these members are. Even a selfish child receiving transfers from his parents would automatically consider the effects of his actions on other siblings as well as his parents. Put still differently, sufficient "love" by one member guarantees that all members act as if they loved other members as much as themselves. (G. Becker [1976], p. 270)

53. Warr (1983) and Bernheim and Bagwell (1988) go further and show that as "propagation requires the participation of two traditionally unrelated individuals ... there will be a proliferation of linkages between families." This gives rise to even stronger neutrality results.

In particular, no government transfer (including those between unrelated members of the same generation) has any real effect, and all tax instruments (including so-called distortionary taxes) are equivalent to lump sum taxes. In essence, the government can affect the allocation of real resources only by altering real expenditures. The efficiency role of government is thus severely limited, and the distributional role is entirely eliminated. More generally ... if all linkages between parents and children are truly operative, then market prices play no role in the resource allocation process: the distribution of goods is determined by the nature of intergenerational altruism. (Bernheim and Bagwell [1988], pp. 309–10)

54. See Kotlikoff and Spivak (1981), Bernheim et al. (1985).

55. They found that the prediction of the pure altruism model that lower-income households will receive higher transfers is not borne out, and that instead, as the exchange model predicts, there is "a positive association between amount remitted and per capita income of the household from other sources" (Lucas and Stark [1985], p. 910). For in the exchange model the "greater wealth of the family should increase its relative bargaining strength" (Ibid., p. 906), and thus leads to a higher demand on its "migrants."

But, as Lucas and Stark recognize, their data—which is cross-sectional—does not allow the altruistic motive for transfers to be tested in a dynamic context. Rosenzweig (1988) does so. In a longitudinal study of six villages in three different agroclimatic regions in the semi-arid tropics of India he found that kinship in a risky world not only tends to bond family members in a single location (in a particular way) but kinship ties are able to be sustained over time and space in implicit insurance-based transfer schemes which contribute to consumption smoothing in the face of covariant income risks. (p. 1167)

It is kinship, and common (family) experiences [which] induce trust, knowledge and altruism among family members,[hence] such income pooling implicit contracts maybe feasible even if spread across wide areas. (p. 1152)

The results of this study can also help explain the difference in systems of marriage and the family between the north and south in both India and China surveyed in Goody (1990). Broadly speaking, there tends to be greater "in-marriage" to close kin in the south than in the north. Goody rightly notes that, this is related to differences in productive systems in the two regions, in both countries, the South being primarily an irrigated rice-producing area, the north a primarily rainfed wheat- and millet-producing area. What he fails to note is that, in addition to the extra demand for female labor in rice cultivation as compared with wheat—which in itself would tend to enhance female status in the south as compared with the north—the differences in village level exogamy in the two regions could also be explained by the differences in climatic uncertainty and its impact on agricultural output and thence household incomes in the two regions. Given the spatial and temporal variability of rainfall, the northern regions in both countries would have a greater risk of a particular village suffering a climate-related fall in output. By marrying their daughters out of the village, the parents would thus ensure that as long as the rains did not fail over a whole region, they would be able to call on her relatives for succor when they suffered a climate-induced fall in output, whereas their daughter's relatives did not. By contrast, this need for insuring against climatic risk would be less acute in the irrigated areas of the South. This, along with the greater demand for female labor in rice cultivation, would provide sufficient incentives to keep daughters in situ by marrying them to close kin, who would be local. The differences in the dowry systems (movables in the north, immovables—mainly land—in the south) as well as differences in the life expectancies of girls (higher in the south than the north), surveyed by Goody would then also follow as part of the appropriate "heirship strategies" in the two different ecological environments.

Furthermore, as the crucible of "high" culture in both India and China was in the north (the Indo-Gangetic plain in India, the hinterland of the Yellow River in China), the domestic customs codified in their great traditions would reflect those deriving from the more climatically challenged regions of their birth. The "looser" customs of their more recent colonized Southern cousins would then appear at odds—and they do—with the respective "grand traditions."

56. As Cox and Jimenez (1990) summarize it:

Some studies find an inverse relation between recipients' resources and transfer amounts received (for instance Kaufman and Lindauer for El Salvador, Kaufman for the Philippines, Ravaillon and Dearden for rural households in Java, and Tomes for bequests in the U.S.) But others (Lucas and Stark for Botswana, Cox for [inter vivos transfers in] the U.S., Ravaillon and Dearden for urban households in Java, and Cox and Jimenez for Peru), find a positive relation, which contradicts the altruism hypothesis. (p. 216)

57. Cox and Jimenez (1992).

58. Cox and Jimenez (1993).

59. As they state:

part of the reason for the low estimates of the degree of crowding out of private transfers by public ones might be due to the fact that the estimates discussed above are derived in environments [in OECD countries] where public transfers are already substantial. These transfers may have already crowded out private transfers to a large extent, rendering the small samples of private recipients uninformative. In contrast, the Philippines has almost no public welfare payments, which makes it an ideal case study for gauging the strength of private transfers. (Cox and Jimenez [1993], p. 6)

60. Ibid., p. 19.

61. Cox and Jimenez (1990), p. 216.

62. See Lal and Wolf (1986).

63. Jimenez (1989).

64. Ibid., p. 114.

65. Evans and Schwab (1995).

66. See also Coleman and Hoffer (1987), Coleman, Hoffer and Kilgore (1982).

67. See Goodin and LeGrand (1987). For references to studies of other Western welfare states see Lal (1994), chap. 15, and Lal and Myint (1996), chap. 9.

68. World Bank (1992a), Box 3.4.

69. Another piece of evidence is provided by a simple regression I ran on the state-level data on per capita public expenditure on health and education between 1976 and 1986 and the changes in literacy rates and life expectancy and infant mortality rates for India, given in Ravallion and Subbarow (1992). In these cross-sections I found that there was no statistically significant relationship between changes in state level health expenditures and health outcomes, and a statistically significant negative relationship between changes in educational expenditure and literacy!

70. See Ahmad (1991) for a representative exemplar of this type of viewpoint.

71. World Bank (1992a), Box A3.5.

72. See Goodin and Le Grand (1987).

73. See Stigler (1970), Meltzer and Richard (1981), Peltzman (1980).

74. See Mesa-Lago (1983, 1990) for Latin America.

75. Posner (1992), p. 324.

76. The econometric evidence for the United States on the effects of the welfare system on incentives is summarized in Danziger et al. (1981) and Moffit (1992). The latter also incorporates many of the findings of the former. Moffits concludes:

The literature on the incentive effects of the U.S. welfare system ... has shown unequivocal evidence of effects on labor supply, participation in the welfare system and on some aspects of family structure.... Yet the review has also shown that the importance of these effects is limited in many respects. The labor supply effects, whilst statistically significant, are not large enough to explain the high rates of poverty among female heads.... In addition the econometric estimates of family structure effects are not large enough to explain long-run declines in marriage rates and, in any case, are incapable of explaining recent upward trends in female headship because welfare benefits have been declining.... Some of the evidence assembled in the review suggests that family-structure issues appear to be at least as important in understanding the economic status of low income female heads as labor supply issues.... Unfortunately, the research on family structure remains in its infancy compared to the voluminous research on labor supply. (pp. 56–57)

77. Magnet, pp. 31–32.

78. Phelps-Brown (1983), pp. 155–56; Scott (1989), p. 475.

79. Scott (1989), p. 522.

80. See Himmelfarb (1995).

81. Himmelfarb (1994), p. 244.

82. Magnet, p. 19.

83. Murray (1994).

84. Lipset (1996), in his Panglossian account of American exceptionalism, underplays the significance of the underclass by saying it only amounts to about 1–2 percent of the U.S. population: about 2–3 million people (p. 134). This is, of course, a number larger than in the U.S. armed forces. If the latter, though less than 1 percent of the populace, were let loose in the inner cities as invading armies often were in the bad old days, even Lipset might, one hopes, have some trepidation.

85. Ahmad (1991), p. 106.

86. It is worth noting that the first people of the Book—the Jews—do not seem to have suffered a breakdown in traditional family values with secularization to the same extent as their Christian cousins. This is due in part to the "ghetto" mentality created by their diaspora. As a beleaguered minority, the family was often the only institution they could look to for support.

87. See O. Harris (1987) and my earlier chapters on India and Japan. Goody (1990), in his survey of the ethnographic material on Chinese and Indian families, notes that, based on surveys of present-day Taiwan, in the Sinic world household size has decreased, but "family size" has increased. "'Family size' refer to the number of persons belonging to the group that in India would be called a Hindu Undivided Family ... which comprises the descendants who still retain joint rights in a particular estate" (p. 87).

88. As we saw in chapter 5, the West is the only civilization to give free play to the basic passion of "romantic love," with all its implications in terms of family breakdown and serial monogamy. For the Western telecommuting elite, a settled family life may not be of great importance, but for others who need to work in one place broken family lives could pose a problem.

89. As the Ayatollah Khomeini's *fatwah* against Salman Rushdie so vividly demonstrated.

Chapter 10

1. This point is also noted by Gellner (1988), who writes,

The only cultures which adopted economic, cognitive and technological rationality "rationally", i.e., instrumentally, did so because the pioneer societies had already shown these to be effective. But for that very reason, they need not be pervaded by the rational spirit in other aspects of their lives. They chose economic and technical rationality as a *means*. It did not in their case emerge as a by-product of a general cast of mind.... Those who adopt the new ways in the opportunistic emulative spirit may maintain or develop cultures quite different from those of disenchantment. The computer and the shrine may be compatible. (p. 222)

2. M. Harris (1989) notes that Donald Johanson, who discovered her skeleton in 1973, named her "Lucy, evoking the then popular Beatles song 'Lucy in the Sky with Diamonds', itself a cryptogram for mind-altering LSD" (p. 15). There is here a serendipitous connection for the theme of these lectures. As I have argued, it is the 1960s LSD culture that has led to that process of "decivilizing" in the West, which is returning significant portions of its inhabitants back to the instinctual behavior of Lucy!

3. See Edgerton (1992).

4. Not to say of a whole host of other "rights" that are still fiercely contested within the West.

5. See Waswo (1996) for a robust statement of this view vis-à-vis Japan, and Rudolph and Rudolph (1967) for India.

6. Hicks (1979), p. 43.

Appendix

1. This can be seen from the differential equation for the growth rate of per capita income $\hat{y}$, which can be derived from the three basic equations describing the model. The first is the production function relating output (Y), to labor input (hours) (H), which is the hours worked per worker (work intensity) b, multiplied by the population L.

$$Y = (bL)^a \tag{1}$$

with diminishing returns to labor $0 < a < 1$.

The second is a definitional equation describing output (and income) per head (y):

$$y = Y/L. \tag{2}$$

The third is a "behavioral" equation that determines the degree of intensification. Pryor and Maurer (1982) posit that this depends upon a reference income per worker z (which is not necessarily "subsistence") and how far current income per worker (y) falls short of this:

$$\hat{b} = c(z - y), \tag{3}$$

where $c > 0$ is a "constant coefficient of response," and ˆ signifies time rates of change.

Finally, in the Boserup model population growth is exogenous say at the rate n. So:

$$\hat{L} = n. \tag{4}$$

Logarithmically differentiating (1) and (2), and through suitable substitutions in (2a): $\hat{y} = \hat{Y} - \hat{L}$, from (1a): $\hat{Y} = a\hat{b} + a\hat{L}$ (3) and (4), the basic differential equation for the model is obtained:

$$\hat{y} = -yA + D, \tag{5}$$

where $A = ac$; and $D = [a(cz) - (1 - a)n]$. A is positive, and as $a < 1$, so is D. Then $\hat{y}$ will asymptotically approach zero and y asymptotically approaches the steady state level $y_s = D/A = z - [(1 - a)n/ac]$. The steady state growth rates of the other variables are:

$$\hat{y}_s = 0; \quad \hat{L}_s = n; \quad \hat{b} = n[(1 - a)c/ac]; \quad \hat{Y}_s = \hat{L}_s.$$

The last condition is the one represented by the Ishikawa curve.

2. The remainder of this section is based on Lal (1988), pp. 297–304.

3. Including capital and management skills in the production function complicates this argument. As Domar shows, landlords will then emerge among those with access to more capital, superior skill, and better than average land. But "until land becomes scarce, and/or the amount of capital required to start a farm relatively large, it is unlikely that a large class of landowner ... could be supported by economic forces alone" Domar (1970), p. 227.

References

Abrahamian, E. (1982). *Iran—Between Two Revolutions*. Princeton, N.J.: Princeton University Press.

Aftalion, F. (1990). *The French Revolution: An Economic Interpretation*. Cambridge: Cambridge University Press.

Ahluwalia, I. J. (1991). *Productivity and Growth in Indian Manufacturing*. New Delhi: Oxford University Press.

Ahmad, E. (1991). "Social Security and the Poor: Choices for Developing Countries." *World Bank Research Observer* vol. 6, no. 1: 105–27.

Ahmad, E., et al., eds., (1991). *Social Security in Developing Countries*. Oxford: Clarendon Press.

Akerloff, G. (1976). "The Economics of Caste and of the Rat Race and Other Woeful Tales." *Quarterly Journal of Economics* vol. 90, no. 4: 599–617.

Akerloff, G. (1980). "A Theory of Social Custom, of Which Unemployment May Be One Consequence." *Quarterly Journal of Economics* vol. 94, no. 4: 749–775.

Akerloff, G. (1983). "Loyalty Filters." *American Economic Review* vol. 73 (March): 54–63.

Alexander, R. D. (1987). *The Biology of Moral Systems*. New York: Aldine de Gruyter.

Almond, G. A. (1980). *The Civic Culture Revisited*. Boston: Little Brown.

Almond, G. A., and S. Verba (1963). *The Civic Culture*. Princeton, N.J.: Princeton University Press.

Anderson, B. (1991). *Imagined Communities: Reflections on the Origin and Spread of Nationalism*. London: Verso.

Anderson, P. (1978). *Passages from Antiquity to Feudalism*. London: Verso.

Anderson, P. (1979). *Lineages of the Absolutist State*. London: Verso.

Anscombe, G. E. M. (1968). "Modern Moral Philosophy." In J. D. Thompson and G. Dworkin, eds., *Ethics*. New York: Harper & Row.

Appelby, R. S. (1993). "Fundamentalism's Modern Origins." *Foreign Affairs* vol. 72, no. 3: 217–18.

Arapura, J. G. (1972). *Religion as Anxiety and Tranquility*. The Hague: Mouton.

Arrow, K. (1974). *The Limits of Organization*. New York: W. W. Norton.

Ashtor, E. (1976). *A Social and Economic History of the Near East in the Middle Ages*. London: Collins.

Axelrod, R. (1984). *The Evolution of Cooperation*. New York: Basic Books.

Badcock, C. (1991). *Evolution and Individual Behavior*. Oxford: Blackwell.

Baechler, J., J. A. Hall, and M. Mann, eds. (1988). *Europe and the Rise of Capitalism*. Oxford: Blackwell.

Barkow, J. H., L. Cosmides, and J. Tooby (1992). *The Adapted Mind: Evolutionary Psychology and the Generation of Culture*. New York: Oxford University Press.

Barr, N. (1992). "Economic Theory and the Welfare State: A Survey and Interpretation." *Journal of Economic Literature* vol. 30, no. 2 (June): 741–803.

Basham, A. L. (1971). *The Wonder That Was India*. London: Fontana.

Bauer, P. T. (1981). *Equality, the Third World and Economic Delusion*. London: Weidenfeld and Nicholson.

Baum, R. (1994). *Burying Mao: Chinese Politics in the Age of Deng Xiaoping*. Princeton, N.J.: Princeton University Press.

Baumol, W. J., E. E. Bailey, and R. D. Willig (1977). "Weak Invisible Hand Theorems on the Sustainability of Multiproduct Natural Monopoly." *American Economic Review* vol. 67, no. 3: 350–65.

Baumol, W. J., and D. Fischer (1978). "Cost Minimizing Number of Firms and Determination of Industry Structure." *Quarterly Journal of Economics* vol. 92, no. 3: 439–467.

Baumol, W. J., and R. Willig (1981). "Fixed Costs, Sunk Costs, Entry Barriers, and Sustainability of Monopoly." *Quarterly Journal of Economics* vol. 96, no. 3: 405–31.

Becker, C. L. (1932). *The Heavenly City of the Eighteenth-Century Philosophers*. New Haven: Yale University Press.

Becker, G. (1974). "A Theory of Social Interactions," *Journal of Political Economy* vol. 82, no. 6: 1063–91.

Becker, G. (1976). *The Economic Approach to Human Behavior*. Chicago: University of Chicago Press.

Becker, G. (1981, 1991). *A Treatise on the Family*, Cambridge, Mass.: Harvard University Press.

Becker, G. (1996). *Accounting for Tastes*. Cambridge, Mass.: Harvard University Press.

Becker, G., and K. M. Murphy (1988). "A Theory of Rational Addiction." *Journal of Political Economy* vol. 96, no. 4: 675–700.

Bean, R. (1973). "War and the Birth of the Nation-State." *Journal of Economic History* 33 (May): 203–21.

Bell, D. (1976). *The Cultural Contradictions of Capitalism*. New York: Basic Books.

Bellah, R. N., R. Madsen, W. M. Sullivan, A. Swidler, and S. M. Tipton (1986). *Habits of the Heart*. New York: Harper & Row.

Benedict, R. (1946). *The Chrysanthemum and the Sword*. Boston: Houghton Mifflin.

Bennett, W. J. (1993). *The Book of Virtues*. New York: Simon & Schuster.

Berg, A., and E. Berg (1991). "The Political Economy of the Military." In G. Psacharopoulos, ed., *Essays on Poverty, Equity and Growth*. New York: Pergamon, pp. 203–265.

Berman, H. J. (1983). *Law and Revolution*. Cambridge, Mass.: Harvard University Press.

Bernheim, B. D. (1994). "A Theory of Conformity." *Journal of Political Economy* vol. 102, no. 5 (October): 841–77.

Bernheim, B. D., A. Shleifer, and L. Summers (1985). "The Strategic Bequest Motive." *Journal of Political Economy* vol. 93, no. 6 (December): 1045–76.

Bernheim, B. D., and K. Bagwell (1988). "Is Everything Neutral?" *Journal of Political Economy* vol. 96, no. 2 (April): 308–38.

Betzig, L. L. (1986). *Despotism and Differential Reproduction: A Darwinian View of History*. New York: Aldine.

Betzig, L. L., M. Borgerhoff Mulder, and P. Turke, eds. (1988). *Human Reproductive Behavior: A Darwinian Perspective*. Cambridge: Cambridge University Press.

Bhagwati, J. (1993). *India in Transition: Freeing the Economy*. Oxford: Clarendon Press.

Bhagwati, J., and T. N. Srinivasan (1993). *India's Economic Reforms*. New Delhi: Ministry of Finance.

Bhalla, A. S. (1992). *Uneven Development in the Third World: A Study of China and India*. London: Macmillan.

Bhattacharji, D. (1974). "India and China: Contrast and Comparison, 1950–1972." *Journal of Contemporary Asia* vol. 4, no. 4: 439–59.

Birdsall, N. (1989). "Economic Analyses of Rapid Population Growth." *World Bank Research Observer* vol. 4, no. 1 (January): 23–50.

Blacking, J., ed. (1977). *The Anthropology of the Body*. New York: Academic Press.

Blejer, M., et al. (1991). *China: Economic Reform and Macroeconomic Management*. Occasional Paper 76. Washington, D.C.: International Monetary Fund.

Bloch, M. (1965). *Feudal Society*. London: Routledge.

Bloch, M. (1983). *Marxism and Anthropology: The History of a Relationship*. Oxford: Blackwell.

Block, H. (1981). *The Planetary Product in 1980: A Creative Pause?* Washington, D.C.: U.S. Department of State Bureau of Public Affairs.

Bonner, J. T. (1980). *The Evolution of Culture in Animals*. Princeton N.J.: Princeton University Press.

Bork, R. H. (1996). *Slouching Towards Gomorrah: Modern Liberalism and American Decline*. New York: HarperCollins.

Boserup, E. (1965). *The Conditions of Agricultural Growth*. London: Allen & Unwin.

Boserup, E. (1970). *Women's Role in Economic Development*. London: Allen & Unwin.

Boyd, R., and P. J. Richerson (1985). *Culture and the Evolutionary Process*. Chicago: University of Chicago Press.

Brain, R. (1996). "Love in the Field." *Times Literary Supplement*, March 15, p. 6.

Bramwell, A. (1989). *Ecology in the 20th Century: A History*. New Haven: Yale University Press.

Brems, H. (1987). "Bertil Gotthaed Ohlin." In J. Eatwell, M. Milgate, and P. Newman, eds. *The New Palgrave* vol. 3,. London: Macmillan, pp. 697–700.

Burguiere, A., C. Klapisch-Zuber, M. Segalen, and F. Zonabend, eds. (1996). *A History of the Family*. 2 vols. Oxford: Polity Press.

Buss, D. (1994). *The Evolution of Desire*. New York: Basic Books.

Byres, T. J., and P. Nolan (1976). *Inequality: India and China Compared, 1950–1970*. London: The Open University.

Cameron, R. (1993). *A Concise Economic History of the World*, 2d ed. New York: Oxford University Press.

Campbell, D. T. (1975). "On the Conflicts Between Biological and Social Evolution and Between Psychology and Moral Tradition." *American Psychologist* vol. 30, no. 12: 1103–26.

Carrithers, M., S. Collins, and S. Lukes, eds. (1978). *The Category of Person: Anthropology, Philosophy, History*. Cambridge: Cambridge University Press.

Carroll, C. D., B. K. Rhee, and C. Rhee (1994). "Are There Cultural Effects on Saving? Some Cross-Sectional Evidence." *Quarterly Journal of Economics* vol. 109 (August): 685–700.

Castaneda, T. (1992). *Combating Poverty*. San Francisco: ICS Press.

Chaudhri, K. N. (1985). *Trade Civilization in the Indian Ocean: An Economic History from the Rise of Islam to 1750*. Cambridge: Cambridge University Press.

Chaudhri, K. N. (1996). "The Economy in Muslim Societies." in F. Robinson, ed., *The Cambridge Illustrated History of the Islamic World*. Cambridge: Cambridge University Press.

Chayanov, A. V. (1966). *The Theory of Peasant Economy*. Homewood, Il.: R. D. Irwin.

Cheung, S. (1986). *Will China Go "Capitalist"?* 2d ed. London: Institute of Economic Affairs.

Cheung, S. (1990). "Privatization vs. Special Interests: The Experience of China's Economic Reform." in J. Dorn and W. Xi, eds., *Economic Reform in China: Problems and Prospects*. Chicago: University of Chicago Press.

Chisholm, G. B. (1946). "The Re-establishment of a Peace-Time Society." *Psychiatry* vol. 6.

Chomsky, N. (1957). *Syntactic Structures*. The Hague: Mouton.

Cohen, H. J. (1970). "The Economic Background and the Secular Occupations of Muslim Jurisprudents and Traditionalists in the Classical Period of Islam." *Journal of Economic and Social History of the Orient* vol. 13: 36–40.

Cohen, H. J. (1977). *The Food Crisis in Prehistory: Overpopulation and the Origins of Agriculture*. New Haven: Yale University Press.

Cohn, B. S. (1987). *An Anthropologist Among the Historians and Other Essays*. Delhi: Oxford University Press.

Coleman, J. S. (1990). *Foundations of Social Theory*. Cambridge, Mass.: Harvard University Press.

Coleman, J. S., T. Hoffer, and S. Kilgore (1982). *High School Achievements: Public, Catholic and Private Schools Compared*. New York: Basic Books.

Coleman, J. S., and T. Hoffer (1987). *Public and Private Schools: The Impact of Communities*. New York: Basic Books.

Colinvaux, P. (1983). *The Fates of Nations*. London: Penguin.

Collier, P., and D. Lal (1986). *Labor and Poverty in Kenya 1900–1980*. Oxford: Clarendon Press.

Cook, M. (1983). *Muhammad*. Oxford: Oxford University Press.

Cook, M. (1988). "Islam: A Comment." In J. Baechler et al., eds., *Europe and the Rise of Capitalism*. Oxford: Blackwell.

Cook, M., ed. (1970). *Studies in the Economic History of the Middle East*. London: Oxford University Press.

Cooley, C. H. (1922). *Human Nature and the Social Order*. New York: Scribner's.

Cox, D. (1987). "Motives for Private Income Transfers." *Journal of Political Economy* vol. 95, no. 3 (June): 508–46.

Cox, D., and G. Jakubson (1989). "The Connection Between Public Transfers and Private Interfamily Transfers." Mimeo. Boston: Boston College.

Cox, D., and E. Jimenez (1990). "Achieving Social Objectives Through Private Transfers: A Review." *World Bank Research Observer* vol. 5, no. 2 (July): 205–18.

Cox, D. and E. Jimerez (1992). "Social Security and Private Transfers in Peru." *World Bank Economic Review* vol. 6, no. 1 (January): 155–69.

Cox, D. and E. Jimerez (1993). "Private Transfers and the Effectiveness of Public Income Redistribution in the Philippines." Mimeo. World Bank Conference on Public Expenditures and the Poor.

Crawford, C. B., B. E. Salter, and K. I. Lang (1989). "Human Grief: Is Its Intensity Related to the Reproductive Value of the Deceased?" *Ethology and Sociobiology* vol. 10: 297–307.

Crone, P. (1980). *Slaves on Horseback: The Evolution of Islamic Polity*. Cambridge: Cambridge University Press.

Crone, P. (1996). "The Rise of Islam in the World." In F. Robinson, ed., *The Cambridge Illustrated History of the Islamic World*. Cambridge: Cambridge University Press.

Crone, P., and M. Cook (1977). *Hagarism: The Making of the Islamic World*. Cambridge: Cambridge University Press.

Crone, P., and M. Hinds (1986). *God's Caliph*. Cambridge: Cambridge University Press.

Daly, M., and M. Wilson (1983). *Sex, Evolution and Behavior*. 2d edition. Belmont, Calif.: Wadsworth.

Danziger, R., R. Haveman, and R. Plotnick (1981). "How Income Transfers Affect Work, Savings, and Income 'Distribution.'" *Journal of Economic Literature* vol. 19 (Sept.): 975–1028.

Darwin, C. (1871). *The Descent of Man*. 2, New York: Appleton.

Darwin, C. (1872). *The Expression of Emotion in Men and Animals.* London: John Murray.

Dawkins, R. (1976). *The Selfish Gene.* Oxford: Oxford University Press.

Dawkins, R. (1986). *The Blind Watchmaker.* New York: W. W. Norton.

de Bary, W. T. (1991). *The Trouble With Confucianism.* Cambridge, Mass.: Harvard University Press.

Deer, N. (1949). *The History of Sugar.* London: Chapman and Hall.

Delumeau, J. (1990). *Sin and Fear: The Emergence of a Western Guilt Culture, 13th–18th Centuries.* New York: St. Martin's Press.

Demos, J. (1996). "Shame and Guilt in Early New England." In R. Harre and W. G. Parrott, eds., *The Emotions.* London: Sage.

Demsetz, H. (1969). "Information and Efficiency: Another Viewpoint." *Journal of Law and Economics* vol. 12: 1–22.

Demsetz, H. (1995). *The Economics of the Business Firm.* Cambridge: Cambridge University Press.

Dennis, N., and G. Erdos (1993). *Families Without Fatherhood.* London: Institute of Economic Affairs.

Deolalikar, A. B. (1993). "Does the Impact of Government Health Spending on the Utilization of Health Services by Children and on Child Health Outcomes Differ by Household Expenditure: The Case of Indonesia." Mimeo. World Bank Conference on Public Expenditures and the Poor.

Dernberger, R. F., and R. S. Eckaus (1987). *Financing Asian Development* vol. 2, *China and India.* Baltimore: University of America Press.

Desai, I. P. (1964). *Some Aspects of Family in Mahwa.* New York: Asia Publishing House.

Desai, P. (1975). "Discussion (of China and India: During the Last 25 Years)." *American Economic Review* vol. 65, no. 2 (May): 365–68.

de Tocqueville, A. (1835a). *Democracy in America.* London: Collins, 1968.

de Tocqueville, A. (1835b). *Memoir on Pauperism.* In S. Drescher, trans. New York: Ivan R. Dee, 1997.

de Tocqueville, A. (1856). *The Old Regime and the Revolution.* Chicago: University of Chicago Press, 1998.

de Tocqueville, A. (1956), *Democracy in America.* 2 vols. New York: Schocken Books.

Dicey, A. V. (1915). *Introduction to the Study of the Law of the Constitution.* London: Mac Millan.

Dick, A. (1995). *Industrial Policy and Semiconductors: Missing the Target.* Washington. D.C.: American Enterprise Institute.

Diwan, I. (1993). "Efficient Severance Payment Schemes." Mimeo, World Bank.

Doi, T. (1973). *The Anatomy of Dependence.* Tokyo: Kodansha International.

Doi, T. (1985). *The Anatomy of Self.* Tokyo: Kodansha International.

Domar, E. (1970). "The Causes of Slavery or Serfdom: A Hypothesis." *The Journal of Economic History*, vol. 30 (March): 18–32.

Domar, E. (1989). *Capitalism, Socialism and Serfdom*. Cambridge: Cambridge University Press.

Domar, E., and M. J. Machina (1984). "On the Profitability of Russian Serfdom." *Journal of Economic History* vol. 14 (December): 919–55.

Dorn, J., and W. Xi, eds. (1990). *Economic Reform in China: Problems and Prospects*. Chicago: University of Chicago Press.

Douglas, M., and A. Wildavsky (1983). *Risk and Culture*. Berkeley: University of California Press.

Dreze, J., and A. Sen (1989). *Hunger and Public Action*. Oxford: Clarendon Press.

Duby, G. (1974). *The Early Growth of the European Economy*. Ithaca, N.Y.: Cornell University Press.

Duby, G. (1978). *Medieval Marriage: Two Models From Twelfth Century France*. Baltimore: Johns Hopkins University Press.

Dull, J. L. (1990). "The Evolution of Government in China." In P. S. Robb, ed., *Heritage of China*. Berkeley: University of California Press.

Dumont, L. (1970). *Homo Hierarchicus*. London: Weidenfeld and Nicholson.

Dumont, L. (1986). *Essays on Individualism*. Chicago: University of Chicago Press.

Eaton, R. M. (1993). *The Rise of Islam and the Bengal Frontier, 1204–1760*. Berkeley: University of California Press.

Edgerton, R. B. (1992). *Sick Societies*. New York: Free Press.

Eisenstadt, S. N. (1996). *Japanese Civilization: A Comparative View*. Chicago: University of Chicago Press.

Eklund, R. B., R. F. Hebert, R. D. Tollison, G. M. Anderson, and A. B. Davidson (1996). *Sacred Trust: The Medieval Church as an Economic Firm*. New York: Oxford University Press.

Ekman, P. (1972). "Universals and Cultural Differences in Facial Expressions of Emotions." In J. Cole, ed., *Nebraska Symposium of Motivation*. Lincoln: University of Nebraska Press.

Ekman, P., and R. J. Davidson, eds. (1994). *The Nature of Emotion*. New York: Oxford University Press.

Elias, N. (1978). *The Civilizing Process*. 2 vols. New York: Pantheon.

Elster, J. (1979). *Ulysses and the Sirens: Studies in Rationality and Irrationality*. Cambridge: Cambridge University Press.

Elvin, M. (1973). *The Pattern of the Chinese Past*. Stanford: Stanford University Press.

Elvin, M. (1978). "Between the Earth and Heaven: Conceptions of the Self in China." In M. Carrithers et al., eds., *The Category of Person*. Cambridge: Cambridge University Press.

Elvin, M. (1984). "Why China Failed to Create an Endogenous Industrial Capitalism: A Critique of Max Weber's Explanation." *Theory and Society* vol. 3, no. 3: 338–360.

Emmott, B. (1989). *The Sun Also Sets: Why Japan Will Not Be Number One*. London: Simon and Schuster.

Engels, F. (1884). *The Origin of the Family, Private Property, and the State*. New York: International Publishers.

Engerman, S. L. (1983). "Contract Labor, Sugar, and Technology in the Nineteenth Century." *Journal of Economic History* vol. 43: 635–59.

Engerman, S., and K. L. Sokoloff (1994). "Factor Endowments, Institutions, and Differential Paths of Growth Among New World Economies: A View From Economic Historians of the United States." *NBER Working Paper Series*, Historical Paper No. 66. Cambridge, Mass.: National Bureau of Economic Research.

Etzioni, A. (1993). *The Spirit of Community*. New York: Simon & Schuster.

Evans, R. (1993). *Deng Xiaoping*. London: Hamish Hamilton.

Evans, W. M., and R. M. Schwab (1995). "Finishing High School and Starting College: Do Catholic Schools Make a Difference?" *Quarterly Journal of Economics* vol. 110, no. 4: 941–974.

Fagan, B. M. (1993). *World Prehistory: A Brief Introduction*. New York: HarperCollins.

Fernandez-Armesto, F. (1995). *Millennium: A History of the Last Thousand Years*. New York: Scribner.

Feuchtwang, S., A. Hussain, and T. Pairault, eds. (1988). *Transforming China's Economy in the Eighties*. Boulder: Westview Press.

Feuerwerker, A. (1984). "The State and the Economy in Late Imperial China." *Theory and Society* vol. 13: 297–326.

Figgis, J. N. (1960). *Political Thought from Gerson to Grotius, 1414–1625*. New York: Harper Torchbooks.

Findlay, R., and J. Wilson (1987). "The Political Economy of Leviathan." In A. Razin and E. Sadka, eds., *Economic Policy in Theory and Practice*. London: Macmillan.

Finley, M. (1974). *The Ancient Economy*. Berkeley: University of California Press.

Fischer, K., and J. Tangney, eds. (1995). *The Self-Conscious Emotions*. New York: Guildford.

Fisher, H. (1992). *Anatomy of Love: The Natural History of Monogamy, Adultery, and Divorce*. New York: W. W. Norton.

Fisher, H. (1995). "The Nature and Evolution of Romantic Love." In W. Jankowiak, ed., *Romantic Passion* pp. 23–41. New York: Columbia University Press.

Fiszben, A. (1992). "Labor Retrenchment and Redundancy Compensation in State Owned Enterprises: The Case of Sri Lanka." South Asia Region, Report No. IDP 121, Washington, D.C.: World Bank.

Fogel, R. W. (1989). *Without Consent or Contract*. New York: W. W. Norton.

Frank, R. H. (1988). *Passions Within Reason*. New York: W. W. Norton.

Frankfort, H. (1948). *Kingship and the Gods*. Chicago: University of Chicago Press.

Freud, S. (1918/1950). *Totem and Taboo*. New York: W. W. Norton.

Freud, S. (1930/1969). *Civilization and Its Discontents*. New York: W. W. Norton.

Friesen, W. V. (1972). *Cultural Differences in Facial Expressions in a Social Situation*. Ph.D. dissertation, University of California, San Francisco.

Fuchs, L. H. (1991). *The American Kaleidoscope*. Hanover, N. H.: University Press of New England.

Fukuyama, F. (1995). *Trust*. New York: Free Press.

Fuller, C. J. (1976). *The Nayar Today*. Cambridge: Cambridge University Press.

Garcin, Jean-Claude (1978). "The Mamluk System and the Blocking of Medieval Moslem Society." In J. Baechler et al., eds, *Europe and the Rise of Capitalism*. Oxford: Blackwell.

Garnovetter, M. (1985). "Economic Actors and Social Structure: The Problem of Embeddedness." *American Journal of Sociology* vol. 91, no. 3: 481–510.

Gay, P. (1988). *Freud: A Life for Our Time*. New York: W. W. Norton.

Gellner, E. (1981). *Muslim Society*. Cambridge: Cambridge University Press.

Gellner, E. (1988). *Plough, Book and Sword: The Structure of Human History*. London: Collins Harvill.

Gellner, E. (1992). *Postmodernism, Reason and Religion*. London: Routledge.

Gellner, E. (1993). *The Psychoanalytic Movement: The Cunning of Unreason*. Evanston, Ill.: Northwestern University Press.

Gibbon, E. (1985). *The Decline and Fall of the Roman Empire*. London: Penguin Classics.

Glass, D. V., and D. E. C. Eversley (1965). *Population in History*. London: E. Arnold.

Glazer, N. (1976). "Social and Cultural Factors in Japanese Economic Growth." In H. Patrick and H. Rosovsky, eds., *Asia's New Giant*. Washington, D.C.: Brookings Institution.

Gluck, C. (1985). *Japan's Modern Myths: Ideology in the Late Meiji Period*. Princeton, N.J.: Princeton University Press.

Goode, W. J. (1963). *World Revolution and Family Patterns*. Glencoe, Ill.: Free Press.

Goodin, R. E., and J. Le Grand (1987). *Not Only the Poor*. London: Allen & Unwin.

Goodwin, R. M. (1967). "A Growth Cycle." In C. Feinstein, ed., *Socialism, Capitalism and Economic Growth*. Cambridge: Cambridge University Press.

Goody, J. (1976). *Production and Reproduction*. Cambridge: Cambridge University Press.

Goody, J. (1983). *The Development of the Family and Marriage in Europe*. Cambridge: Cambridge University Press.

Goody, J. (1990). *The Oriental, the Ancient and the Primitive*. Cambridge: Cambridge University Press.

Goody, J. (1996). "Comparing Family Systems in Europe and Asia." *Population and Development Review* vol. 22, no. 1 (March): 1–20.

Goody, J., and G. A. Harrison (1976). "The Probability of Family Distributions." In J. Goody, J. Thirsk, and E. P. Thompson, eds., *Family and Inheritance: Rural Society in Western Europe 1200–1800*. Cambridge: Cambridge University Press.

Green, D. G. (1986). *Challenge to the NHS*. Hobart Paperback 23. London: Institute of Economic Affairs.

Green, D. G. (1988). *Everyone a Private Patient*. Hobart Paperback 27. London: Institute of Economic Affairs.

Green, D. G. (1993). *Reinventing Civil Society*. Choice in Welfare Series 17. London: Institute of Economic Affairs.

Greif, A. (1994). "Cultural Beliefs and the Organization of Society: A Historical and Theoretical Reflection on Collectivist and Individualist Societies." *Journal of Political Economy* vol. 102, no. 5: 912–50.

Guha, A. (1981). *An Evolutionary View of Economic Growth*. Oxford: Clarendon Press.

Gur, C. R., and H. A. Sackem (1979). "Self-Deception: A Concept in Search of a Phenomenon." *Journal of Personality and Social Psychology* vol. 37: 147–69.

Gurevich, A. (1995). *The Origins of European Individualism*. Oxford: Blackwell.

Gurley, J. G. (1975). "Discussion (of China and India: During the Last 25 Years)." *American Economic Review* vol. 65, no. 2 (May): 368–71.

Hahn, F. (1973). *On the Notion of Equilibrium in Economics*. Cambridge: Cambridge University Press.

Hajnal, J. (1965). "European Marriage Patterns in Perspective." In D. V. Glass and D. E. C. Eversley, eds., *Population in History*.

Hajnal, J. (1982). "Household Formation Patterns in Historical Perspective." *Population and Development Review* vol. 8, no. 3 (September): 449–94.

Hale Jr., N. G. (1995). *The Rise and Crisis of Psychoanalysis in the United States*. New York: Oxford University Press.

Hall, J. (1985). *Power and Liberties*. Oxford: Blackwell.

Halliday, F. (1996). *Islam and the Myth of Confrontation*. London: I. B. Taurus.

Hallpike, C. R. (1986). *The Principles of Social Evolution*. Oxford: Clarendon Press.

Hansen, B. (1991). *The Political Economy of Poverty, Equity and Growth: Egypt and Turkey*. New York: Oxford University Press.

Harding, H. (1987). *China's Second Revolution: Reform After Mao*. Washington, D.C.: Brookings Institution.

Hare, R. M. (1952). *The Language of Morals*. Oxford: Clarendon Press.

Harre, R., and W. G. Parrott, eds. (1996). *The Emotions*. London: Sage.

Harris, M. (1969). *The Rise of Anthropological Theory: A History of Theories of Culture*. London: Routledge.

Harris, M. (1989). *Our Kind: The Evolution of Human Life and Culture*. New York: Harper & Row.

Harris, O. (1987). "Extended Family." In J. Eatwell, M. Millgate, and P. Newman, eds., *The New Palgrave: A Dictionary of Economics*. London: Macmillan.

Harris, R. (1988). *Beyond the Welfare State: An Economic, Political and Moral Critique of Indiscriminate State Welfare and a Review of Alternatives to Dependency*. Occasional Paper No. 77. London: Institute of Economic Affairs.

Harrison, L. E. (1992). *Who Prospers: How Cultural Values Shape Economic and Political Success.* New York: Basic Books.

Hayek, F. (1944). *The Road to Serfdom.* London: Routledge.

Hayek, F. (1978). *The Three Sources of Human Values.* London: London School of Economics.

Hayek, F. (1978a). *Denationalization of Money: The Argument Refined.* Hobart Paper Special 70, 3d ed. London: Institute of Economic Affairs.

Hayek, F. (1979). *Law, Legislation and Liberty.* Chicago: University of Chicago Press.

Heckscher, E. (1955). *Mercantilism.* London: Allen and Unwin.

Hegel, G. W. F. (1820/1967). *Philosophy of Right.* London: Oxford University Press.

Hegel, G. W. F. (1832/1991). *The Philosophy of History.* Buffalo, N.Y.: Prometheus Books.

Herlihy, D. (1961). "Church Property on the European Continent, 701–1200." *Speculum* 36: 81–105.

Hicks, G. L., and S. G. Redding (1983). "The Story of the East Asian 'Economic Miracle'" parts. I and II. *Euro-Asia Business Review* vol. 2, no. 3, and vol. 2, no. 4: 18–22.

Hicks, J. R. (1969). *The Theory of Economic History.* Oxford: Oxford University Press.

Hicks, J. R. (1979). *Causality in Economics.* Oxford: Blackwell.

Himmelfarb, G. (1994). *The De-moralization of Society.* New York: Knopf.

Himmelfarb, G. (1995). *On Looking Into the Abyss.* New York: Vintage.

Hirschman, A. O. (1977). *The Passions and the Interests.* Princeton, N.J.: Princeton University Press.

Hirshleifer, J. (1984). "The Emotions as Guarantors of Threats and Promises." In J. Dupre, ed., *The Latest on the Best: Essays in Evolution and Optimality.* Cambridge, Mass.: MIT Press, pp. 307–26.

Hirshleifer, J., and J. C. Martinez Coll (1988). "What Strategies Can Support the Evolutionary Emergence of Cooperation?" *Journal of Conflict Resolution* vol. 32, no. 2: 367–98.

Hodgson, M. (1974). *The Venture of Islam.* Chicago: University of Chicago Press.

Hume, D. (1740/1985). *A Treatise on Human Nature,* London: Penguin Classics.

Hume, D. (1750/1975). *An Enquiry Concerning the Principles of Morals.* London: Oxford University Press.

Hume, D. (1777/1987). *Essays,* Indianapolis: Liberty Classics.

Hume, D. (1779/ 1948). *Dialogues Concerning Natural Religion.* New York: Hafner Press.

Huntington, S. P. (1993). "The Clash of Civilizations." *Foreign Affairs* vol. 72, no. 3: 22–49.

Huxley, T. H., and J. Huxley (1947). *Evolution and Ethics: 1893–1943.* London: Pilot Press.

Ibn Khaldun (1379/1967). *The Muqaddimah: An Introduction to History.* Princeton, N.J.: Princeton University Press.

Iliffe, J. (1987). *The African Poor*. Cambridge: Cambridge University Press.

Inalcik, H. (1994). "The Ottoman State: Economy and Society, 1300–1600." In H. Inalcik and D. Quateret, eds., *An Economic and Social History of the Ottoman Empire 1300–1914*. Cambridge: Cambridge University Press.

Ishikawa, S. (1967). *Economic Development in Asian Perspective*. Tokyo: Kinokuniya.

Issawi, C. (1981). *The Arab World's Legacy*. Princeton, N.J.: Darwin Press.

Issawi, C. (1982). *An Economic History of the Middle East and North Africa*. New York: Columbia University Press.

Jankowiak, W., ed. (1995). *Romantic Passion: A Universal Experience?* New York: Columbia University Press.

Jankowiak, W., and E. Fischer (1992). "A Cross-Cultural Perspective on Romantic Love." *Ethnology* vol. 31, no. 2: 149–55.

Jefferson, G. H., T. G. Rawski, and Y. Zheng (1992). "Growth, Efficiency, and Convergence in China's State and Collective Industry." *Economic Development and Cultural Change* vol. 40, no. 2 (January): 240–66.

Jefferson, G. H., and T. G. Rawski (1994). "Enterprise Reform in Chinese Industry." *Journal of Economic Perspectives* vol. 8, no. 2: 47–70.

Jenner, W. J. F. (1992). *The Tyranny of History: The Roots of China's Crisis*. London: Penguin.

Jimenez, E. (1989). "Social Sector Pricing Revisited: A Survey of Some Recent Contributions." *Proceedings of the World Bank Annual Conference on Development Economics*. pp. 109–38.

Jimenez, E., M. E. Lockheed, and V. Paqueo (1991). "The Relative Efficiency of Private and Public Schools in Developing Countries." *World Bank Research Observer* vol. 6, no. 2 (July): 205–18.

Jones, E. L. (1981). *The European Miracle*. Cambridge: Cambridge University Press.

Jones, E. L. (1988). *Growth Recurring*. Oxford: Oxford University Press.

Kant, I. (1788/1958). *Critique of Practical Reasoning*. London: Penguin Classics.

Kapadia, K. M. (1956). "Rural Family Pattern: A Study in Urban-Rural Relationship." *Sociological Bulletin*, vol. 5, no. 2 (September): 111–26.

Kaufman, W., ed. (1954). *The Portable Nietzsche*. New York: Viking Penguin.

Keegan, J. (1993). *A History of Warfare*. New York: Vintage.

Keightley, D. N. (1990). "Early Civilization in China: Reflections on How it Became Chinese." In P. S. Ropp, ed., *Heritage of China*, pp. 15–54. Berkeley: University of California Press.

Kertzer, D. I., and R. P. Saller (1991). *The Family in Italy: From Antiquity to the Present*. New Haven Yale University Press.

Kindleberger, C. P., and G. di Tella (1982). *Economics in the Long View*. 3 vols. London: Macmillan.

Kitcher, Patricia (1995). *Freud's Dream*. Cambridge, Mass.: MIT Press.

Kitcher, Philip (1985). *Vaulting Ambition: Sociobiology and the Quest for Human Nature*, Cambridge, Mass.: MIT Press.

Knowles, J. C., and R. Anker (1981). "An Analysis of Income Transfers in a Developing Country." *Journal of Development Economics* vol. 8 (April): 205–6.

Kolenda, P. M. (1968). "Region, Caste and Family Structure: A Comparative Study of the Indian 'Joint' Family." In M. Singer and B. S. Cohn, eds., *Structure and Change in Indian Society*. Chicago: University of Chicago Press.

Kotkin, J. (1991). *Tribes: How Race, Religion and Identity Determine Success in the New Global Economy*. New York: Random House.

Kotlikoff, L. J., and A. Spivak (1981). "The Family as an Incomplete Annuities Market." *Journal of Political Economy* vol. 89 (April): 372–91.

Kroeber, A. L. (1948). *Anthropology*. New York: Harcourt, Brace and World.

Kumar, D. (1992). "The Chinese and Indian Economies From ca 1914–1949." Research Program on the Chinese Economy, CP No. 22, STICERD. London: London School of Economics.

Kuper, A. (1994). *The Chosen Primate*. Cambridge, Mass.: Harvard University Press.

Kupperman, K. O. (1993). *Providence Island, 1630–1641: The Other Puritan Colony*. Cambridge: Cambridge University Press.

Kuran, T. (1993). "Fundamentalisms and the Economy." In M. E. Marty and R. Scott Appelby eds, *Fundamentalisms and the State*, 289–301. Chicago: University of Chicago Press.

Kuran, T. (1995). *Private Truths, Public Lies*. Cambridge, Mass.: Harvard University Press.

Kuran, T. (1997). "Islam and Underdevelopment: An Old Puzzle Revisited." *Journal of Institutional and Theoretical Economics* vol. 153, no. 1 (March): 41–72.

La Fontaine, J. S. (1978). "Person and Individual: Some Anthropological Reflections." In M. Carrithers et al., eds., *The Category of Person*. Cambridge: Cambridge University Press.

Lal, D. (1981). *Prices for Planning*. London: Heinemann Educational Books.

Lal, D. (1988, 1989). *The Hindu Equilibrium*. 2 vols. Oxford: Clarendon Press.

Lal, D. ed. (1992). *Development Economics*. 4 vols. Aldershot: Edward Elgar.

Lal, D. (1993a). *The Repressed Economy*. Aldershot: Edward Elgar.

Lal, D. (1993b). "The Role of the Public and Private Sectors in Health Financing." HRO Working Paper No. 33. Washington, D.C.: World Bank.

Lal, D. (1994). *Against Dirigisme*. San Francisco: ICS Press.

Lal, D. (1995a). "Eco-fundamentalism." *International Affairs* vol. 71 (July): 22–49.

Lal, D. (1995b): "India and China: Contrasts in Economic Liberalization?" *World Development* vol. 23, no. 9: 1475–1494.

Lal, D. (1996). "Participation, Markets and Democracy." In M. Lundahl and B. J. Ndulu, eds., *New Directions in Development Economics*, pp. 299–322. London: Routledge.

Lal, D., and M. Wolf, eds. (1986). *Stagflation, Savings and the State*. New York: Oxford University Press.

Lal, D., and H. Myint (1996). *The Political Economy of Poverty, Equity and Growth: A Comparative Study*. Oxford: Clarendon Press.

Lancaster, J. B., and C. S. Lancaster (1983). "Parental Investment: The Hominid Adaptation." In D. J. Ortner ed., *How Humans Adapt: A Biocultural Odyssey*. Washington, D.C.: Smithsonian Institution Press.

Lane-Fox, R. (1988). *Pagans and Christians*. London: Penguin.

Lardy, N. R. (1983). *Agriculture in China's Modern Economic Development*. Cambridge: Cambridge University Press.

Lardy, N. R. (1992). *Foreign Trade and Economic Reform in China: 1978–1990*. Cambridge: Cambridge University Press.

Laslett, P. (1977). *Family Life and Illicit Love in Earlier Generations*. Cambridge: Cambridge University Press.

Laslett, P. (1983). "Family and Household as Work Group and Kin Group: Areas of Traditional Europe Compared." in R. Wall et al., eds., *Family Forms in Historic Europe*. Cambridge: Cambridge University Press.

Laslett, P. (1989). "Marriages Ups and Downs." *Times Literary Supplement*, August 4, p. 843.

Laslett, P., and R. Wall, eds. (1972). *Household and Family in Past Time*. Cambridge: Cambridge University Press.

Lebra, T. S. (1992). "Self in Japanese Culture," in N. R. Rosenberger, ed., *Japanese Sense of Self*. Cambridge: Cambridge University Press.

Lebra, T. S., and W. P. Lebra, eds. (1974). *Japanese Culture and Behavior: Selected Readings*. Honolulu: University of Hawaii Press.

LeDoux, J. (1996). *The Emotional Brain*. New York: Simon and Schuster.

Levine, R., and D. Renelt (1992). "A Sensitivity Analysis of Cross-Country Growth Regressions." *American Economic Review* vol. 82, no. 4 (September): 942–63.

Lévi-Strauss, C. (1969). *The Elementary Structures of Kinship*. Boston: Beacon Press.

Lewis, B. (1958, 1993). *The Arabs in History*. Oxford: Oxford University Press.

Lewis, B. (1973). *Islam in History*. London: Alcove Press.

Lewis, B. (1982). *The Muslim Discovery of Europe*. New York: W. W. Norton.

Lewis, B. (1993). *Islam and the West*. New York: Oxford University Press.

Lewis, B. (1994). *The Shaping of the Modern Middle East*. New York: Oxford University Press.

Lewis, H. B. (1971). *Shame and Guilt in Neurosis*. New York: International Universities Press.

Lewis, H. B. (1976). *Psychic War in Men and Women*. New York: New York University Press.

Lewis, M. (1992). *Shame: The Exposed Self*. New York: Free Press.

Lewis, W. A. (1955). *The Theory of Economic Growth*. London: Allen & Unwin.

Liebowitz, M. R. (1983). *The Chemistry of Love*. Boston: Little, Brown.

Lin, J. Y. (1990a). "Collectivization and China's Agricultural Crisis in 1959–1961." *Journal of Political Economy* vol. 98 (December): 1228–52.

Lin, J. Y. (1990b). "Institutional Reforms in Chinese Agriculture: Retrospect and Prospect." In J. Dorn and W. Xi, eds., *Economic Reform in China*. Chicago: University of Chicago Press.

Lin, J. Y. (1992). "The Needham Puzzle: Why the Industrial Revolution Did Not Originate in China." Dept. of Economics Working Paper No. 650. Los Angeles: University of California at Los Angeles.

Lin, J. Y., F. Cai, and Z. Li (1994). "Why China's Economic Reforms Have Been Successful: Implications for Other Reforming Economies." Mimeo. Beijing: Dept. of Rural Economy, Development Research Center.

Lindbeck, A. (1990). "The Swedish Experience." Seminar Paper No. 482. Stockholm: Institute for International Economic Studies.

Lindholm, C. (1995). "Love as an Experience of Transcendence." In W. Jankowiak, ed., *Romantic Passion*, pp. 57–71. New York: Columbia University Press.

Lipset, S. J. (1996). *American Exceptionalism: A Double-Edged Sword*. New York: W. W. Norton.

Little, I. M. D. (1981). "Comment on Kuznets, Driving Forces of Economic Growth: What Can We Learn From History?" In H. Giresch, (ed.), *Towards an Explanation of Economic Growth*. Tubingen: J. C. B. Mohr.

Little, I. M. D. (1994). "Trade and Industrialization Revisited." Iqbal Memorial Lecture, Pakistan Institute of Development Economics.

Locay, L. (1989). "From Hunting and Gathering to Agriculture." *Economic Development and Cultural Change* vol. 37, no. 4: 737–756.

Locke, J. (1690/1947). *An Essay Concerning Human Understanding*. London: J. M. Dent.

Lucas, R. E., and O. Stark (1985). "Motivations to Remit: Evidence From Botswana." *Journal of Political Economy*, vol. 93 (October): 901–18.

Lynch, J. (1973). *The Spanish-American Revolutions, 1808–1826*. New York: Norton.

Ma, G., and R. Garnaut (1992). "How Rich is China: Evidence From the Food Economy." Working Paper, Dept. of Economics. Canberra: Research School of Pacific Studies, Australian National University.

Macfarlane, A. (1979). *The Origins of English Individualism*. Oxford: Basil Blackwell.

Macfarlane, A. (1986). *Marriage and Love in England: Modes of Reproduction, 1300–1840*. Oxford: Blackwell.

MacIntyre, A. (1990). "Individual and Social Morality in Japan and the United States: Rival Conceptions of the Self." *Philosophy East and West* vol. 40, no. 4: 489–97.

Maddison, A. (1971). *Class Structure and Economic Growth: India and Pakistan since the Moghuls*. London: Allen & Unwin.

Maddison, A. (1991). "Postwar Growth and Slowdown: A Global View." In G. Gahlen, H. Hesse, and H. G. Ramser, eds., *Wachstumstheorie und Wachstumpolitik*. Tübingen: J. C. B. Mohr.

Magnet, M. (1993). *The Dream and the Nightmare: The Sixties Legacy of the Underclass.* New York: Quill/Murrow.

Makus, H. R., and S. Kitayama (1991). "Culture and The Self: Implications for Cognition, Emotion, and Motivation." *Psychological Review* vol. 98: 224–53.

Malenbaum, W. (1959). "India and China: Contrast in Development." *American Economic Review* vol. 49, no. 3 (June): 284–309.

Malenbaum, W. (1982). "Modern Economic Growth in India and China: The Comparison Revisited, 1950–1980." *Economic Development and Cultural Change* vol. 31, no. 1 (October): 45–84.

Malenbaum, W. (1990). "A Gloomy Portrayal of Development Achievements and Prospects: China and India." *Economic Development and Cultural Change* vol. 38, no. 2 (January): 391–406.

Mann, M. (1986). *The Sources of Social Power* vol. 1. Cambridge: Cambridge University Press.

Marty, M. E., and R. Scott Appelby, eds. (1993). *Fundamentalisms and the State.* Chicago: University of Chicago Press.

Masao, M. (1964). "Japanese Thought." *Journal of Social and Political Ideas in Japan* 7, April: 41–48.

Matson, J., and M. Selden (1992). "Poverty and Inequality in China and India." *Economic and Political Weekly* (April 4): 701–15.

Matsumoto, D. (1989). "Cultural Influences on the Perception of Emotion." *Journal of Cross-Cultural Psychology* vol. 20: 92–105.

Matsumoto, D. (1992). "American-Japanese Cultural Differences in the Recognition of Universal Facial Expressions." *Journal of Cross-Cultural Psychology* vol. 23: 72–84.

Matsumoto, D. (1996). *Unmasking Japan: Myths and Realities About the Emotions of the Japanese.* Stanford: Stanford University Press.

McClelland, J. S. (1996). *A History of Western Political Thought.* London: Routledge.

McDougall, W. (1980). *An Introduction to Social Psychology.* London: Methuen.

McEvedy, C., and R. Jones (1978). *Atlas of World Population History.* London: Penguin Books.

McKinnon, R. I. (1992). "Macroeconomic Control in Liberalizing Socialist Economies: Asian and European Parallels." Pacific Basin Working Paper Series, No. PB92-05. San Francisco: Federal Reserve Bank of San Francisco.

McManners, J., ed. (1993). *The Oxford History of Christianity.* Oxford: Oxford University Press.

McNeill, W. H. (1963). *The Rise of the West.* Chicago: University of Chicago Press.

McNeill, W. H. (1979). *A History of the World,* 3d ed. New York: Oxford University Press.

McNeill, W. H. (1983a). *The Pursuit of Power.* Oxford: Blackwell.

McNeill, W. H. (1983b). *The Great Frontier: Freedom and Hierarchy in Modern Times.* Princeton, N.J.: Princeton University Press.

McNeill, W. H. (1984). "Migration in Historical Perspective." *Population and Development Review* vol. 10, no. 1: 1–18.

Mead, M. (1967). *Cooperation and Competition among Primitive Peoples*, Boston: Beacon Press.

Meerman, J. (1979). *Public Expenditure in Malaysia: Who Benefits and Why*. New York: Oxford University Press.

Meltzer, A., and S. Richard (1981). "A Rational Theory of the Size of Government." *Journal of Political Economy* vol. 89: 914–27.

Mesa-Lago, C. (1983). "Social Security and Extreme Poverty in Latin America." *Journal of Development Economics* vol. 12: 83–110.

Mesa-Lago, C. (1989). *Ascent to Bankruptcy: Financing Social Security in Latin America*. Pittsburgh: Univ. of Pittsburgh Press.

Mill, J. S. (1848/1970). *Principles of Political Economy*. London: Penguin Books.

Mill, J. S. (1874/1969). "Nature." In J. M. Robson, ed., *Collected Works of John Stuart Mill*, vol. 10. Toronto: University of Toronto Press.

Mill, J. S. (1910). *On Liberty*. London: J. M. Dent.

Minogue, K. (1995). *Politics*. Oxford: Oxford University Press.

Moffitt, R. (1992). "Incentive Effects of the U.S. Welfare System: A Review." *Journal of Economic Literature* vol. 30, no. 1: 1–16.

Mohammed, J., and J. Whalley (1984). "Rent Seeking in India: Its Costs and Policy Significance." *Kyklos* vol. 37, no. 3: 387–413.

Mokyr, J. (1990). *The Lever of Riches*. New York: Oxford University Press.

Money, J. (1980). *Love and Love Sickness: The Science of Sex, Gender Difference, and Pair Bonding*. Baltimore: Johns Hopkins University Press.

Moore Jr., B. (1966). *Social Origins of Democracy and Dictatorship: Lord and Peasant in the Making of the Modern World*. Boston: Beacon Press.

Morgan, L. H. (1877). *Ancient Society*. New York: New York Labor News.

Morishima, M. (1982). *Why Has Japan "Succeeded"?* Cambridge: Cambridge University Press.

Morris, C. (1972). *The Discovery of the Individual, 1050–1200*. Toronto: University of Toronto Press.

Murdock, G. P. (1967a). "Ethnographic Atlas: A Summary." *Ethnology* vol. 6: 305–26.

Murdock, G. P. (1967b). *Ethnographic Atlas*. Pittsburgh: University of Pittsburgh Press.

Murray, C. (1984). *Losing Ground: American Social Policy, 1950–1980*. New York: Basic Books.

Murray, C. (1996). *Charles Murray and the Underclass: The Developing Debate*, IEA Health and Welfare Unit, Choice in Welfare no. 33, Institute of Economic Affairs, London.

Myrdal, G. (1964). *An American Dilemma*. 2 vols. New York: McGraw Hill.

Nakane, C. (1972). *Japanese Society*. Berkeley: University of California Press.

Needham, J. (1956). *Science and Civilization in China* vol. 2, *History of Scientific Thought*. Cambridge: Cambridge University Press.

Needham, J. (1963). "Poverties and Triumphs of the Chinese Scientific Tradition." In A. C. Crombie, ed., *Scientific Change*. London: Heinemann.

Needham, J. (1969). *The Grand Titration: Science and Society in East and West*. London: Allen & Unwin.

Needham, J. (1978). *The Shorter Science and Civilization in China*. 3 vols. Cambridge: Cambridge University Press.

Nesse, R. M. (1990). "Evolutionary Explanations of Emotions." *Human Nature* vol. 1, no. 3: 261–89.

Nietzsche, F. (1954). *The Portable Nietzsche*. New York: Viking Press.

Nietzsche, F. (1967). *The Will to Power*. New York: Vintage.

Nietzsche, F. (1881/1982). *Daybreak: Thoughts on the Prejudices of Morality*. Cambridge: Cambridge University Press.

North, D. (1981). *Structure and Change in Economic History*. New York: W. W. Norton.

North, D. (1989). "Institutions and Economic Growth: An Historical Introduction." *World Development* vol. 17, no. 9 (September); 1319–32.

North, D. (1990). *Institutions, Institutional Change and Economic Performance*. Cambridge: Cambridge University Press.

North, D., and R. P. Thomas (1973). *The Rise of the Western World*. Cambridge: Cambridge University Press.

Nussbaum, M. C. (1990). *Love's Knowledge*. New York: Oxford University Press.

Oakeshott, M. (1973). *On Human Conduct*. Oxford: Clarendon Press.

Oakeshott, M. (1993). *Morality and Politics in Modern Europe*. New Haven: Yale University Press.

Oberai, A. S., and H. K. M. Singh (1980). "Migration, Remittances and Rural Development." *International Labor Review* (Mar.–Apr.): 229–41.

Ohly, F. (1992). *The Damned and the Elect: Guilt in Western Culture*. New York: Cambridge University Press.

Owen, R. (1981). *The Middle East in the World Economy, 1800–1914*. London: Methuen.

Parker, W. N. (1982). "European Development in Millennial Perspective." In C. P. Kindleberger and G. di Tella, eds., *Economics in the Long View* vol. 2. London: Macmillan.

Patrick, H., and H. Rosovsky, eds. (1976). *Asia's New Giant: How the Japanese Economy Works*. Washington, D.C.: Brookings Institution.

Peltzman, S. (1980). "The Growth of Government." *Journal of Law and Economics* vol. 25, no. 3: 209–87.

Pepper, D. (1984). *The Roots of Modern Environmentalism*. London: Routledge.

Peristiany, J., ed. (1965). *Honor and Shame: The Values of a Mediterranean Society*. London: Weidenfeld and Nicholson.

Peristiany, J. G., and J. Pitt-Rivers, eds. (1992). *Honor and Grace in Anthropology*. Cambridge: Cambridge University Press.

Perkins, D. (1969). *Agricultural Growth in China 1368–1968*. Chicago: Aldine.

Perkins, D. (1994). "Completing China's Move to the Market." *Journal of Economic Perspectives* vol. 8, no. 2: 23–46.

Phelps-Brown, E. (1983). *The Origins of Trade Union Power*. Oxford: Clarendon Press.

Pinker, S. (1994). *The Language Instinct*. London: Penguin.

Pintner, W. (1995). "The Future of Russia in Historical Perspective." Working Paper No. 9. Center for International Relations, University of California, Los Angeles.

Pipes, D. (1981). *Slave Soldiers and Islam: The Genesis of a Military System*. New Haven: Yale University Press.

Platteau, J. P. (1991). "Traditional Systems of Social Security and Hunger Insurance: Past Achievements and Modern Challenges." In E. Ahmad et al. eds., *Social Security in Developing Countries*. Oxford: Clarendon Press.

Pocock, J. G. A. (1975). "Early Modern Capitalism: The Augustan Perception." In E. Kamenka and R. S. Neale, eds., *Feudalism, Capitalism and Beyond*. London: Arnold.

Ponnuru, R. (1995). *The Mystery of Japanese Growth*. Rochester Paper 4, Trade Policy Unit. London: Center for Policy Studies, and Washington, D.C.: American Enterprise Institute.

Posner, R. A. (1992). *Sex and Reason*. Cambridge, Mass.: Harvard University Press.

Postan, M. M. (1975). *The Medieval Economy and Society*. London: Penguin.

Pryor, F. L. (1977). *The Origins of the Economy: A Comparative Study of Distribution in Primitive and Peasant Economies*. New York: Academic Press.

Pryor, F. L., and S. B. Maurer (1982). "On Induced Economic Change in Pre-Capitalist Societies." *Journal of Development Economics* vol. 10, no. 3 (June): 325–53.

Putnam, R. D. (1993). *Making Democracies Work*. Princeton, N.J.: Princeton University Press.

Putnam, R. D. (1995). "Bowling Alone: America's Declining Social Capital." *Journal of Democracy* vol. 6: 65–78.

Pye, L. W. (1985). *Asian Power and Politics: The Cultural Dimensions of Authority*. Cambridge, Mass.: Harvard University Press.

Rahman, F. (1979). *Islam*. 2d ed. Chicago: University of Chicago Press.

Ravallion, M., and K. Subbarow (1992). "Adjustment and Human Development in India." *Journal of Indian School of Political Economy* vol. 4, no. 1: 55–79.

Rawski, T. G. (1989). *Economic Growth in Prewar China*. Berkeley: University of California Press.

Redding, G. S. (1990). *The Spirit of Chinese Capitalism*. Berlin and New York: de Gruyter Press.

Reischauer, E. O. (1997). *The Japanese Today*. Cambridge, Mass.: Harvard University Press.

Rempel, H., and R. Lobdell (1978). "The Role of Urban-to-Rural Remittances in Rural Development." *Journal of Development Studies* vol. 14 (April): 324–41.

Renfrew, C. (1973). *Before Civilization*. London: Penguin.

Renfrew, C. (1987). *Archaeology and Language*. Cambridge: Cambridge University Press.

Reynolds, L. G., (1985). *Economic Growth in the Third World 1850–1980*. New Haven: Yale University Press.

Riasanovsky, N. (1993). *A History of Russia*. 5th ed. New York: Oxford University Press.

Ridley, M. (1996). *The Origins of Virtue*. London: Penguin.

Riskin, C. (1987). *China's Political Economy: The Quest for Development since 1949*. New York: Oxford University Press.

Rodinson, F., ed. (1996). *The Cambridge Illustrated History of the Islamic World*. Cambridge: Cambridge University Press.

Rodinson, M. (1971). *Mohammed*. London: Penguin.

Robinson, M. (1974). *Islam and Capitalism*. London: Penguin.

Roland, A. (1988). *In Search of Self in India and Japan: Towards a Cross-Cultural Psychology*. Princeton, N.J.: Princeton University Press.

Rosen, G. (1990): "India and China: Perspectives on Contrasting Styles of Economic Reform." *Journal of Asian Economics* vol. 1, no. 2: 273–90.

Rosen, G. (1992). *Contrasting Styles of Industrial Reform: China and India in the 1980s*. Chicago: University of Chicago Press.

Rosenberg, N., and L. E. Birdzell Jr. (1986). *How the West Grew Rich*. New York: Basic Books.

Rosenberger, N. R., ed. (1992). *The Japanese Sense of Self*. Cambridge: Cambridge University Press.

Rosenzweig, M. (1988). "Risk, Implicit Contracts and the Family in Rural Areas of Low Income Countries." *Economic Journal* vol. 98 (December): 1148–70.

Rowe, W. T. (1990). "Modern Chinese Social History in Comparative Perspective." In P. S. Ropp, ed., *Heritage of China*, pp. 242–62. Berkeley: University of California Press.

Roy, O. (1994). *The Failure of Political Islam*. Cambridge, Mass.: Harvard University Press.

Rubin, B. R. (1986). "Journey to the East: Industrialization in India and the Chinese Experience." In D. Basu and R. Sissons, eds., *Social and Economic Development in India: A Reassessment*, pp. 67–88. New Delhi: Sage Publishers.

Rudolph, L. I., and S. H. Rudolph (1967). *The Modernity of Tradition*. Chicago: University of Chicago Press.

Rudra, A. (1981). "Against Feudalism." *Economic and Political Weekly* vol. 16, no. 52:

Ruthven, M. (1991). *Islam in the World*. London: Penguin.

Ruttan, V. (1988). "Cultural Endowments and Economic Development: What Can We Learn from Anthropology? *Economic Development and Cultural Change*, vol. 36, no. 3, supplement, ps. S247–S271.

Said, E. (1994). *Orientalism*. 2d ed. New York: Vintage.

Sala-i-Martin, X. (1994). "Cross Sectional Regressions and the Empirics of Economic Growth." *European Economic Review* vol. 8, nos. 3–4 (April): 739–47.

Samuelsson, K. (1961). *Religion and Economic Action*. New York: Basic Books.

Sanderson, A. (1978). "Purity and Power among the Brahmans of Kashmir." In M. Carrithers et al., eds., *The Category of Person*. Cambridge: Cambridge University Press.

Sartre, J.-P. (1944/1958). *Huis Clos*. Translated as "In Camera" in *Three European Plays*. London: Penguin.

Scheff, T. J. (1990). *Microsociology*. Chicago: University of Chicago Press.

Schelling, T. (1978). "Altruism, Meanness, and Other Potentially Strategic Behaviors." *American Economic Review* vol. 68: 229–30.

Scherer, K. R., and H. G. Wallbott (1994). "Evidence for Universality and Cultural Variation of Differential Emotion Response Patterning." *Journal of Personality and Social Psychology* vol. 6, no. 2: 310–28.

Schlesinger, A. M. (1992). *The Disuniting of America*. New York: W. W. Norton.

Schumpeter, J. A. (1918). "The Crisis of the Tax State." *International Economic Papers*, no. 4.

Scott, M. Fg. (1989). *A New View of Growth*. Oxford: Clarendon Press.

Scruton, R. (1982). *Kant*. Oxford: Oxford University Press.

Searle, J. R. (1992). *The Rediscovery of the Mind*. Cambridge, Mass.: MIT Press.

Searle, J. R. (1995). *The Reconstruction of Social Reality*. New York: Free Press.

Selowsky, M. (1979). *Who Benefits from Public Expenditure? A Case Study of Colombia*. New York: Oxford University Press.

Sen, A. K. (1977). "Rational Fools: A Critique of the Behavioral Foundations of Economic Theory." *Philosophy and Public Affairs* vol. 6: 317–44.

Sen, A. K. (1982). *Poverty and Famines*. Oxford: Clarendon Press.

Sen, A. K. (1985). "Goals, Commitments and Identity." *Journal of Law Economics and Organization* vol. 1: 341–55.

Sen, A. K. (1992). *Inequality Reexamined*. Oxford: Clarendon Press.

Seton-Watson, H. (1977). *Nations and States*. Boulder: Westview Press.

Shah, A. M. (1974). *The Household Dimension of the Family in India*. Berkeley: University of California Press.

Shepher, J. (1983). *Incest: A Biosocial View*. New York: Academic Press.

Shepherd, G. M. (1988). *Neurobiology*. New York: Oxford University Press.

Shorter, E. (1975). *The Making of the Modern Family*, New York: Basic Books.

Siedentop, L. (1996). "The Western Malaise." *Times Literary Supplement*, March 15, pp. 3–4.

Singer, I. (1984, 1987). *The Nature of Love*. 3 vols. Chicago: University of Chicago Press.

Singer, P. (1983). *Hegel*. Oxford: Oxford University Press.

Singh, Y. (1986). *Modernization of Indian Tradition*. Jaipur: Rawat Publications.

Skidelsky, R. (1995). *The Road from Serfdom: The Economic and Political Consequences of the End of Communism*. London: Allen Lane.

Skinner, Q., ed. (1985). *The Return of Grand Theory in the Human Sciences*. Cambridge: Cambridge University Press.

Smith, A. (1759/1984). *The Theory of Moral Sentiments*. Indianapolis: Liberty Classics.

Smith, A. (1776/1991). *The Wealth of Nations*. Buffalo, N.Y.: Prometheus Books.

Smith, J. P., and F. Welch (1986). *Closing the Gap: Forty Years of Economic Progress for Blacks*. Santa Monica: Rand Corporation.

Smith, R. M. (1979). "Some Reflections on the Evidence for the Origins of 'European Marriage Pattern' in England." In C. Harris, ed., *The Sociology of the Family*. Keele: Keele University Press.

Smith, V. (1975). "The Primitive Hunter Culture, Pleistocene Extinction, and the Rise of Agriculture." *Journal of Political Economy* vol. 83 (August): 165–274.

Solomon, R. C., and K. M. Higgins, eds. (1988). *Reading Nietzsche*. New York: Oxford University Press.

Solow, B. L. (1991). "Slavery and Colonization." In B. L. Solow, ed., *Slavery and the Rise of the Atlantic System*. Cambridge: Cambridge University Press.

Southern, R. W. (1953). *The Making of the Middle Ages*. New Haven: Yale University Press.

Southern, R. W. (1970). *Western Society and the Church in the Middle Ages*. London: Penguin.

Spear, T. G. P. (1965). *A History of India* vol. 2. London: Penguin.

Spengler, O. (1932, 1991). *The Decline of the West*. Abridged ed. New York: Oxford University Press.

Squire, L. (1993). "Fighting Poverty." *American Economic Review* vol. 83 (May): 377–82.

Srinivas, M. N. (1965). "Social Structure." *The Gazetteer of India*, vol. 1. New Delhi: Publications Division, Government of India.

Srinivas, M. N. (1966). *Social Change in Modern India*. Berkeley: University of California Press.

Srinivasan, T. N. (1993). "Overview" and "Economic Liberalization and Future Prospects." In T. N. Srinivasan et al., eds., *Agriculture and Trade in China and India: Policies and Performance since 1950*. San Francisco: ICS Press.

Staten, H. (1990). *Nietzsche's Voice*. Ithaca, N.Y.: Cornell University Press.

St. Augustine (427/1984). *The City of God*. London: Penguin.

Stigler, G. (1970). "Director's Law of Public Income Distribution." *Journal of Law and Economics* vol. 13, no. 1: 1–10.

Stigler, G., and G. Becker (1977). "Degustibus Non Est Disputandum." *American Economic Review* vol. 67, no. 2: 76–90.

Stone, L. (1977). *The Family, Sex and Marriage in England, 1500–1800*. London: Wiedenfeld and Nicholson.

Strathern, A. (1977). "Shame on the Skin?" In J. Blacking, ed., *The Anthropology of the Body*. New York: Academic Press.

Sugden, R. (1993). "A Review of *Inequality Re-examined* by Amartya Sen." *Journal of Economic Literature* vol. 31, no. 4 (December): 1947–86.

Summers, R., and A. Heston (1991). "The Penn World Table (Mark 5: An Expanded Set of International Comparisons, 1950–1988)." *Quarterly Journal of Economics* vol. 106, no. 2 (May): 327–68.

Swamy, G. (1981). "International Migrant Workers' Remittances: Issues and Prospects." World Bank Staff Working Paper No. 481. Washington, D.C.: World Bank.

Swamy, S. (1973). "Economic Growth in China and India, 1952–1970: A Comparative Appraisal." *Economic Development and Cultural Change* vol. 21, no. 4, pt. 2: 1–84.

Swamy, S. (1977). "The Economic Distance between China and India, 1955–1973." *China Quarterly* vol. 70 (January): 371–81.

Swamy, S. (1989). *Economic Growth in China and India—A Perspective by Comparison*. New Delhi: Vikas Publishers.

Symons, D. (1992). "On the Use and Misuse of Darwinism in the Study of Human Behavior." in Barkow et al., ed., *The Adapted Mind*. New York: Oxford University Press.

Tanner, M. (1994). *Nietzsche*. Oxford: Oxford University Press.

Tawney, R. H. (1926). *Religion and the Rise of Capitalism*. London: John Murray.

Tennov, D. (1979). *Love and Limerence: The Experience of Being in Love*. New York: Stein and Day.

Tobin, J. (1992). "Japanese Preschools and the Pedagogy of Selfhood." In N. R. Rosenberger, ed., *The Japanese Sense of Self*. Cambridge: Cambridge University Press.

Tobin, J., D. Wu, and D. Davison (1989). *Preschool in Three Cultures: Japan, China and the United States*, New Haven: Yale University Press.

Tooby, J., and L. Cosmides (1989). " Evolutionary Psychology and the Generation of Culture, Part I." *Ethology and Sociobiology* vol. 10: 29–49.

Tooby, J., and L. Cosmides (1990). "The Past Explains the Present—Emotional Adaptations and the Structure of Ancestral Environments." *Ethology and Sociobiology* vol. 11: 375–424.

Toulmin, S. (1990). *Cosmopolis*. Chicago: University of Chicago Press.

Trevor-Roper, H. (1965). *The Rise of Christian Europe*. London: Thames and Hudson.

Triandis, T. C. (1995). *Individualism and Collectivism*. Boulder: Westview Press.

Trivers, R. (1985). *Social Evolution*. Menlo Park, Calif.: Benjamin Cummings.

Troeltsch, E. (1931). *The Social Teachings of the Christian Churches and Groups*. 2 vols. London: Allen & Unwin.

Tsuru, S. (1993). *Japan's Capitalism*. Cambridge: Cambridge University Press.

Tucker, M. B., and C. Mitchell-Kernan, eds. (1995). *The Decline in Marriage among African Americans*. New York: Russell Sage Foundation.

Ullmann, W. (1966). *The Individual and Society in the Middle Ages*. Baltimore: Johns Hopkins University Press.

van de Walle, D. (1992). "The Distribution of the Benefits from Social Services in Indonesia, 1978–87." Mimeo, Policy Research Working Paper, Country Economics Dept. Washington, D.C.: World Bank.

van Wolferen, K. (1989). *The Enigma of Japanese Power*. London: Macmillan.

Vogel, E. F. (1991). *The Four Little Dragons*. Cambridge, Mass.: Harvard University Press.

Wakefield, E. G. (1829/1929). *A Letter from Sydney*. In F. M. Lloyd Pritchard, ed., *Collected Works*. London: Dent.

Wall, R., et al., eds. (1983). *Family Forms in Historic Europe*. Cambridge: Cambridge University Press.

Wallbott, H. G., and K. R. Scherer (1995). "Cultural Differences in Experiencing Shame and Guilt." In K. Fischer and J. Tangney, eds., *The Self-Conscious Emotions*. New York: Guilford.

Ware, K. (1993). "Eastern Christendom." In J. McManners, ed., *The Oxford History of Christianity* pp. 131–66. Oxford: Oxford University Press.

Warr, P. G. (1983). "The Private Provision of a Public Good is Independent of the Distribution of Income." *Economic Letters* vol. 13: 207–11.

Waswo, A. (1996). *Modern Japanese Society, 1868–1994*. Oxford: Oxford University Press.

Weber, M. (1958). *The Protestant Ethic and the Spirit of Capitalism*. New York: Scribners.

Webster, R. (1995). *Why Freud Was Wrong*. London: HarperCollins.

Weiming, T. (1990). "The Confucian Tradition in Chinese History." In P. S. Ropp, ed., *Heritage of China*, pp. 112–37. Berkeley: University of California Press.

Weiner, M. (1991). *The Child and State in India*. Princeton, N.J.: Princeton University Press.

Wen, J. G. (1993). "Total Factor Productivity Change in China's Farming Sector, 1952–1989." *Economic Development and Cultural Change* vol. 42, no. 1 (October): 1–41.

Werner, E. E. (1979). *Cross Cultural Child Development*, Monterey, Calif.: Brooks/Cole.

Westermarck, E. (1922). *The History of Human Marriage*. 3 vols. New York: Allerton Book Co.

White, L. (1978). *Medieval Religion and Technology*. Berkeley: University of California Press.

Whyte, M. K. (1996). "The Chinese Family and Economic Development: Obstacle or Engine?" *Economic Development and Cultural Change* vol. 45, no. 1: 1–30.

Wickler, W. (1972). *The Biology of the Ten Commandments*. New York: McGraw Hill.

Williams, B. (1993). *Shame and Necessity*. Berkeley: University of California Press.

Wilson, B. (1982). *Religion in Sociological Perspective*. Oxford: Oxford University Press.

Wilson, J. Q. (1993). *The Moral Sense*. New York: Free Press.

Wilson, W. J. (1987). *The Truly Disadvantaged: The Inner City, The Underclass, and Public Policy*. Chicago: University of Chicago Press.

Wittfogel, K. A. (1957). *Oriental Despotism*. New Haven: Yale University Press.

Wolf, A. P. (1995). *Sexual Attraction and Childhood Association: A Chinese Brief for Edward Westermarck*. Stanford: Stanford University Press.

Wolf, A., and Chieh-Shan Huang (1980). *Marriage and Adoption in China*. Stanford: Stanford University Press.

Wong, C. (1991). *Economic Reform in China*. Manila: Asian Development Bank.

World Bank (1983). *China: Socialistic Economic Development* vol. 1. Washington, D.C.: World Bank.

World Bank (1985). *China: Long Term Issues and Options*. Baltimore: Johns Hopkins University Press.

World Bank (1992a). *Poverty Reduction Handbook*. Washington, D.C.: World Bank.

World Bank (1992b). *China: Reform and the Role of the Plan in the 1990s*. Washington, D.C.: World Bank.

World Bank (1993). *The East Asian Miracle*. New York: Oxford University Press.

Wright, G. A. (1971). "Origins of Food Production in South Western Asia." *Current Anthropology* vol. 12, no. 4: 447–77.

Wright, R. (1994). *The Moral Animal*. New York: Pantheon.

Wrigley, E. A. (1977). "Reflections on the History of the Family." *Daedalus* vol. 106, no. 2 (Spring): 71–85.

Wrigley, E. A. (1978). "Fertility Strategy for the Individual and the Group." In C. Tilly, ed., *Historical Studies of Changing Fertility*. Princeton, N.J.: Princeton Univ. Press.

Wrigley, E. A. (1988). *Continuity, Chance and Change: The Character of the Industrial Revolution in England*. Cambridge: Cambridge University Press.

Wrigley, E. A., and R. S. Schofield (1981). *The Population History of England, 1541–1871*. Cambridge: Cambridge University Press.

Yi, Z. et al. (1993). "Causes and Implications of the Increase in China's Reported Sex Ratio At Birth." *Population and Development Review* vol. 19 (June): 283–302.

Young, A. (1992). "A Tale of Two Cities: Factor Accumulation and Technical Change in Hong Kong and Singapore." In O. Blanchard and S. Fischer, eds., *NBER Macroeconomic Annual 1992*. Cambridge: MIT Press.

Index

Conscience, 93
Constantine I, 76, 95
Construction of Social Reality, The (Searle), 8, 9
Contemptus Mundi, De (Innocent III), 92
Cook, M., 61
  Hagarism, 50–51
Cornwallis, Charles, 33
Cosmological beliefs, 10–11, 16–17, 81, 99, 202–203n49
  Chinese, 44–47, 141–142
  Indian, 35, 37–39
  Islamic, 56–59
  Japanese, 145–146, 149–150
  Near Eastern, 24–25
  Western, 100–101
Costa Rica, 164
Creoles, 115, 118
Critique of Practical Reason (Kant), 105
Crone, Patricia, 49
  Hagarism, 50–51
Cultural Revolution, 135–136
Culture, 45, 100, 213n72
  anthropologists and, 14–16
  defining, 6–8
  and economics, 1–2, 5–6, 205n61
  guilt, 91–92, 93–94, 154
  and welfare state, 165–171

Darwin, Charles, 9–10, 11, 13, 109, 119, 175, 202n48, 224n75
Darwinism, 8, 105, 200n34, 205n57
Death, 92–93, 227n124
Delumeau, Jean, 91–92
Democracy, 31, 73–74, 124, 164, 177
Demographic transition, 110
Demos: political nationalism and, 115–119
Deng Xiaoping, 47, 134–135
Dervishes, 61
Descartes, René, 119
Designer goods, 141, 236–237n17
Development of the Family and Marriage in Europe, The (Goody), 83–84, 85, 87, 89
DGTD. *See* Directorate General of Technical Development
Dialogues Concerning Natural Religion (Hume), 104, 106
Diderot, Denis, 104
Directorate General of Technical Development (DGTD), 133–134
Divorce, 90, 150, 151

Douglas, M., 121
Dumont, Louis, 75, 77, 78–79

East Asia, 1–2, 6, 11. *See also various countries*
  economies of, 137–142
Eastern Europe, 96. *See also* Russia
Ecofundamentalism, 108–110, 176–177
Ecology, 29, 45, 79
  of Greece, 73, 74
  of Himalayan foothills, 31–32
  of Islam, 53–54
  and Near Eastern civilization, 24–25
  and polities, 70–71
Economic development, 66, 70–71, 128–29
Economic growth, 69, 70, 127
  in China, 39–40, 42, 46, 234–235n17
  in Europe, 79–86
  Islamic world, 54–55
  in Japan, 142–143, 147–148, 238n47
  types of, 19–21
Economic liberalism, 114–115, 232n60
Economic liberalization, 131, 132, 133, 134
Economic Principle, 14–15, 177–178
Economic reform, 130
  in China, 134–136
  in India, 131–134
Economies, 72, 87, 100, 129–130
  Chinese, 39–43, 233–234n11, 235–236nn31, 32
  East Asian, 137–142
  globalization of, 121–124, 176
  Indian, 34–35, 36–37(figs.), 234n16, 235n21
  Islamic, 54–56, 65–66
Education, 33, 66, 108, 128, 156, 198n20, 236n34, 246n69
  public, 162–163
Egypt, 45, 66
  ancient civilization in, 22, 23–26, 53
Einstein, Albert, 120
Ekman, P., 13
Elias, Norbert: *The Civilizing Process*, 153
Elizabethan Poor Law, 159
Elster, Jon, 5
Elvin, M., 43, 44
Emmott, Bill, 147
Emotions, 12–13, 148, 199n25, 200nn28, 30, 202–203nn44, 49. *See also* Guilt; Love; Shame
Energy economics, 20, 110
Engels, Frederick, 86

Qing regime, 44
Qin regime, 44

Ramsey prices, 189
Rao, Narasimha, 132, 235n21
Rationalism, 119
Reason: and morality, 106
Reformation, 93, 100–101, 231n51
Reincarnation, 38
Religion, 25–26, 50, 74, 212n52
  environmental movement as, 108–110
  Freudianism as, 107–108
  and guilt, 91–92
  Indian, 31, 32, 38–39
  in Japan, 145–146
  modernization in, 170–171
  origins of, 37–38
  in United States, 155–156, 241nn22, 23, 28
Religious movements: anticaste, 31, 32
Renaissance, 79, 119
Renouncer, 77
Rent seeking, 18
Retirement contracts, 88
Reynolds, Lloyd, 2
Rise of Christian Europe, The (Trevor-Roper), 80
Roh Tae Woo, 139
Roman Catholic Church, 96, 99, 174, 221–222n45, 223n65. See also Church; Church-state
Romanov dynasty, 117
Romanticism, 100
Rome, 70, 103, 220n18
Rosovsky, Henry, 147
Rousseau, Jean-Jacques, 9, 198n20
Russia, 117
  and orthodox Christianity, 95–97
Russian Revolution, 107

Sakarov, Andrei, 97
Sakoku, 142
Sala-i-Martin, X., 3
Salvation: in Hinduism, 37, 38
Samurda Gupta, 32
Sartre, Jean-Paul, 108
Sassanian empire, 49
Savings, 137
Scale economies, 140–141
Schumpeter, Joseph, 121–122, 206n4
Science, 44, 74
  Islamic, 54, 63–64
  in Japan, 144–145

Scottish Enlightenment, 9, 113, 124, 230n34
Searle, John, 16–17
  The Construction of Social Reality, 8, 9
Sects: Indian, 31, 32
Self: in Japan, 149–150
Self-consciousness, 8–9
Selowsky, M., 162
Serfdom, 70, 71, 97, 228nn140, 142
Seventeen Article Constitution, 142
Sex, sexuality, 91, 92–93
Sexual Revolution, 165
Shakespeare, William, 119
Shame, 13, 39, 59, 75, 102, 141, 154, 157, 176, 177, 201n37, 202n48, 203–205nn50, 55, 210–211n27, 240n3, 242n27
  in Japan, 148, 238–239nn49, 54
Shame and Necessity (Williams), 75
Shang dynasty, 39
Sharia, 57, 62, 63
Shias, 52
Shintoism, 145–146
Shradha, 32
Sicily, 86
Sin, 75
  original, 58–59, 67, 91, 92, 103, 178
Singapore, 137, 138
Singh, Mammohan, 132
Slouching Towards Gomorrah (Bork), 103
Smiles, Samuel, 10
Smith, Adam, 7, 10, 100, 232n81
  The Moral Sentiments, 113
  The Wealth of Nations, 20
Smithian growth, 20, 34, 42, 46, 54–55, 69, 142
Social facts, 16–17
Social hierarchy: in India, 28–29, 30, 33
Socialism: Fabian, 128–129, 132
Socialization, 148, 153–154, 200n33, 201n36
  in China, 46–47
  in Greece, 74–75
  Islam and, 59, 67
  and religion, 38–39
  in United States, 155–158, 176
Social safety nets, 159, 243n40
Social spending, 163–164
Social system, 81, 128, 242n25
  Hindu, 28–39
  Western absolutism and, 153–154
Solzhenitsyn, Aleksandr, 97
South America, 115, 116, 206n67